OFF THE BEATEN PATH® SERIES

TENTH EDITION

MAINE

OFF THE BEATEN PATH®

DISCOVER YOUR FUN

TARYN PLUMB

Globe
Pequot
Guilford, Connecticut

All the information in thie guidebook is subject to change. We recommend that you call ahead to obtain current information before traveling.

Globe
Pequot

An imprint of The Rowman & Littlefield Publishing Group, Inc.
4501 Forbes Blvd., Ste. 200
Lanham, MD 20706
www.rowman.com

Distributed by NATIONAL BOOK NETWORK

Maps by Equator Graphics

British Library Cataloguing in Publication Information available

Library of Congress Cataloging-in-Publication Data available

ISBN 978-1-4930-3757-5 (paperback)
ISBN 978-1-4930-3758-2 (e-book)

∞™ The paper used in this publication meets the minimum requirements of American National Standard for Information Sciences—Permanence of Paper for Printed Library Materials, ANSI/NISO Z39.48-1992

Printed in the United States of America

Contents

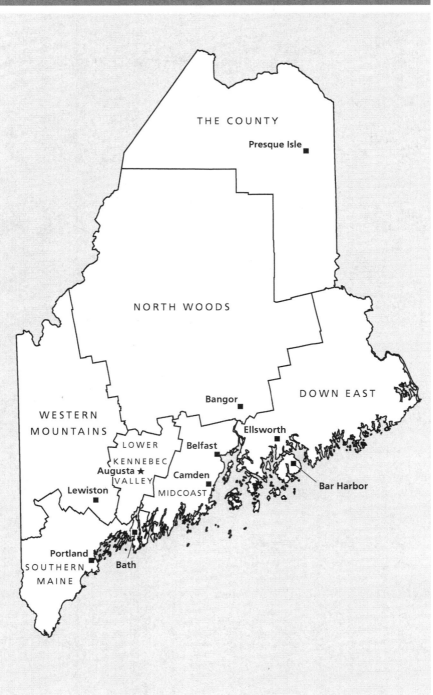

THE COUNTY

Presque Isle ■

NORTH WOODS

DOWN EAST

Bangor ■

WESTERN
MOUNTAINS

Ellsworth

LOWER   Belfast

KENNEBEC

Augusta ★   Camden

VALLEY

Lewiston ■   MIDCOAST

Bar Harbor

Portland ■   Bath

SOUTHERN
MAINE

Acknowledgments

No one person can know all the locales off the beaten path, so this book wouldn't have been possible without the help of dozens of people offering tips and feedback (and sometimes sending the writer on wild goose chases, but those can be fun, too). Thanks to friends, family, locals, editors, and many an old-time Mainer for their input and advice. Particularly of note are the dedicated staff members and volunteers at the state's numerous museums, historical attractions, historical and preservation societies, tourism organizations, and chambers of commerce. And don't believe the stereotype of the stodgy and off-putting Mainer—they are a proud and often reserved bunch, but they are among the most hospitable you'll find anywhere.

Introduction

Maine has an idyllic sense about it; it evokes images of rock-strewn beaches, rustic woods, unspoiled mountains. Then there are the clichés of moose, lobster, and the local colloquialism sprinkled with expressions of "ayuh."

Ultimately, there's a reason it's called "Vacationland." People from all over the U.S. and Canada converge on Maine throughout the year—and particularly en masse in the summer. Maine is their getaway place, their great escape. And Maine people, too, when given the opportunity, travel to other parts of the state for their holidays and time off. After all, Maine is expansive, and it would take several lifetimes to see, appreciate, and experience all that it has to offer.

Fall is a particularly splendid time to visit the Pine Tree State (some would say even more so than summer). So-called "leaf peepers" flock to Maine by the carload and busload to view the gorgeous blazing hues of autumn color. Maine's foliage dazzles because of its great variety of hardwoods, such as red maple, sugar maple, white and yellow birch, ash, and oak. These trees produce the various tints of red, yellow, orange, and purple that set Maine's fall-foliage treetop high above that of other states.

Want to experience Maine off the beaten path on an up close and personal level? That's the goal of this book. With it, you can meticulously plan out your itinerary months in advance—or if you're so inclined, you can travel on a whim, allowing Maine to reveal itself to you as you go. In either case, a copy of DeLorme's beloved *Maine Atlas & Gazetteer* will help ensure that you won't get lost.

As with any state, change has come to much of Maine, some good, some bad (depending on who you ask). Coastal communities, especially, can tend to lose their identity by embracing the beach-magnet mentality. Likewise, many saw the upgrade of US 1 as a disaster, especially residents of the small towns it bypassed altogether. But what was once considered a curse is now in some cases looked at as a blessing.

Still, many of the smaller places retain their old-time charm. Several even appear much the same as they did twenty, forty, or even fifty years ago. These are ripe for exploring and well worth anybody's time.

Lots of communities have also achieved a pleasant balance with the years, maintaining the traditional and embracing the new. Many dozens of places remain, for the most part, off the beaten path. To find and explore them, take out a map and choose virtually any town or village east of US 1 and west of the sea. The many points, capes, and peninsulas that have thus far escaped the thundering herd beckon to the inquisitive.

Likewise, the farther Down East you travel, the less commercial influence you'll see. Down East, by the way, is a term held over from the days of the booming maritime trade, when the prevailing winds made for smooth sailing in that direction—that is, "downward and to the east." Today, when traveling by road, Down East can either mean east or northeast, so be sure to pay attention.

didyouknow?

Maine is the only state that shares a border with just one other state. And, Maine is the only state with just one syllable.

And while there is no official designation for where Down East begins and ends, it is generally agreed to include all of Hancock and Washington Counties. (But you're sure to find people in other areas who will disagree.)

Northern Maine, the "Great North Woods," has long been the setting of some controversy. This area is primarily huge commercial woodland, complete with untold miles of private roads and many small but long-established working communities. A plan to turn this area (which makes up about half of the state) into a North Woods national park has gone back and forth for years. You'll see support (largely by non-residents of the expansive area) boasted on bumper stickers and signs announcing NORTH WOODS NATIONAL PARK 100 MILES.

On the other hand, people who live and work in the North Woods are not necessarily amenable to the idea of being displaced and seeing their homes and communities turned into a park. Many feel that the area is a healthy, working forest and that the local industries are based on a self-sustaining concept that has worked for generations.

In any case, it's a dispute that's not likely to be settled anytime soon. It's a fact that Maine is the most thickly forested state in the lower forty-eight and has been for some time. Regardless of whether or not it becomes the setting of a dedicated park, Maine's North Woods remains a place of singular peace and wildness.

Here's a word on paper-company roads in the North Woods. Most of them are open to the public, some for free and others for a slight fee. For the most part, they are better maintained than many unpaved roads in the organized townships to the south. As such, it's tempting to drive fast and watch the thick clouds of dust that swirl up and trail your path. It's hard to see much of the countryside this way, though. And it's also a good way to collide with a moose or deer—this is their home and they're known for their lack of ability (or desire) to yield. Better to slow down and appreciate the vastness and serenity of this remarkable place. Remember, too, that the roads are made for logging vehicles: They drive fast, with a purpose and they have the right-of-way.

Speaking of woods and forests in general, Maine has more forested land now than it did a hundred years ago. Much of what was once farmland is now forested, adding many hundreds of acres to the biomass each year.

Meanwhile, on to a different topic: Food. Restaurants aplenty are listed in this book, not only the fine and elegant type, but the true, off-the-beaten-path places where locals go to enjoy their favorite dishes. Lobsters, clams, and scallops aside, Maine offers plenty of other fine regional, seasonal, and delicious treats.

Fiddleheads, the immature fronds of young ostrich ferns, are Maine's most ephemeral delicacy. The tasty fronds are ripe from late April in the south to late May in the north. Buying their produce from local pickers, restaurants offer fiddleheads in various forms, from steamed fiddleheads to fiddlehead quiche. When the season is over and they're crossed off the menu for another year, you can find the canned variety in many Maine stores and supermarkets. (But as with anything, canned is a poor replacement for the fresh variety.)

Blueberries, raspberries, and strawberries are prominent seasonal favorites (blueberries in particular are a proud Maine harvest) and when in season are featured on menus and in all manner of recipes in both homes and restaurants the length and breadth of Maine. If you're partial to fresh seasonal desserts (who isn't?), be sure to check out **Helen's Restaurant**, on Lower Main Street in **Machias**. Helen's is justly famous for its cakes, puddings and especially its pies—its "famous" baked wild blueberry pie has been featured in the likes of *National Geographic Traveler*, *Life Magazine* and *Every Day with Rachael Ray*. In fact, most locals and visitors make it a special point to visit Helen's when in the area (some even making a special side trip when not). Recently reopened after a restaurant rebuild, Helen's is open from 6 a.m. to 8 p.m. Mon through Sat, and from 7 a.m. to 2 p.m. on Sun, Thanksgiving

Mysteries of the Earliest Inhabitants

Little is known of the first people who lived in what is now Maine. Today, they are simply known as the **"Red Paint People,"** a name ascribed due to the fact that they were known to bury quantities of red ochre, or powdered hematite, with their dead. Their graves also contained knives and spear points—but they apparently had no knowledge of the bow and arrow (at least as far as historians and archaeologists have been able to determine). They pre-dated the Algonquians, one of the most populous and widespread native groups in New England and the Atlantic Canada region, but as of yet, no one can say definitively where they came from, how long they stayed in what would eventually become Maine, and when they finally vanished.

Fact Block

Maine Office of Tourism
59 State House Station, Augusta 04330
(888) 624-6345
visitmaine.com

Maine Tourism Association
327 Water St., Hallowell 04347
(800) 767-8709
mainetourism.com

Major newspapers: *Portland Press Herald, Bangor Daily News, Lewiston Sun Journal, Morning Sentinel*

Recommended reading for kids:

- *ABC's of Maine* by Harry W. Smith

- *Charlotte's Web* by E. B. White

- *Abbie Against the Storm: The True Story of a Young Heroine and a Lighthouse* by Marcia K. Vaughn

- *Blueberries for Sal* by Robert McCloskey

- *Lost Trail: Nine Days Alone in the Wilderness* by Donn Fendler

Public transportation:

Concord Coach Lines
(800) 639-3317
concordcoachlines.com

Amtrak Downeaster
(800) 872-7245
amtrakdowneaster.com

Average high/low temperatures (Fahrenheit) in Portland: Jan 31/13, Feb 34/15, Mar 42/25, Apr 53/34, May 64/44, June 73/53, July 79/59, Aug 78/58, Sept 70/50, Oct 59/39, Nov 48/31, Dec 37/20
(*Source: National Oceanic and Atmospheric Administration*)

Population: 1,335,907 (2017 Census estimate)

Size: 33,265 square miles (about the size of the rest of New England combined)

Famous Mainers: 15th vice president Hannibal Hamlin; movie director John Ford; actress Anna Kendrick; actor Patrick Dempsey; retailer L.L. Bean; poet Henry Wadsworth Longfellow; novelist Stephen King; painters Marsden Hartley and Winslow Homer; marathoner Joan Benoit Samuelson; activist Dorothea Dix; legendary logger Jigger Johnson

State bird: black-capped chickadee

State tree: eastern white pine

State animal: moose (of course!)

Highest point: Mount Katahdin (5,267 feet)

and Christmas excepted (and check ahead of time if you're uncertain about other major holidays). Call (207) 255-8423 or visit helensrestaurantmachias .com for more information.

Throughout this book, restaurant cost categories refer to prices of entrees without beverages, desserts, taxes, or tips. Those listed as inexpensive are $10 or less; moderate, between $10 and $15; and expensive, $20 and over. Accommodations that are listed as inexpensive are up to $100 per double per night; moderate, $101 to $200 per night; and expensive, $201 and up per night.

When is the best time to seek Maine off the beaten path? You'll find that many places listed here and elsewhere are open only in the summer—with abbreviated hours sometimes stretching into the early fall. Traditionally, Maine summer begins on Memorial Day weekend and ends the day after Labor Day.

But many people (including the author) find the off-season much more appealing. For example, the four weeks from mid-April to mid-May are often cool but not cold and can be warm but hardly ever hot. This is also before the May flies and other biting bugs have grown into marauding swarms. Springtime in Maine is nothing short of glorious: Migrating birds, including many colorful warblers, fill backyards, woodlands, and hedgerows with sweet songs, and spring wildflowers are at their peak.

Another good time to explore Maine off the beaten path is from late October to early November (that is, after the tour bus-toting leaf peepers have departed back south). It's cool, with steely gray skies, and there's just a hint of crisp winter in the air. The leaves have mostly fallen from the trees, allowing for long-distance views across a newly stark landscape. The bugs are mostly gone, too—so for those with an artistic bent, this is the time to paint or photograph coastal scenery at your leisure.

Winter, of course, also has its charms. Locals have found ways to endure the bitter cold and snow for thousands of years; today you'll find skiing, ice-fishing, snowshoeing, snowmobiling and snow tubing aplenty. Because of its breadth of space and tradition, Maine offers more high-quality opportunities for these winter pastimes than any other New England state. So grab some warm clothes, "cramp-ons" and embrace the invigorating colder months.

At the end of the day, even Mainers whose families go back many generations can't tell you *all* the hidden nooks and crannies and secret treasures to be found; we only hope this book does those places justice and keeps the reader searching for more.

So when is the best time to visit Maine off the beaten path? Every chance you can get, of course! (Did you expect us to say anything else?)

Southern Maine

While you could look for a greater range of terrain and regional character than you'll find in southern Maine, you'd be hard pressed to find it. Southern Maine has everything: From small coastal harbors and beaches, to mountains and woods. It is the bucolic quiet of the country and the state's most populous and bustling city wrapped up in one. And, as is the case with much of the state, the bulk of the population is clustered along the coast. It is here where European ships first deposited early settlers, and, later, where highway construction made it most convenient to live. The main arteries—such as US 1 and the turnpike—run parallel to the shoreline, creating a broad transportation corridor with links to Boston and southward. By contrast, traveling east to west (or vice versa) can sometimes present more of a challenge (Maine, after all, just wouldn't be Maine without its windy, bumpy and often heavily frost-heaved secondary and back roads).

Historical attractions are a chief draw of the southern region—those who delight in the quiet serenity of early homesteads and the cluttered comfort of antiques stores will find contentment here. Likewise, this is prime beach territory; in the warmer months, locals and tourists alike congregate to its miles

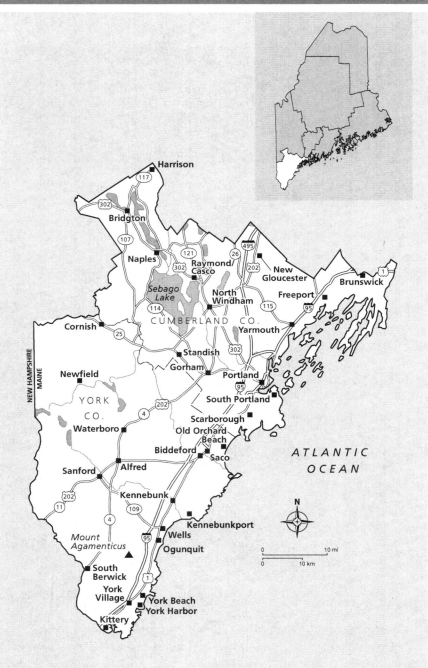

Harrison
117
302
Bridgton
107
121
Naples
302
Raymond/
Casco
26
495
202
New
Gloucester
Freeport
Brunswick
1
North
Windham
115
95
Sebago
Lake
CUMBERLAND CO.
114
Cornish
25
Yarmouth
Standish
302
NEW HAMPSHIRE
MAINE
Newfield
Gorham
Portland
95
YORK
CO.
South Portland
Waterboro
202
Scarborough
4
Old Orchard
Beach
Biddeford
Saco
ATLANTIC
OCEAN
Sanford
Alfred
Kennebunk
202
11
109
4
Kennebunkport
95
Wells
Mount
Agamenticus
Ogunquit
N
South
Berwick
0   10 mi
York
Village
York Beach
0   10 km
1
York Harbor
Kittery

of sandy shorefront. With or without the crowds, it's a great place to walk, relax and of course swim—but keep in mind that the ocean temperature doesn't get much warmer than 60 degrees on even the balmiest of days.

did you know?

Despite its size, Maine has one of the slowest population growth rates in the country. Some would say this adds to its charm.

York County

Some would argue that **York County** should be entirely eliminated from this guide. After all, it is one of the state's greatest tourist hamlets (due largely to its southernmost nature and easily-accessible diversity of terrain). Few places here remain undiscovered by visitors, and many cater exclusively to tourists (one of Maine's most significant trades). Due to that fact, as well as its large population of summer-only residents, some Mainers disavow the county altogether (if good-naturedly). In fact, one prominent Maine newspaper once quipped that the state should just gift York County to New Hampshire in exchange for toll-free travel on the Granite State's turnpike. Maine never did act on this unsolicited advice, but the idea hits upon the popular notion that York County has been engulfed by the megalopolis that spreads north from the cultural and economic powerhouse of Boston.

Still, York County is a delightful spot with plenty to offer (particularly if you can avoid the bustle, clatter, and gridlock of US 1). The region has a strong historical tradition with roots tracing to the 17th and 18th centuries and many attractions reflecting this early history. Visitors might also be surprised to find that, just driving a tad bit inland, the townships and forests are as peaceful, inviting and remote as any to be found in the state.

Kittery and Vicinity

If you're driving north, your first encounter with Maine will be **Kittery**, the state's oldest town located just over the I-95 bridge after Portsmouth, New Hampshire. Veer off at exit 3 if you've got an urge to spend some money. A growing number of factory outlets cluster along both sides of US 1, creating a sort of Scylla and Charybdis of consumer culture. Dozens of stores hawk brand-name merchandise ranging from Coach to Calvin Klein, Movado to Swarovski. Bostonians and many others seeking out a bargain (or two or three) throng here all year long, which often results in gridlock and lots of frustration (not to mention many a beeping horn) along this busy stretch of road. And if you're trying to take a left? Be prepared for a long wait. If you'd prefer outlet shopping on foot in a village setting, stay on the highway and head for **Freeport**,

POPULAR ATTRACTIONS

Hamilton House, Salmon Falls River

Museums of Old York buildings and the Old Burying Ground, York

Perkins Cove, Ogunquit

Ogunquit Museum of American Art, Ogunquit

Seashore Trolley Museum, north of Kennebunkport

Biddeford Pool

The inland town of Cornish

Eastern Promenade Trail, Portland

Sabbathday Lake Shaker Community, New Gloucester region

Maine's other well-known outlet destination. You'll come upon it about an hour north of Kittery.

One of the shops that launched the Kittery retail boom is the eponymous **Kittery Trading Post**, and it's worth a visit even if you're not partial to shopping. It is Maine in a nutshell, filled with rugged merchandise and all manner of hunting, fishing, camping, and outdoor gear. You'll find it on US 1 on your left as you head north past the chain stores and strip malls. It's open daily; call (888) 587-6246 or (207) 439-2700 (local) for hours and information or visit kitterytradingpost.com.

In contrast to the outlet area, Kittery's small downtown (referred to as "Kittery Foreside") has a sleepy, backyard feel, seemingly overlooked by both travelers and time. Dominating the town is the venerable **Portsmouth Naval Shipyard**. It was established on Dennett's Island in 1806 as the Navy's first yard, then in 1866, expanded to neighboring Seavey Island (the names are now interchangeable, depending on who you're talking to). The main entrance is in the middle of Kittery, just beyond the Rice Library, a stately manse of elaborate Victorian brickwork.

Kittery's rich naval and shipbuilding heritage comes alive in the **Kittery Historical and Naval Museum**. It features a large collection of shipbuilding tools, ship models, lighthouse artifacts and examples of the age-old art of scrimshaw. There are also displays from "bygone" eras, a digital timeline of Kittery, as well as an authentic reproduction of a 17th-century garrison house, a fortified farmstead offering protection from raids by Native Americans during the Colonial days. The museum is open seasonally on Wed and Sat from 10 a.m. to 4 p.m. and on Sun from 1 to 4 p.m. Admission is $5 for adults and $3 for children. A family plan, which must include at least one child, is available for $10. Discounted rates are also available, including

Island Wrangle

One of New England's more enduring disputes is the battle over who owns the **Portsmouth Naval Shipyard**, which is in Kittery, (according to Maine and the U.S. Supreme Court). But New Hampshire claims otherwise, and efforts to bring the shipyard under its jurisdiction erupt periodically and very often during election years.

The dispute dates back to Colonial days, when New Hampshire's border was set at the high-water mark of the Piscataqua River on the Maine side. New Hampshire claims the shipyard is on an island and, therefore, in New Hampshire territory. Nonsense, says Maine; it's an extension of the mainland and part of Maine. And the Pine Tree State has the U.S. Supreme Court to back it up: The country's highest judicial body ruled in favor of Maine in 2002 after New Hampshire filed suit over the matter.

It's more than an idle point of debate, however. New Hampshire workers who commute to the shipyard are required to pay Maine state income tax, which they resent mightily. (New Hampshire has no state income tax.) Wresting control of the shipyard would put an end to this "taxation without representation," according to Granite Staters. In one of the more colorful protests in recent memory, disgruntled workers hung a giant tea bag made of bed sheets from the bridge, declaring the start of a new Boston tea party to fight for their rights.

for AAA members. For more information call (207) 439-3080 or visit kitterymuseum.com. Be sure to check out the museum's variety of special events, including historical presentations and neighborhood block parties. To get there, drive north on I-95 and take exit 2 to ME 236. Follow the route south to the rotary, then take US 1 north. The museum is on the immediate right, next to Kittery Town Hall.

A pair of historic coastal forts along ME 103 on the Maine side of Portsmouth Harbor likewise invites exploration. ***Fort McClary*** has gone through a number of permutations and additions since the bluff was first fortified in 1715. The original fort was expanded and strengthened during the American Revolution, the War of 1812, the Civil War, and then again during the 1898 Spanish-American War. The most prominent building on the 27-acre site—located amid a labyrinth of earthworks—is a handsome hexagonal wooden blockhouse atop a fieldstone and granite foundation. Built in 1844, it has the distinction of being the last blockhouse constructed in the state. The unique building and the surrounding property are administered as a state historic site and are open from Memorial Day to Columbus Day, 10 a.m. to sunset (unless otherwise posted at the gate). Admission is $3 for adult Maine residents, $4 for adult nonresidents, $1 for senior nonresidents, $1 for children (ages 5-11), and free for children under 5 and seniors over 65. For more information call (207) 439-2845 or, in the off-season, (207) 490-4079.

TOP ANNUAL EVENTS

JANUARY

**Old Orchard Beach Lobster Dip
(to benefit Special Olympics Maine)**
Old Orchard beachfront, Mid-Jan
oldorchardbeachmaine.com
(207) 879-0489

MARCH

Maine Maple Sunday
Across Maine, fourth Sunday In March
mainemapleproducers.com

JUNE

Old Port Festival
Portland, early June
portlandmaine.com/old-port-festival
(207) 772-6828

Kennebunkport Festival
Kennebunkport downtown and
waterfront, early June
kennebunkportmainelodging.com/
kennebunkport-festival

Portland Schoonerfest and Regatta
Portland Harbor, late June
tallshipsportland.org
(207) 619-1842

**La Kermesse Franco-Americaine
Festival**
Biddeford, late June
lakermessefestival.com

South Berwick Strawberry Festival
Downtown Brunswick, late June
southberwickstrawberryfestival.com

JULY

Yarmouth Clam Festival
Yarmouth, "always the third Friday in
July!"
clamfestival.com
(207) 846-3984

Wells Harbor Fest
Wells, mid-July
wellstown.org
(207) 646-5113

Maine Open Farm Day
Across Maine, late July
maine.gov/dacf
(207) 287-7620

The remains of *Fort Foster* on nearby *Gerrish Island* (which is visible from Fort McClary) are of a more contemporary vintage. This early fort was expanded during World War II, when it was used to anchor one end of a massive net that stretched across Portsmouth Harbor as a means to keep inquisitive German submarines from prowling around the naval yard. The 90-acre former stronghold is now operated as a park by the town of Kittery. Explore its hulking concrete walls and towers, attractive pebbly beaches, and long fishing pier. Picnic tables and sweeping lawns provide dramatic views of the Portsmouth Harbor, nearby and far-off lighthouses and an old offshore Coast Guard station—which lends the whole area a fine sense of Gothic melodrama.

The town-run park is on the southern tip of Gerrish Island on the historically-titled Pocahontas Road, which is accessible from the mainland by crossing a small

AUGUST

Topsham Fair
Topsham Fairgrounds, early Aug
topshamfair.net
(207) 729-1943

Maine Highland Games
Topsham Fairgrounds, mid-Aug
mainehighlandgames.org

Brunswick Outdoor Arts Festival
Downtown Brunswick, mid-Aug
brunswickdowntown.org
(207) 729-4439

Wells Chili-Fest
Late Aug
wellschilifest.com
(207) 646-2451

SEPTEMBER

Maine Open Lighthouse Day
Weekends, throughout Maine
lighthousefoundation.org
(207) 594-4174

OCTOBER

Harvest on the Harbor
Portland waterfront, mid-Oct
harvestontheharbor.com

York HarvestFest
Throughout York, mid-Oct
yorkharvestfest.com
(207) 363-4422

Kennebunk HarvestFest
Throughout Kennebunk, mid-Oct
kennebunkmaine.us

NOVEMBER

Maine International Beer Festival
Thompson's Point in Portland, early Nov
visitportland.com

The Annual Lighting of the Nubble
Nubble Light in York, early Nov
nubblelight.org

bridge. Look for a sign on ME 103 just north of Kittery Point village, then make the first right over the bridge. The park is open May through Labor Day, 10 a.m. to 8 p.m. (weekends only in May and September). Admission is $10 per vehicle. Walk-in or bike-in rates for day use are $5 per adult and $1 per child. Contact the town public works department for more information at (207) 439-0333.

While in Kittery, don't forget to check out its restaurants, boutiques, cafés and art galleries. It's also worth meandering around just to view the gorgeous examples of Colonial and Georgian architecture—including the **Lady Pepperell House** on Kittery Point—and the local flair, such as colorful buoys serving as all manner of lawn ornaments and house adornments. Likewise, take a drive along the town's "gourmet mile" on US 1, where you'll come across a nice selection of organic markets.

Salmon Falls River Valley

It's both Maine's blessing and its curse: Out-of-towners, as well as many transplants, become so smitten with the coast that they overlook the inland areas (which ultimately comprise the bulk of Maine's land mass—just look at a map).

Don't make the same mistake.

A good place to start off is ***Vaughan Woods Memorial***, a 250-acre park 12 miles inland; it provides solace from the relative crowding and congestion of the coast. The park is located on a quiet, unspoiled stretch of the ***Salmon Falls River*** near ***South Berwick***. You'll find a quiet pine and hemlock grove near the parking area, and feel free to wander the trails down a gentle hill through hemlocks and maples to ***Cow Cove***. Where'd that name come from? This is where the first cattle in Maine were landed off a ship from Denmark in 1634 (Maine's first permanent settlement was just upstream). From a riverside bench, take the time to enjoy the picture-perfect view across the cove of what is arguably Maine's most outstanding example of Georgian architecture.

That splendid manor home across the way is the ***Hamilton House***. While it's open to the public, it is not accessible from along the shore, so as you leave the park, take the first left onto Vaughan Lane, then drive to the end and find a parking spot along the expansive rolling fields. Built in 1787 by Colonel Jonathan Hamilton—a successful West Indies trader and merchant from Portsmouth—his self-named house passed through various hands before being acquired by Historic New England in 1949. With its regal quality, wonderful proportions, and picturesque setting, this historical gem is sure to impress even those without a propensity for architecture or history. Its grounds are immaculately maintained and feature a hedge-enclosed garden complete with a sundial and classical statuary. Guided tours of the house, which are offered throughout the summer, reveal a fine collection of Chippendale and Sheraton furniture, as well as hand-painted wallpaper murals, hand-hooked rugs, and numerous other elegant period antiques.

To reach Vaughan Woods and the Hamilton House, turn onto US 101 (heading south toward New Hampshire) from ME 236, then make an immediate right. Vaughan Woods is 2.7 miles on the left. The park is open daily from 9 a.m. to sunset from Memorial Day to Labor Day (visitors are also welcome during daylight hours in the off season; they can park outside the gate and walk in). For more information call (207) 384-5160 or (207) 490-4079 (off-season). Hamilton House is open June 1 through Oct 15, Wed through Sun from 11 a.m. to 4 p.m. Guided tours are offered on the hour, the last beginning at 3 p.m. Admission is $10 for adults, $9 for seniors, and $5 for students. Entry is free for members of Historic New England. Call (207) 384-2454 or visit historic newengland.org.

As you head back into civilization in the center of **South Berwick**, be sure to stop at the **Sarah Orne Jewett House**, which presides over the town's main intersection. Jewett, who died in 1909, is widely regarded as one of Maine's most accomplished writers and has risen in stature in academia in recent years. Indeed, novelist Willa Cather once wrote that Jewett's *Country of the Pointed Firs* would take its place alongside Mark Twain's *Huckleberry Finn* and Nathaniel Hawthorne's *The Scarlet Letter* on the shelves of great American literature. Published in 1896, *Country of the Pointed Firs* is a collection of tales of Maine coastal life (Jewett summered in Martinsville in Knox County up north). It remains in print and is available in paperback in many Maine bookstores, as well as online, and is widely accepted as her greatest work. Jewett also wrote the novel *The Tory Lover*, which is set at the aforementioned Hamilton House. While it is no longer in print, copies can be found online and at many used booksellers.

The Jewett House, built in 1774, has been fully restored and furnished to reflect the period from 1849 to 1909, when the author lived and worked. It features classically Georgian detailing, including a wide staircase with a large landing and a presiding window overlooking the yard, fine early wood paneling, and examples of the flamboyant and colorful "flocked" style of 18th-century wallpaper. Like the Hamilton House, the Jewett House is owned by Historic New England (it was bequeathed in 1930 by the family), and offers tours during the summer.

Located at 101 Portland St., it is open June 1 through Oct 15, Fri through Sun from 11 a.m. to 5 p.m. (the last guided tour beginning at 4 p.m.) and 1st and 3rd Sat, Nov through May. Admission (which includes the guided tour) is $8 for adults, $7 for seniors, and $4 for students. As is the case with the Hamilton House, it is free for members of Historic New England. For more information call (207) 384-2454 or visit historicnewengland.org.

And don't forget to duck into the newer Greek Revival house next door, which serves as a visitor center and museum shop, and features rotating exhibits by local artists.

If you're planning to stay in town for a while, don't miss the unique performances put on at the **Hackmatack Playhouse**. Since 1972, the venue on 538 School St. has presented everything from *Fiddler on the Roof* to *Little Shop of Horrors*. Visit their website, hackmatack.org, for information on upcoming shows and pricing. And while you're enjoying the performances from local thespians, take a stroll out back to the **Hackmatack Buffalo Farm**. Located directly behind the playhouse, the bison roam a span of 30 acres. This happens to be some of the oldest cultivated land in the U.S., with the Guptill family (founders of the theater, a self-described "seacoast summer tradition") having raised crops here since the mid-1600s.

As you get your bearings en route back to the coast, consider a detour to the *Bauneg Beg Mountain Conservation Area* in *North Berwick*. The 89-acre site is located off Fox Farm Hill Road. Traced with roughly two miles of lightly-traveled trails (including a large bouldered area ominously referred to as "Devil's Den"), the summit of its tallest peak (866 feet) offers views as far as the grand Mount Washington in New Hampshire. Visit the Great Works Regional Land Trust website at gwrlt.org for maps and details.

Another nice diversion is *Mount Agamenticus*, a 692-foot hill that can be climbed by foot or car. It is located within the greater *Mount Agamenticus Conservation Region*, which consists of 10,000 contiguous acres spanning several towns. Long a navigational landmark for sailors, the small mountain bump has a diverse and intriguing history. *Aspinquid*, a revered Pawtucket Indian who died at the age of 94 in 1692, was said to be buried on the mound in a funeral ceremony that involved the sacrifice of more than 6,000 animals. In more recent years Agamenticus has served more prosaic functions as the "Big A" ski area in the 1960s and early '70s, as well as a site for many a radio tower. In the warmer months, its summit can be a bit cluttered for nature purists. But try to look past that by taking in the spectacular views—westward toward New Hampshire's White Mountains; eastward along the coast spanning from Cape Ann in Massachusetts up Maine's vast southern shoreline.

There is also a "learning lodge" at the hilltop that is open on weekends, 11 a.m. to 3 p.m., from Memorial Day through Columbus Day. If you're into hiking and biking, check out the numerous other trails in this conservation area; visit agamenticus.org for more details, directions, and weather and trail condition reports. The park and trails are open year-round from dawn to dusk. The summit access road gate is open April to Sept, 6 a.m. to sunset, and Oct through March, 7 a.m. to sunset.

The Yorks

Head on back east to the coast and you'll find yourself in the Yorks. There's technically only one York, which was named after the walled city in England and incorporated in 1652, making it Maine's second-oldest town (Kittery being the first). But it is composed of three areas with distinct identities and separate names: York Village, York Harbor, and York Beach. It doesn't take long to discover that each has its own particular personality.

Those with an affinity for history—both academics and amateurs alike—are invariably drawn to *York Village*, where they can find what is arguably one of the finest collections of historic buildings open to the public in the state of Maine. First settled around 1630, York Village is a peaceful town of tree-lined streets, with few intrusions from this modern age. Don't miss the ***Museums of Old York*** (formerly the Old York Historical Society), which maintains several buildings dotting the landscape between the York River and York Street, each with its own unique flavor and intriguing past.

mainefirsts

The first water-powered corn-grinding mills in New England were located in southern Maine. They were on the property of farmer John Mason, and in full operation by 1635.

Start at the visitor center located in the Parsons Education Center on 3 Lindsay Road; it's just off RT 1A and not far from the classically New England white-steepled First Parish Church. Here you can pick up maps of the area, explore an adjacent tavern and one-room schoolhouse (complete with original woodwork and student "graffiti" from the time), and view exhibits featuring artifacts from the organization's permanent collection. These include restored, elaborately-detailed bed hangings, portraits, and documents from the Colonial Period, as well as Queen Anne-style furniture.

Of particular note is the ***Old Gaol***, built in 1719 and considered to be the oldest jail in the U.S. While it might not look like it from the outside (it maintains a certain Colonial charm—far different than the prisons of today) it was erected to house both low-level criminals, such as debtors, as well as more hardened felons. Constructed of fieldstone walls more than 2 feet thick, it was in use until 1860, with its cells and dungeons located right next to the living quarters of the jailkeeper and his family. The building was saved by local

April Greening

The "greening" of Maine heralds many a local's favorite time of year: Spring (also marking a time to breathe a sigh of relief after successfully surviving another winter). Beginning sometime in late Apr and lasting into early May—weather always depending, of course—fields and meadows become positively verdant, many taking on a striking emerald green. Hillsides, meanwhile, brown and barren from the dormant months, come alive with strips of pastel green as poplar leaves unfurl with the strengthening sunlight. It's an ephemeral visual treat; soon enough more powerful shades of green take over as maple, oak, and beech trees leaf out, and the underlying grass grows taller and darkens with age. But those first, tentative greens of early spring are what many a Mainer dreams about during the long winter. Nothing else in nature equals it in the state of Maine.

preservationists as a "museum for colonial relics" in 1900, and visitors today can learn about the criminals incarcerated here and the crimes they committed.

Boasting a less seedy past is the **Emerson–Wilcox House** next door, a post-road tavern originally built in the mid-18th century. Many additions were tacked on over the years; a knowledgeable guide can help you trace the history of early American architecture.

Meanwhile, along the York River stands the **John Hancock warehouse and wharf**, once owned by the famous signer of the Declaration of Independence whose name has become synonymous with the very signature itself. In the words of one historian, Hancock was "more successful in politics than in business," and visitors can explore that notion at this wharf, restored in 1950 after a long and rather lackluster history. It holds the distinction of being one of York's only remaining commercial buildings from the Colonial period. Just across the waterway is the completely furnished and recently renovated **Elizabeth Perkins House**. Originally home to many ferrymen and sea captains, it is named for Mary Perkins and her daughter, Elizabeth, who summered here starting in 1898. Maintaining the Perkins' decorating style and belongings, it is one of the most complete and finest examples of Colonial Revival architecture on display in the region.

For an additional dose of history, take a respectful walk around the **Old Burying Ground**, one of Maine's oldest cemeteries. Small and pastoral and flanked by tumbling stone walls, it is on the property of the **First Parish Church**—itself dating to 1747 and having endured a number of transitions (including being lifted up, set back 20 feet, and turned to face the road). The cemetery is the final resting place of some of the town's earliest and most notable residents, and showcases the evolution of gravestone carving in the 18th and 19th centuries.

Intrigued by the paranormal? Seek out the unusual grave of **Mary Nasson**, who died on August 18, 1774. Although her tombstone itself is decidedly benign and features a simple epitaph describing her as a loving mother and wife, it presides over a giant rectangular slab covering the area where her body would have been buried. Some argue that this was a means to keep the purported witch and exorcist—said to have attracted her own murder of crows—from rising out of her grave. More likely, it was what's known as a "wolf stone," intended to ensure that bodies were left undisturbed by rooting wild or domestic animals. (At one time they would have been found all over the cemetery, but have since been removed or, more likely, repurposed when building materials became scarce.) Either way, it is a rare and unique find.

As you make your way around Old York, you can set your own pace of exploration, wandering either by foot or car with self-guided tours; there are also limited guided tours at the Emerson-Wilcox and Perkins properties. Call ahead for schedules.

The Old York buildings are open Tue through Sat, 10 a.m. to 5 p.m., and Sun, 1 to 5 p.m., late May through early Sept, and the same hours on Thurs, Fri, Sat, and Sun through early Oct. Tickets may be purchased at any of the properties. Cost to visit one building is $8 for adults and $5 for children under 16, and all-day tickets for all buildings are $15 for adults and $10 for children under 16. For more information call (207) 363-1756 or visit oldyork.org.

While you're in the village center, be sure to check out the array of boutiques, including **Woods to Goods** (woodstogoods.com), a unique store featuring items such as ship models, decorative anchors, and even heirloom-quality furniture, crafted by inmates from the state's prisons.

didyouknow?

If you unkinked and unfurled Maine's coastline, it would span a straight line of roughly 3,500 miles. Yet a mere 35 miles of those are beach—the majority of which are located in southern Maine.

Heading downstream from York Village (or driving east on US 1A), you'll come to **York Harbor**, which is slightly more modern when it comes to both tone and architecture. A great way to take in the scenery and stretch your legs is with a stroll along the waterfront walking path.

Meanwhile, if you head south on ME 103, you'll find one of the area's more quirky attractions: **Wiggly Bridge**. It's said to be the smallest suspension bridge in the world, and those who venture across it will testify that it lives up to its name. Park along the road and follow the path across the footbridge to enjoy a quiet walk through the woods. The trail loops back along Barrel Mill Pond; more ambitious hikers may continue on, traversing dirt roads headed back towards Lindsay Road near Hancock Wharf in York Village.

Heading in the other direction will take you along York Harbor's waterfront to Harbor Beach, where the modern **Stage Neck Inn** resort dominates a bluff overlooking the harbor's mouth. You'll find that the path is narrow and quiet, a world removed from the present day. If you're eager for more history, visit the **Sayward–Wheeler House**, another property owned and maintained by Historic New England. Its well-maintained grounds are the first you cross when heading east on the path off ME 103. The fine merchant's home was built in the 1760s and offers a magnificent view of the harbor. Owned by captain, judge, and businessman Jonathan Sayward, it is filled with items such as Chippendale-style chairs and a grandfather clock said to have been Sayward's most cherished possession, as well as chinaware he brought back from the successful 1745 battle against the French at Louisbourg during King George's

War. The building is open June 1 through Oct 15 on the 2nd and 4th Sat of each month. Tours are held on the hour from 11 a.m. to 4 p.m. Admission is $5 for adults, $4 for seniors, and $2.50 for students. For more information call (207) 384-2454 or visit historicnewengland.org.

If you're enjoying the scenery thus far, continue past Harbor Beach to the **Cliff Walk**, a dramatic shoreline trail that hugs rocky crags and provides excellent views of the harsh coastline and the splendid 19th-century summer homes overlooking it. The roughly mile-long trail crosses private land but is open to the public within certain limitations (that is, no picnicking, no bus tours, no boisterous activity). The trail, which may be rough going for those with unsure footing, also provides access to several small pebbly beaches. It starts at the end of Harbor Beach Road, where you'll find limited parking.

Northward up the coast, **York Beach** is a pleasant seaside town—but you'll find it is more raucous, less polished, and more tourist-oriented than other parts of the York area. Even so, it has a more laid-back feeling than other popular stretches of beach in the southern region. The area just off the beach retains a honky-tonk feel, with neon and fried dough aplenty; although this has been tempered a bit by recent gentrification efforts.

For an additional dose of mainstream fun, just a short walk from the beach is **York's Wild Kingdom** a combined zoo and amusement park. It has a variety of wild animals from around the world, a 5,500-square-foot butterfly garden, a selection of amusement park rides, including a bumper car pavilion and a small roller coaster, batting cages, and a mini golf course. General admission (including the zoo and all rides) costs $23.75 for adults, $18.50 for youths (4-12), and $5.25 for children (3 and under). Ticket packages are also available for separate admission to rides or the zoo. The park is open May through Sept. For specific hours, call (207) 363-4922 or visit yorkswildkingdom.com.

For a more authentic encounter with finned, furred, and clawed natives of the area, check out the **Center for Wildlife** on **Cape Neddick**. Founded in 1986, the private nonprofit provides medical care and sanctuary to sick, injured, and orphaned wildlife—including hawks, hummingbirds, waterfowl, beaver, porcupines, frogs, snakes, and toads (to name a few)—until they are ready to be released back into the wild. Visitors can pick up a map and venture around on their own, or participate in regular guided tours. The facility also offers regular education programs, walks and "myth-busting" events, and hosts monthly volunteer workdays. The Center is open from 9 a.m. to 5 p.m. every day, including weekends and holidays. Tours are offered on Tue, Sat, and Sun in the summer months. Suggested donation is $5 per person; all money received goes back to animal care and rescue. Visit thecenterforwildlife.org for details and to take a virtual tour.

The world-famous Nubble Light is close by (be on the lookout for its quintessential profile as you drive up US 1A), flanked by **Long Sands Beach** to the south and **Short Sands Beach** to the north. As you'll find at many of the beaches in the state, parking can tend to be problematic; keep an eye out for metered spots.

Ogunquit and Wells Area

North of York Beach you'll find **Ogunquit**, a pleasant seaside town that was "discovered" by urban artists from New York and Boston. Over the past century, it has been transformed into quite the art mecca, abounding with galleries, restaurants, boutiques, and self-styled "resorts." To its credit, it has managed to retain much of its character—but be warned that during the peak season you'll find yourself stewing in traffic and dodging crowds. A trip in the "shoulder season" of spring and fall is positively lovely and relaxing; this is when you'll also find great lodging and dining deals.

The best way to experience Ogunquit is to park your car, leave it where it is for the duration of your stay, and opt instead to travel by foot or bicycle. Likewise, the best way to see and experience the ocean is along **Marginal Way**, a winding footpath donated to the town in 1923 by a farmer who used it to usher his cattle back and forth to summer pasture. These days, you're not likely to see too many cows, but you're sure to come upon a fair number of hikers and sunbathers. Get up early or stick around 'til dusk to avoid "gridlock" on the trail.

Parking can be found near the town police station on Cottage Street (there's a fee charged). More ambitious walkers could make a day of it by parking farther up the coast at **Footbridge Beach** (turn off US 1 on Ocean Street) and ramble south along the sandy edge for about a mile to the main beach. Crossing the bridge on Beach Street into Ogunquit's center, feel free to explore the eating options, then pick the main pathway up again on Shore Road (across from Seacastles Resort). From here, the route meanders away from the sandy strand and along the twisting, rocky shoreline, with well-placed benches available for resting, reading, or relaxing. In some places you'll find yourself surrounded by wild roses or walking beneath a delicate canopy of cedar trees. Take the time to scramble down to the shore's edge, where you can explore tide pools and the rugged coastal geology.

The pathway ends at the picturesque and well-protected harbor of **Perkins Cove**, what some consider the loveliest little harbor in Maine. As such, it is a popular tourist destination, boasting more than its fair share of jewelry stores, crafts shops, and restaurants. As with many other waterside locales, parking is a perpetual problem. Be sure to investigate the pedestrian footbridge crossing the harbor entrance, the only double-leaf draw-footbridge in the U.S. If you're lucky, you'll see a tall-masted sailboat and get a unique-to-Ogunquit experience: Should it need to enter or exit the cove, it will blast its horn to alert the harbormaster, his deputy, or whoever else happens to be nearby. Don't hesitate to help out by raising the narrow bridge with the aid of a crank and a series of buttons; you'll be participating in a longtime maritime tradition.

But a trip to Ogunquit wouldn't be complete without taking in its cultural side. Check out a show in the heart of town at *John Lane's Ogunquit Playhouse* (ogunquitplayhouse.org), which presents musical theater seasonally out of its retro-styled 1937 building on Main Street. Or visit the *Ogunquit Museum of American Art*, tucked away on the narrow and windy Shore Road. The only museum in Maine dedicated exclusively to American art, it features a robust collection from notable Maine artists such as Marsden Hartley, Peggy Bacon, and Edward Betts, as well as rotating exhibits. But perhaps its most striking feature is its expansive outdoor sculpture garden; its impeccably landscaped property rolling down to the sea is pockmarked with granite breaching whales,

From the Chippendale-Quality to the Downright "Chipped"

The 50-mile stretch of US 1 between York and Scarborough is a mecca of sorts for shoppers who aren't satisfied unless they come away with something a half-century old (or older). There are some two dozen antiques shops along this route, ranging from the ineffably classy to the kitschy.

On the higher end of the scale is the wonderful **R. Jorgensen Antiques**, which displays fine examples of early American and European furniture in an impeccably restored 1685 home with a modern outbuilding. The shop is open Mon through Sat from 10 a.m. to 5 p.m., and Sun noon to 5 p.m. It is located at 502 Post Rd. (US 1) in Wells. For more information call (207) 646-9444 or visit rjorgensen.com.

Another great spot for browsing—albeit with a selection less upscale than that at Jorgensen's—is farther north at **Antiques USA**, on US 1 in Arundel. Dozens of dealers stock this sprawling, Walmart–sized shop with all manner of items, from sublime to silly. This is a must-visit if you like rooting around for undiscovered deals. It's open all year (except major holidays) from 10 a.m. to 5 p.m. Call (207) 985-7766 or visit antiquesusamaine.com.

At the northern end of this antiques row is the fine **Centervale Farm** on US 1 in Scarborough. Unlike many other US 1 shops, which are mini-malls offering merchandise from various dealers, Centervale is a single but sizable shop. Its offerings include early American and Mission-style furniture, along with a whole slew of other collectibles. It's open Thur through Sat 10 a.m. to 4 p.m. year-round. For more information call (207) 883-3443.

entwined marble figures and "dancers" of welded steel. It is worth the visit simply to see the unique juxtaposition (and, in some cases, blending) of nature and art. The museum is open May 1 through Oct 31, seven days a week from 10 a.m. to 5 p.m. Visit ogunquitmuseum.org or call (207) 646-4909.

Traveling north out of Ogunquit, you'll quickly hit **Wells**. The self-described "friendliest town in Maine" bustles like many hamlets that clutter the southern Maine coast; in the summer months especially, it is difficult to find respite here.

Difficult, but not impossible. Seek out the **Wells Reserve at Laudholm**, whose coastal marsh and forested uplands are managed both as a wildlife sanctuary and for scientific research. Born of a public-private partnership between the National Estuarine Research Reserve and the Laudholm Trust, the property features 7 miles of trails traversing 2,250 acres of salt marsh, a quiet barrier beach, forest, and fields.

Laudholm Farm provides the setting for an enchanting walk through not only complex ecosystems, but a long-gone era. Once maintained as a summer residence by prominent New England railroad tycoon George C. Lord, this historic saltwater farm was saved in perpetuity as a Trust in 1986, thanks to donations from nearly 2,500 people. Its centerpiece is a majestic Victorian farmhouse with graceful barns and outbuildings. The farm complex perches on a gentle rise amid open fields, providing views down the coast. Nature guides and trail maps are available in the visitor center, located inside the farmhouse. Be sure to pick up an interpretive pamphlet for the *Knight Trail*, which provides an introduction to the local habitat, flora, and fauna. Birders will be delighted with the mix of terrain here: Some 250 avian species have been observed just within the reserve itself. The site also offers a wide range of guided walking tours, kayak tours, summer day camps for children, and educational and historical programs. Find a complete list, as well as loads more info about the property at wellsreserve.org.

From Memorial Day weekend through mid-Oct, admission is $5 for adults (over 16), $1 for children (ages 6-16), and free for those under 6. Trails are always open 7 a.m. to sunset. The visitor center is open from Memorial Day weekend through mid-Oct, every day from 10 a.m. to 4 p.m.; and in April, May, Oct, and Nov, Mon through Fri, 10 a.m. to 4 p.m. You're on your own from December to March, when the center is closed. To reach the Reserve, turn right off US 1 onto Laudholm Farm Road at the blinking light, just after the Maine Diner. Turn left at the fork, then make the next right at the farm's entrance.

Located just north of Laudholm Farm is the expansive *Rachel Carson National Wildlife Refuge*. It is named for the crusading biologist, ahead-of-her-time-environmentalist, and author of the landmark *Silent Spring*, who spent many of her summers in Maine exploring tidal waters. Appropriately enough, Carson, who died in 1964, worked for the U.S. Fish and Wildlife Service, which manages the property. The refuge was established in 1966 to protect salt marshes and estuaries for migratory birds. It is a work in progress made up of several parcels of land; the hope is that it will one day span 14,600 protected acres in York and Cumberland counties.

Starting at the refuge headquarters on Port Road, you'll find a mile-long nature trail offering a good introduction to the salt-marsh ecosystem. The *Carson Trail* skirts the edge of a pleasant marsh, with informative educational stations along the way. Stop at the main kiosk near the parking area to pick up a free trail map and brochure. For more information, contact refuge headquarters at (207) 646-9226 or visit fws.gov/refuge/rachel_carson.

The Kennebunks

Kennebunkport embraces its image as a slumbering, upscale seaside town long known for its elegant inns, bed-and-breakfasts, tony waterfront area, and numerous art galleries. It secured its vibrant, moneyed status in the first half of the 19th century, when it was host to a booming shipbuilding trade that transformed it into one of the wealthiest towns in New England. Later, it was ultimately styled as an "ideal vacation spot": In the late 1800s, as the railroad boom facilitated travel north from Boston, a group of well-to-do locals and out-of-towners formed the Kennebunkport Seashore Company, buying up more than 700 acres of farmland that hugged the coastline and building hotels, resorts, and spas along it.

Today, the area remains a top vacationing destination—but it is perhaps most famous for its connection with the Bush family; namely former Presidents George H.W. Bush and George W. Bush. Although the Bushes have been part of the Kennebunkport social scene for generations, their favorite summering spot wasn't illuminated in the national spotlight until the elder Bush was elected president in 1988. The thenceforth-nicknamed "Summer White House" became host to such political luminaries as Margaret Thatcher and Vladimir Putin. The family still summers at the dramatic "Bush Compound," as it's also called, which stands stately on *Walker Point*, a sliver of land jutting out into the Gulf of Maine and named for family patriarchs and builders, David Davis Walker and George H. Walker.

The Bush element continues to draw tourists to Kennebunkport—the property itself is guarded by Secret Service officers, but visitors can snap photos from a vantage point across the bay with the picturesque property as a backdrop. Whether the political family is in town or not, though, be prepared for cramped streets in the warmer months; in particular, available parking can tend

St. Anthony's Franciscan Monastery and Guest House

In 1947, Lithuanian Franciscan friars fleeing war-ravaged Europe acquired the 66-acre Rogers estate. Located at 28 Beach Ave. and named "Fairfield," it was designed by Buffalo, New York, architects Edward Broadhead Green and William Sydney Wicks. In addition to its centerpiece Tudor manse, **St. Anthony's Franciscan Monastery and Guest House** features grounds landscaped in the English garden tradition by Fredrick Law Olmsted and Associates.

Today the friars occupy the house, but the gardens and trails are open to the public year-round, from sunrise to sunset. All are welcome to enjoy the quiet serenity of riverside walking paths, woodlands, and outdoor chapels. A walking tour brochure is available at the front desk of the Guest House, and a gift shop below the chapel is open from March 1 to Dec 31, 10 a.m. to noon and 1 to 4 p.m. If you're looking for overnight accommodations, rooms are available in the Guest House, three accompanying Tudor-style buildings, and a single-story cottage. Prices are listed as inexpensive. You can find all the expected amenities here, as well as an outdoor saltwater pool. Be sure to book early, as spots fill up quickly. For more information call (207) 967-4865 or visit franciscanguesthouse.com. For details on the friary, visit framon.net.

to be nonexistent near Dock Square in the center of town, so check along side streets. (And snag whatever available spot you can get!)

As you start out on Main Street looking down toward Dock Square, you'll find **White Columns**. Constructed in 1853, this impressive, Greek Revival home is named for the dramatic columns that wrap around its two-story, open-air front porch. It was home to the same family for 130 years, who continually maintained its mid-19th century look, feel, and furnishings as they passed it down from generation to generation. That proviso continued when it was bequeathed to the local historical society in 1983—ancestor Elizabeth Nott stipulated that it was not to be changed. And it hasn't: Serving as an architectural time capsule, it features its original Victorian-era French carpeting, furniture, and intricate French wallpaper.

The stately building also hosts the **_First Families Kennebunkport Museum_**, where you can learn not only about the Bush dynasty, but the numerous other merchants, sea captains, shipbuilders, and vacationers who have called the seaside town both permanent and temporary home. Likewise explore the philanthropic efforts of the town's most famous summer residents in the new installation, "The Bush Family: A Legacy of Giving."

Eager for more history? Head on down to the **_Pasco Center_** on North Street, the headquarters of the **_Kennebunkport Historical Society_**. There, you can see a working 19th-century-era blacksmith shop; a small clapboard circa-1850 shipwright's office (the last remaining in town); and the studio of Louis D. Norton, a Paris-trained artist who settled here and painted murals on the walls of the landscape around him.

The Pasco Center is open year round, Mon through Fri, 9 a.m. to 3 p.m. White Columns, meanwhile, is open Memorial Day through Columbus Day, Mon through Sat, 10 a.m. to 4 p.m. Guided tours last thirty to forty minutes and are offered on the hour, the last of the day leaving at 3 p.m. Admission is $10 for adults and children under 12 are free. Tickets include admission to the First Families Museum. The historical society also offers historic walking tours of Kennebunkport by appointment only and typically geared toward groups of eight or more. Cost is $10 per person, or $15 when combined with a ticket for the house tour. For more information, visit kennebunkporthistoricalsociety .com or call (207) 967-2751.

Looking for a more rustic experience? You can find that at *Sandy Pines Campground*—sort of. Located just a few minutes from both Dock Square and the beautiful Goose Rocks Beach, it offers what's known as "glamping"— several steps removed from traditional camping and oh-so-Kennebunkian. Picture what are essentially palatial tents, huts, and wheeled "camp carriages" outfitted with lighting, air conditioning, mini-fridges and bath amenities. Visit sandypinescamping.com or call (207) 967-2483 for details or to book a spot.

Tom's Better Tube of Toothpaste

As the story goes, when US troops invaded Panama in 1989 to oust dictator and on-again, off-again American ally Manuel Noriega, they found a tube of Tom's of Maine toothpaste in the disgraced general's palace. Such is the wide-reaching influence (and appeal) of the Maine company's unique products.

Founded in 1970 by Philadelphia natives Tom and Kate Chappell, the socially responsible subsidiary of Colgate-Palmolive (since 2006) specializes in a growing array of personal care items that are made without artificial ingredients. The Chappells introduced the first natural toothpaste in the US market; today the company's offerings have expanded to deodorant, shampoo, lip balm, and baby care items. But its enduring legacy is its toothpaste, which is available in expected flavors such as peppermint and spearmint—and the not-so-expected, like herbal mint, cinnamint, and fennel. It can take a little getting used to at first, but many a commoner—and a dictator, as well—finds it hard to go back to traditional brands once they've tried Tom's. Find Tom's products in stores across the state or at tomsofmaine.com (which features a locator tool). Want to see its team in action? Tom's offers tours of its green, state-of-the-art factory in Sanford (just a few miles inland from the Kennebunks). Reservations are required, so call ahead at (207) 985-2944.

Just north of Kennebunkport, on the quaint-sounding Log Cabin Road, you'll run into the **Seashore Trolley Museum**. It's a lively, thriving scrap yard where still-operating streetcars wind their way through heaps of rusting metal and old railroad ties; feel free to wander and wonder.

Founded in 1939, the trolley museum is home to the world's largest collection of streetcars, and is also the largest and oldest-known museum dedicated to public transportation. You'll see streetcars from a number of towns in Maine that once had trolley systems; others have found their way here from as far away as Glasgow, Budapest, and Nagasaki, as well as New Orleans and San Francisco (where they are as synonymous with the city identity as the lighthouse is to Maine). There are about 200 or so cars on the lot, many of them restored and maintained by a cadre of 200 volunteers. It's nostalgic, to be sure, and you can revel in the experience by wandering around the hulking giants by foot, or by taking unlimited rides on a 1.5-mile interpretive railway boasting authentically restored cars.

Be sure to also visit the **Town House Shop**, where new streetcars are overhauled when they arrive (anything from welding, to upholstering, to electrical work). Exhibits are also scattered throughout the visitor center, barns, and the vehicles themselves, and the gift shop offers an unrivaled selection of postcards, books, and everything else streetcar-related.

The Museum is open from 10 a.m. to 5 p.m. daily from May through Oct; from 10 a.m. to 5 p.m., weekends only, in early May and late October; and on Fri, Sat, and Sun the first two weekends in December. The last trolley of the day departs at 4:15 p.m. Admission is $12 for adults, $10 for seniors (over age 60), $9.50 for youths (ages 6-15), and $5 for children (ages 3-5). Children under 3 get in free. For more information visit trolleymuseum.org or call (207) 967-2712.

The handsome inland town of **Kennebunk**, located 3.5 miles from the port on ME 35 and ME 9A, offers a slower pace and less of a seasonal ebb and flow. Between the port and the town, on Summer Street, you'll pass through the **Kennebunk Historic District** with its fine examples of grand 19th-century architecture. Be sure to pull over and take in the flamboyant grandeur of the "wedding cake house," a bright yellow building with ornate Gothic-style flourishes that looks just as its name would suggest. So the story goes, a local, newly married sea captain rushed to sea before his new bride received a proper wedding cake. Upon his return, he had the house built as a means to appease his new wife. Don't worry: As you're driving through this welcoming town with its otherwise Colonial and Victorian architecture, you can't miss it.

Also downtown, on 117 Main St., you'll find **The Brick Store Museum**. Formerly Lord's Store, the building is unique in the fact that it was crafted in 1825 from locally-kilned brick—as opposed to Maine timber, which was (and remains) plentiful. Edith Cleaves Barry founded the museum in 1936, running it at first as a tiny operation confined to the second floor. It has since expanded down the block, and provides a modest, intimate look at the arts, history, and culture of the Kennebunks and the surrounding area. Its permanent collection includes maritime paintings, ship models, and early-19th-century portraits and furnishings; there are also three to four special rotating exhibits a year. The Brick Store holds the distinction of being one of the only privately-funded museums in the state that is open year round (while so many others close up shop as locals fly south or hunker down for the winter). Hours are Tues, Thurs, and Fri from 10 a.m. to 5 p.m.; Wed from 10 a.m. to 6 p.m.; Sat from 10 a.m. to 4 p.m.; and Sun from 12 to 4 p.m. Admission is $7 for adults, $6 for seniors, and $3 for children (ages 6-16) and students with a valid ID. There are also family and family weekend passes available, at $20 and $10, respectively. Be sure to ask about special discount rates. For more information, visit brickstoremuseum .org or call (207) 985-4802.

One of southern Maine's most idyllic beaches is located a short drive south. You can reach **Parsons Beach** by driving down its self-named road, a lovely ride in and of itself—it is flanked by Maple trees and feels a world apart from the more crowded areas. This white-sanded expanse has been passed down through the Parsons family for generations, and they have fought to keep it open to the public. Admittedly, it isn't the best beach for swimming (it's a bit rocky because this is where the 30-mile-long Mousam River flows into the sea), but it's a gorgeous and welcoming spot, hard to beat in this region when it comes to relaxing, reading, or just letting oneself go with the flow of the summer. To find it, head south on ME 9 from Kennebunkport; you'll soon cross a marsh and the Mousam River. Make your first left (Parson's Beach Road) and continue to the end. There's limited parking, so you may have to walk a little (and please be respectful of any "Resident Parking Only" signs).

If you're looking for more of a woodsy oasis, you don't have to go far to find it. The aptly named **Secret Garden**, property of the Kennebunk Land Trust, is hidden away behind the town's Evergreen Cemetery. Follow Summer Street 2 miles from the intersections of US 1 and ME 35 in the center of town; enter at the main gate, drive to the rear and park near an old woods road. A 1.5-mile trail leads you through forest, boggy areas, and sun-dappled groves carpeted with ferns. Another option is **Wonder Brook/Murphy Preserve**, composed of adjacent town and trust-owned properties totaling roughly 80 acres. The 2.5 miles of trail are picturesque and wooded, with rustic brook and river crossings throughout. It is a welcome haven to pileated woodpeckers and warblers, so be sure to keep an eye out (and ear open) during the migratory season. Once you get walking, you'd never know this beautiful, peaceful property is a mere half-mile from downtown (just at the end of Plummer Lane). For details and maps (of these and other Trust properties), visit kennebunklandtrust.org.

Old Orchard Beach and Vicinity

Located near the "twin towns" (they're really cities, but we'll get to that later) of Saco and Biddeford, *Old Orchard Beach* isn't quite what you'd call a hidden gem. Still, it's worth a quick diversion for its lively, honky tonk atmosphere. Thousands of locals and out-of-towners flock to this beach town and its 7 miles of sandy oceanfront every year; it is particularly popular for pilgrimages by French Canadians, so you're likely to hear just as much French spoken here as English. A mini Jersey Shore of sorts, it is best known for its profusion of amusements, dizzying rides, greasy foods, and the perennial mating dance on display among its younger crowds. One of the attractions just off the beach is *Palace Playland*, dating to 1902 and claiming to be New England's largest pinball and video arcade. If you're an aficionado of the garish, plan to stroll after dark, when the beachfront fully displays its brilliant neon plumage and the Ferris wheel rotates in silhouette against the night sky.

Just a mile to the south of Old Orchard on ME 9, you'll come to a suburb with a decidedly different disposition. *Ocean Park* was founded in 1881 by the *Centennial Conference of Free Will Baptists* as an educational summer resort. Also known as Chautauqua-by-the-sea, it offers a non-denominational, interfaith setting modeled after the self-same adult-education movement of the late 19th and early 20th centuries. (Bear-riding preservationist president Theodore Roosevelt even called Chautauqua the "most American thing in America.")

In a stately grove of pines several blocks from the ocean, you'll find the three pleasing buildings dating to the colony's early days. Clustered on the north side of Temple Street near the intersection of Royal Street, is the *Temple*,

Carousel Lost

Until 1996 Old Orchard Beach was famous for its antique carousel, which was the centerpiece of Palace Playland, the amusement park just off the beach. The vintage 1910 merry-go-round was built by the world-famous Philadelphia Toboggan Company (one of the oldest existing amusement ride manufacturers in the world) and provided endless hours of amusement for the very young, the very old, and pretty much everyone in between. But in the end, the attraction succumbed to the mania for collecting. With skyrocketing prices for circus memorabilia, its owners sold off its handsome, hand-carved wooden horses. Happily the old building remains and is now home to a new herd of characteristic and vibrantly colored fiberglass animals.

an octagonal wooden structure of white clapboard and green shutters representing a once highly popular architectural style. Based on plans purchased for $27, it was dedicated in August 1881 and has been in continuous use by congregants ever since. Today, the Ocean Park Association continues to offer a variety of spiritual, cultural, educational, and recreational offerings in the Chautauqua tradition. Stop by its visitor center at 14 Temple Ave. for more details. Its administrative offices are open year-round, 9 a.m. to 4 p.m., Mon through Fri. Visit oceanpark.org or call (207) 934-9068.

Nearby, the small former mill cities of **Biddeford** and Saco are revitalizing downtowns that once hummed with industrial activity. Visitors can learn about this rich history at the **Biddeford Mills Museum**, which formerly housed Pepperell Manufacturing. The once sizable textile operation was sited along the banks of the Saco River as a means to harness the power of the 136-mile-long waterway—which ultimately flows down from the White Mountains in New Hampshire into and across Maine before joining with the Atlantic Ocean. Guided tours explore the expansive building and its unique underground canals, focusing on the industry, history, and day-to-day lives of its hundreds of workers. The roughly two-hour historic tours are offered from June to Sept on Thurs and Sat at 10 a.m. They meet in front of **Portland Pie Company** on 40 Main St. at 9:45 a.m. and are limited to the first 25 registrants. Reserve a spot by calling (207) 284-8520. Cost is $15 for adults, $12 for seniors (age 65 and over), and $10 for students under age 18. Visit biddefordmillsmuseum.org for more information.

Meanwhile, **Saco** hosts its self-named **Saco Museum**, arguably one of the region's best small museums. Displays highlight early life in southern Maine, with a particular emphasis on the late 18th and early 19th centuries. Founded in 1870, it features a colonial kitchen, an 18th-century bedroom, and an early printing press. It also boasts an exceptional collection of paintings including portraits; examples of the early technique of silhouetting that essentially served as a "snapshot" of a person before the camera was invented; and period items such as a mahogany clock and decorative fire buckets that were lined along the streets should flames erupt (an ever-present danger). The museum is located at 371 Main St. in Saco. Admission is $5 for adults, $3 for seniors, and $2 for students (with valid ID) and children (ages 7-18); children under 7 get in free. Hours are Tues, Wed, and Thurs from noon to 4 p.m.; Fri from noon to 8 p.m.; Sat from 10 a.m. to 4 p.m.; and Sun (June to Dec only) from noon to 4 p.m. Admission is free every Fri night between 4 to 8 p.m.. For more information visit sacomuseum.org or call (207) 283-3861.

The twin cities are also home to a number of beaches (along both the ocean and the banks of the Saco), as well as two vintage water and amusement parks: *Funtown Splashtown USA* (funtownsplashtownusa.com), which has roots in the 1960s, and the 40-year-old *Aquaboggan* (aquaboggan.com), which identifies itself as Maine's original water park.

Not to be missed for a stay, an afternoon visit, or just a nice, leisurely, scenic drive, is *Biddeford Pool*. Year-round residents try to keep "the Pool" a secret—and understandably so. There's only one way in and out of this snug beachfront village: ME 208, which twists and turns as it runs along the coast and past welcoming cottages and bungalows in the cedar-shingled style. The beach and small town center are largely underdeveloped and feature few amenities, so bring all the gear and snacks you think you'll need. And keep hyper-vigilant when driving, as pedestrians and cyclists rule the roads here. Be sure to take in the subtle grandeur of the beachfront *Marie Joseph Spiritual Center*, which offers one-day, weekend and week-long religious retreats (more on that at mariejosephspiritual.org). Take the time for a stroll (once you can find a parking spot, that is) both around the quiet streets and neighborhoods and along the water. At the very tip of the Pool you'll find *East Point Audubon Sanctuary*. Its short but stunning scenic trail around the point's perimeter offers a unique and rare view of this section of coast; the striated rocks greet the crashing waves, and *Wood Island Lighthouse* stands guard off in the distance. You'll have the opportunity to encounter a variety of shore birds, so bring binoculars. Especially in this fast-paced world, it is a welcoming spot to refresh and unwind, and take in the beauty and serenity of the natural realm.

Inland York County

Since the majority of visitors cluster along York County's coastal boundaries, it's fair to say that some of the region's best hidden gems lie inland. Heading west, travelers pass through the mostly rural and residential towns of Sanford, Alfred, and Waterboro. The latter is home to the *Taylor/Frey/Leavitt House Museum*, located on 6 Old Alfred Rd not far from the intersection with the busy Sokokis Trail. It was built in 1850 for its wealthy namesake merchant James Leavitt (who was also a paterfamilias, fathering 12 children). Although classically simple outside, the two-story Greek Revival home is notable for its dramatic interior finishes; these include elaborate molding, wallpaper, and wood-graining, as well as carved corner blocks that are rare to New England homes. Meanwhile, its barn and ell contain antique cobbler, optician, and barber shops, and its outbuildings (among the quaintest and most adorable historical sites you're likely to find anywhere in the state) include an 1817 Deering schoolhouse and a 19th century blacksmith shop. Run by the Waterboro Historical Society and listed on the National Register of Historic Places, the museum is open on Saturdays from late May through late Sept, from 9 a.m. to noon. For more information, call (207) 247-5878.

For a more immersive historical experience, head on up ME 5 toward Limerick, then follow ME 11 into the small town of Newfield. Here, in this wooded valley near the New Hampshire border, is the *19th Century Curran Homestead Village at Newfield*, (formerly Willowbrook at Newfield). The sprawling historic village offers visitors a glimpse of late-19th-century Maine; it contains more than three dozen structures, including both original homes and replicas of early buildings. Its collections are extensive and broad, with virtually everything originating from within 100 miles of the museum. This includes an extensive number of carriages and horse-drawn sleighs, a tandem bicycle, an opulent 1849 Concord coach commissioned by a Bath sea captain, and an 1894 Armitage–Herschell carousel (still operating) with its original organ. The centerpiece of the village is the 1835 *William Duggin House*, furnished in the busy Victorian style preferred by better families everywhere in the late 19th century. There is also a tiny one-room post office, country store, a print shop, carriage house, granary and cider mill, an 1890s basketball court, and a working 18th century hand-cranked "washing machine."

Owned and run as Willowbrook since 1970, the museum recently changed hands to Curran, which also operates a historic village at 372 Fields Pond Rd. in Orrington. As such, its hours are subject to change, so be sure to call ahead at (207) 205-4849 or visit its website at curranhomestead.org. Admission is $12 for adults and $10 for seniors and veterans. Children under 18 get in free. Visitors get a free ride on the carousel with admission.

Heading back up ME 11 to ME 5 will bring travelers into *Cornish*, a delightful little town that has experienced a Renaissance over the last decade. ("Cozy" and "picturesque" are apt adjectives to describe it.) Its once-empty downtown "strip" is now filled with small boutiques, gift and toy shops, jewelers, and antique stores. It has particularly become a destination for small-scale antiquers; its largest store in this category is Cornish Trading Company (cornish trading.com), a multi-dealer shop located in a three-story building on Main Street next to the tiny town green.

Just across the street is the popular and upscale (for the laid-back environs here, at least) *Krista's* restaurant, whose entrée offerings include gorgonzola chicken, char-grilled swordfish, and a seasonally-changing, market-priced "special hunk of meat" (ask your server). Dinner plates range around $20; Krista's also serves breakfast and lunch. Visit kristasrestaurant.com or call (207) 625-3600.

The local favorite, *Bay Haven Lobster Pound* (bayhavenlobsterpound .com; 207-625-7303) is just down the street, as is the recently introduced (and increasingly popular) *Fairgrounds Pizza and Pub* (fairgroundstavern.com; 207-625-9523), which serves hearty sandwiches, burgers and salads and heaping seafood dishes.

Want to stay the night? You have a couple of options right in town: There's the *Perkins House Bed and Breakfast* at 3 Old School St. (207-625-9033); and the *Inn at Cornish* at 2 High Rd., featuring 16 rooms and an on-site Lincoln Pub. Visit cornishinn.com or call (207) 625-9499.

The burgeoning, proud community hosts numerous activities and annual events, as well, including a strawberry festival in May; a New England vintage baseball festival in June (players wear circa-1860s uniforms and follow the rules according to that time); a harvest and bazaar in July; and an apple festival in late September. Visit cornish-maine.org for more information.

Cumberland County

Cumberland County is Maine's most populous (just shy of 300,000 residents), wealthiest, and densely-settled region (plus it is home to the thriving hub of Portland, arguably its busiest and trendiest city, with no shortage of the "hipster" type here). Many consider it a state gem because it features all that Maine has to offer within its zigzag of borders. It is all at once urban, suburban, and rural; spotted with beaches and lakes (including the state's second-largest water body, *Sebago Lake*); carpeted with woods and overseen by mountains; chock full of history; and overflowing with culture, nightlife, and restaurants.

Portland

As you'll read here and see and hear plenty elsewhere, *Portland* is the state's largest city. But don't be fooled by this "state's largest" business: It's still a small city, always a pleasure to visit, and a fine place to live. The city proper has a population of just around 67,000, making it about a tenth of the size of Boston to the south. Despite its relatively low head count, though, Portland has a brisk urban feel that eludes many cities several times its size. That's due in large part to its location on a peninsula, which forced early builders to think innovatively for their time and grow upward rather than outward. Especially in the warmer months, you can't beat a leisurely walk around its plentiful historic neighborhoods. And Portland's urbanity transcends mere appearances. Today the

portlandtrivia

New England's largest stand of European linden trees is located in Portland. Nearly 400 of the stately shade trees were planted in a large arc around Back Cove in 1921 as a tribute to the Maine soldiers who fought in World War I.

city boasts its own symphony, a first-class art museum, several theater groups, and an array of art galleries side-by-side with excellent restaurants.

Visitors invariably gravitate first to the charming **Old Port** near the waterfront. This picturesque area with its uneven brick sidewalks and cobblestoned streets is lined with boutiques, bars, T-shirt shops, and ice-cream emporiums aplenty. These narrow streets blossomed during rediscovery and renewal in the late 1970s, when the formerly run-down, derelict area was spruced up from sidewalk to cornice. Take some time to walk around the Old Port and investigate the extravagant late-19th-century brickwork. If your impression is that it's rather uniform and planned, you'd be right. Portland's downtown was devastated by fire in 1866 and rebuilt shortly afterward (a detail you'll note on the date plaques of many buildings, which read 1867 or thereabouts). It's here that you'll also find the vibrant Old Port Festival (held in June), as well as other educational events such as "Walk the Working Waterfront," which essentially serves as a meet-and-greet for the variety of businesses that line the wharves and piers on Commercial Street.

While the Old Port is outwardly charming, you'll find that other parts of the city are somewhat more subtle in their intrigue. On upper **Congress Street**, Portland's main artery of commerce and culture, be sure to visit the **Neal Dow Memorial**, a wonderful 1829 brick home preserved in memory of the so-called "Father of Prohibition." Dow was born in Portland in 1804, when the city thrived on the rum trade emanating from the West Indies. The obvious ill effects of "demon rum" on the city streets led Dow to become a lifelong temperance leader, and he was ultimately responsible for bringing prohibition to Maine (love it or hate it). An outspoken and effective lobbyist, he singlehandedly ushered a bill that banned the sale of spirits in Maine through the state legislature in 1851. The campaign brought him political prominence and propelled him into the office of mayor of Portland. Still, it's no surprise that his anti-alcohol efforts also earned him a number of enemies. Tour his one-time home and remember to ask where local agitators tried to beat down the rear door to discuss their "grievances" with the pious Mr. Dow.

When he died in 1897, the "Napoleon of Temperance," as he was also known, bequeathed his mansion and its contents to the **Maine Women's Christian Temperance Union**. Established in 1874 and still operating out of offices on the building's second floor, the organization promotes alcohol abstinence and has broadened its focus to anti-marijuana efforts, as well. The union offers tours of the first floor, which is kept up much as it was during Dow's day. Bookshelves are lined with titles devoted to the evils of alcohol and the house is decorated with a fine collection of priceless antiques. Another small room contains relics such as Dow's death mask, as well as artifacts from his time as a Union general in the Civil War.

The Neal Dow Memorial, at 714 Congress St., is open for tours by appointment. Cost is $10 for adults, $7 for seniors (ages 62 and older), and free for active military personnel and children under 6. Visit nealdowmemorial .org or call (207) 773-7773.

If you're intrigued by the city's range of architecture, consider a walking tour through one of its several historic neighborhoods. One particularly elegant area is the **Western Promenade**, where the city's grandest homes stand on a bluff looking west to the distant **White Mountains**. These mansions range from Gothic to Italianate to Shingle-style, making the area a virtual catalog of 19th-century architecture. Around Bowdoin Street, take note of the several homes in the unique Shingle-style, the specialty of renowned Portland architect **John Calvin Stevens**.

Meanwhile, the nonprofit historic preservation group **Greater Portland Landmarks** offers guided walks of the area. These focus on the **Spring Street Historic District**, which has been on the Register of Historic Places since 1971; the city's 1872 **Custom House** (open only to the public via tour); and the India Street neighborhood, the city's oldest street and home to the **Abyssinian Meeting House**, the country's third-oldest African-American meeting house. These guided tours are offered June through October. Cost is $10 for adults and $8 for group members. Be sure to check the website, portlandlandmarks.org, for specific details on dates, as well as information on special, in-depth historic tours that are offered sporadically throughout the summer.

The group also has a wealth of materials online for the self-directed stroller, encouraging exploration of the Munjoy Hill neighborhood, the Congress Street

dry maine

Maine was a leader in the temperance movement that had such a significant impact on the country's political and social landscape in the 19th and 20th centuries. The world's first "total abstinence society" formed in Portland in 1815, and a statewide group was established in 1834. In 1838, these organizations won a victory with the statewide "Fifteen Gallon Law," which banned the sale of liquor in amounts less than fifteen gallons; it was followed up by an 1846 law prohibiting the sale of spirituous liquors except for medicinal and industrial use. However, these were never strictly enforced. Still, the issue persisted, becoming a political stumbling block throughout Maine and elsewhere.

Since the end of Prohibition in 1933, Maine cities and towns have reserved the right, by local referendum, to prohibit the sale of alcohol within their borders. To this day, some Maine towns remain "dry"—meaning residents have to go elsewhere to get their beer, wine, and liquor.

and Old Port historic districts, as well as 15 unique houses of worship across the city.

Also of note is the Greater Portland Landmark headquarters, the *Safford House*, at 93 High St. Dating to 1858, it is one of the last Renaissance Revival-style homes built in its neighborhood, and served as a home, a business and a classroom space over the generations. Since purchasing the brick-and-brownstone building in 2005, the group has embarked on an intensive, multi-phase preservation plan that has included replacing the roof and restoring its original windows.

Easily the most extravagant home in Portland is the Morse–Libby House, known locally as the *Victoria Mansion*. This gorgeous brownstone mansion was built as an exuberant interpretation of the Italianate villa style. It was constructed between 1859 and 1863 for Ruggles Sylvester Morse, a Maine native who made his fortune in the New Orleans hotel trade (those familiar with the southern, historically rich city will no doubt be able to identify the architectural similarities). The exterior is solid and imposing, a layered grouping of towers and blocks with overhanging eaves—and inside, virtually no space has been left unadorned. Eleven Italian artists were employed to paint murals and trompe l'oeil scenes on the walls and ceilings; the staircases contain 400 hand-carved mahogany balusters; dark, brooding rooms are filled with marble fireplaces and ornate chandeliers and punctuated by colorful, fractured shafts of light from stained glass. Preservationists managed to forestall demolition of this gem (to make room for a gas station, no less) in 1940; the house is now administered by its self-named Victoria Mansion institution.

Guided tours are offered daily from early May to the end of October. Hours are Mon through Sat from 10 a.m. to 3:45 p.m.; Sun from 1 to 4:45 p.m. Special tours are also offered during the Christmas holiday season (closed Christmas Day and New Year's Day); call ahead or visit the website for details. Admission is $16 for adults, $14 for AAA members and seniors over 62, and $5 for students (ages 6-17). Children under 6 are admitted free. There is also a family rate that includes admission for two adults and up to five children for $35. The mansion is at 109 Danforth St. between State and High Streets. For more information call (207) 772-4841 or visit victoriamansion.org.

You'll find a decidedly less opulent homestead not far away on busy Congress Street near Monument Square. The *Wadsworth–Longfellow House* was built in 1785 by General Peleg Wadsworth, a Revolutionary War officer and grandfather of Portland's most celebrated native son, Henry Wadsworth Longfellow. The renowned poet spent his childhood in this house, which is as austere and simple as the Victoria Mansion is unrestrained. This was originally a two-story house, but its gabled roof was destroyed and a third story and hip roof were added in 1815, creating a solid Federal appearance. Virtually all of its furnishings and antiques are original to the Wadsworth and Longfellow families, and also serve as a timeline of the changing styles of the 19th century. The garden behind the house is not to be missed; small and punctuated by meandering paths, it offers a quiet respite amid the hubbub of Portland's downtown.

The library and offices of the *Maine Historical Society* are located just next to the historic home. (Incongruously boxy, modern, and built in the 1980s by a bank, the structure tends to crop up in surveys of Portland's least favorite buildings.) The historical society offers changing exhibits featuring artifacts and documents from more than 12 centuries of Maine history; it also welcomes inquisitive minds, both professional and amateur, to explore its *Brown Research Library*.

The Longfellow House and Maine Historical Society are located at 485–489 Congress St. The house is open in May daily from 12 to 5 p.m., and from June to Oct, Mon through Sat 10 a.m. to 5 p.m., and Sun 12 to 5 p.m. The museum is open year-round with varying hours. Cost to visit both sites is $15 for adults, $13 for students and seniors, and $4 for children (ages 6-17). Children under 5 get in free. For more information call (207) 774-1822 or visit mainehistory.org.

warfeverhits maine

On June 26, 1863, the Civil War's northernmost naval battle was waged just off Portland's shores. Confederate raiders captured and destroyed the *US Revenue Caleb Cushing* as it was moored in Portland Harbor. This event sparked the building of fortifications and batteries up and down Maine's coast.

Meanwhile, for a different kind of historical experience, take a walk through the nearby *Eastern Cemetery*, located at the intersection of Congress Street and Washington Avenue. Dating to 1668, this is not only the oldest historic landscape in Portland, but one of the oldest public burial grounds in the country. More than 4,000 marked stones representing the evolution of tombstone artistry scatter its five acres; Longfellow ancestors are buried here, as are city founders and soldiers of the Revolutionary War. The citizen group Spirits Alive! at Eastern Cemetery took over its preservation and stewardship in 2006; for information on their work and special events, visit spiritsalive.org.

Continuing eastward on Congress Street you'll begin a climb up Munjoy Hill. At its crest, you can't miss the unique *Portland Observatory*. This handsome conical building topped with a cupola was constructed in 1807 by Captain Lemuel Moody, and today it is the only remaining historical maritime signal station in the US. Manned for many years by Moody himself, the wooden observatory was used to sight incoming cargo ships well before they pulled

Maine, Last Stop

For many residents of the lower 48, Maine represents the northernmost apex of their travels. This is true for many plants and animals, too: Maine serves as either the extreme southern or northern terminus of their ranges. For instance, flowering dogwood, mountain laurel, and sassafras are all common south of Maine, but are only found in a few southern and coastal locations within the state. The same goes for the Virginia opossum, a species that is only now beginning to wander into southern Maine. Conversely, Maine represents the southernmost range of the lynx, the gray jay, and the gray wolf, whose roaming and breeding grounds are typically in remote areas of Canada.

into the harbor. Once the ships were spotted with a powerful telescope, the observer would hoist the ships' flags atop the building to alert the town of their impending arrival. When it was built, the 86-foot-high observatory occupied an open, treeless hill previously used for anything from circuses, to political rallies, to public hangings. Today this lighthouse doppelganger (sans the light, of course) provides quite the contrast as it hugs the sidewalk along a busy street and juts above an otherwise unassuming neighborhood of low apartment buildings and small shops.

The observatory suffered from extensive insect damage over the years. Thankfully, it was restored by the Greater Portland Landmarks and reopened in 2000. It offers magnificent sweeping views—the best you'll find in town—of the flurry of the city, the tranquility of the harbor, and the outlying islands of Casco Bay. Located at 138 Congress St., it is open daily from Memorial Day to Columbus Day from 10 a.m. to 4:30 p.m. Admission is $10 for adults; $8 for seniors, students and AAA members; and $3 for children (ages 6-16); children under 6 are admitted free. Contact (207) 774-5561 or visit portlandlandmarks .org for more information.

Getting up above the city limits may have stirred some curiosity about the islands just off Portland's docks. Although several of them are home to year-round inhabitants—including Chebeague, Peaks, and Cliff—and are within Portland city limits, the pace is decidedly slower and the landscape far more rural than urban.

Most of the islands enjoyed their heyday as summer destinations for middle-class vacationers a century ago, and the architecture reflects that heritage. You'll find the quaint backdrop of a general store and maybe a small restaurant on each isle, but little else besides residences. Most are still predominantly summer destinations with the exception of **Peaks Island**, which has become something of a trendy island suburb; many of its inhabitants commute twenty minutes by ferry to jobs in the city. *Chebeague Island*, at 2,400 acres, is the largest and offers fine bicycling terrain. *Cliff Island* is the farthest from town (getting to it takes over an hour by ferry) but it's well worth the visit, offering the most convincing lost-in-time atmosphere.

Mackworth Island, a 100-acre island in the southern part of Casco Bay, is a part of Maine's Public Reserved Lands. The hiking path that circles the island offers superb views of the bay and the opportunity to visit some small and intimate beaches. It is an active bird sanctuary and also home to the Governor Baxter School for the Deaf. Road access is via Andrews Avenue, directly off busy US 1. It is open year-round, daily from 9 a.m. to sunset, and costs $4 for adult nonresidents and $1 for senior nonresidents. For more information call (207) 688-4712.

Frequent ferry service is offered throughout the summer to all islands. Visitors can disembark with a picnic lunch to wander and return on a later boat, or can simply enjoy the passing water view from benches on the ship's upper deck. You can hop a ferry via *Casco Bay Lines* (cascobaylines.com) or *Chebeague Transportation Company* (chebeaguetrans.com).

Meanwhile, water lovers and landlubbers alike will find a striking recreational pathway along the waterfront on the city's eastern end. The aptly named *Eastern Promenade Trail* curves a little over a mile around the base of flinty cliffs with great views out toward the islands and *Fort Gorges*, a hulking stone fortress that rises out of the harbor just offshore. It's a popular spot for strolling or bike riding, and links to the equally popular *Back Cove Pathway*, which loops around a tidal cove for 3.5 miles. You'll find the latter teeming with runners, walkers, and strollers at any time of day.

See those train tracks that parallel the promenade trail? They're part of the *Maine Narrow Gauge Railroad Co. and Museum*. It features a collection of locomotives and coaches dating from the early 20th century, when a number of "two-footer" rail lines were built to link communities that couldn't justify a

asandwichfirst

According to legend, Giovanni Amato devised the now-famed "Maine Italian" sandwich in 1899. The Portland baker sold his unique creation to workers on the Portland docks. Today, his namesake chain of Maine restaurants (and numerous other bakeries and delis across the state) carry on the tradition. The uninitiated luncher, expecting a typical sub roll filled with a variety of meats, cheese, and vegetables, is often surprised by its simplicity: A soft roll filled with ham, cheese, onions, pickles, tomatoes, green pepper and black olives, with salt and pepper and plenty of oil. Likewise, Mainers sampling Italian subs in other parts of the country insist that their version is the only "true" Italian. Let your taste buds judge.

full-size train line. You can learn about the history of the small trains (in an equally fitting small museum) followed by a short ride out along the tracks.

The museum is open daily from 9:30 a.m. to 4 p.m. from early May to late Oct, with trains running daily from 10 a.m. to 3 p.m. Train rides are $10 for adults, $9 for seniors, and $6 for children (ages 3-12), and tickets include admission to the museum. To visit the museum only, cost is $5 for adults, $4 for seniors, and $3 for children (ages 3-12). For details, visit mainenarrow-gauge.org or call (207) 828-0814. Narrow Gauge also offers a "Polar Express" on select dates from Thanksgiving to Christmas; visit the website for information and to purchase tickets (which is strongly encouraged, as the event sells out quickly).

Looking for some pastoral respite? Bet you didn't know there's a natural waterfall practically in the heart of downtown. Perhaps Portland's greatest hidden gem is the ***Fore River Sanctuary***—the unsuspecting visitor would never imagine that these 85 acres quietly trace the blustery confines of the city. The sanctuary boasts nearly 6 miles of trails featuring rustic wooden bridge crossings and the tucked-away ***Jewell Falls***, which, while small by waterfall standards, can rush quite mightily when waters are high. Its subtly marked trailheads are an easy jaunt from the main drag: One is located around 1621 Congress Street as you cross the Fore River heading out of the city; another is located at the end of Rowe Avenue, which is off Brighton Avenue before it passes under the Maine Turnpike. There's limited parking, so be sure to adhere to signage. Visit trails.org/our-trails/fore-river-sanctuary for maps, directions and details on parking. The sanctuary is open year-round from dawn to dusk.

Adjacent to these trailheads is the ***Tate House Museum***, a charming clapboard home built by namesake Captain George Tate. Owned by the Maine chapter of the National Society of the Colonial Dames of America, it is

One Ducky Time

The adventurous (and the aquatically-inclined) won't want to miss the 60-minute, fully narrated tour of Portland and Casco Bay by land and sea aboard **The Downeast Duck**. The 38-foot-long amphibious vehicle, built in Maine and US Coast Guard approved, winds its way through city streets before plunging into the ocean to continue the tour from the water. Along the way it takes in such sights as Portland Headlight, Spring Point Lighthouse, the Calendar Islands, and Fort Gorges. Visitors are required to check-in at 177 Commercial St.; tours then depart directly across the street. Rates are $31 for adults; $28 for seniors (ages 65 and older); and $22 for children (ages 4-12); "Wee ones" (under age 4) ride for free. The first tour begins at 10 a.m. and the last tour leaves at 2:30 p.m. Advanced booking is suggested, as tours typically fill up quickly. Book online at maineducktours.com or call (207) 774-3825.

an elegant, well-preserved example of a pre-Revolutionary home. Tate, who emigrated to the colonies with his family in 1750, served as a "senior mast agent" for the British Royal Navy—meaning he was in charge of the cutting and shipping of white pine to his home country of England. The three-story structure offers a simple elegance with its unpainted clapboards and pale yellow trimmed windows and doorways. It is unique in the fact that it is one of just two structures in Maine with the unusual architectural characteristic of a subsumed dormer in its gabled roof. The society offers tours from its cellar to its attic, the extensive herb garden out back, and the nearby Stroudwater Cemetery where several members of the Tate family keep their final rest.

The house is open June through Oct, Wed through Sat 10 a.m. to 4 p.m., and Sun 1 to 4 p.m. Tours begin on the hour, with the last departing at 3 p.m. Admission is $15 for adults, $12 for seniors, and $7 for children (ages 6-12). Extensive architectural tours are offered by appointment, and cost $18 for adults and $10 for children (ages 6-12). Tickets can be purchased at the society's Means House museum, directly across the street from the house. Visit tatehouse.org or call (207) 774-6177.

For a completely out of this world experience, (and we mean that quite literally), the **International Cryptozoology Museum** is a must-visit. The small nonprofit is located at 11 Avon Street, not far from the Portland Transportation Center. Cryptozoology, for the uninitiated, is the study of hidden or unknown animals, such as Bigfoot, the Loch Ness monster, Mothman and assorted sea serpents and lake monsters. Founder Loren Coleman is a foremost expert on the subject—having written more than 40 books, and been featured in numerous TV shows and documentaries—and the museum is the first of its kind in the world. You can't miss the giant Bigfoot statue guarding its entrance. Inside, you'll find art, movie props, and what is claimed to be evidence of unexplained creatures in the way of scat and hair samples. The museum also offers a rotation of exhibits dedicated to the obscure study. Hours are Mon, Wed, Thurs, and Sun, 11 a.m. to 4 p.m.; and Fri and Sat from 11 a.m. to 6 p.m. Cost is $10 for adults, $8 for seniors (65 and older), and $5 for kids (ages 12 and younger). Visit cryptozoologymuseum.com for more details.

Meanwhile, back to a more mainstream vibe, the **Old Port** is your best bet in the city to browse boutiques—you'll find everything from vintage clothing to beach sand jewelry to culinary salt, body, and spa products. Among the notable long-standing shops here is **Maine Potters Market** (376 Fore St.; 207-774-1633; mainepottersmarket.com) right in the heart of the Old Port. In operation since 1978, this artists' cooperative sells a variety of handcrafted functional items as well as intricate art pieces. Not far away are some fascinating finds at **Portland Architectural Salvage** (portlandsalvage.com). It's much like it sounds; the 20,000-square-foot warehouse space at 131 Preble St. is crammed with items from around the world and across the decades—anything from vintage neon signs, to cupboards and cabinets charmingly scuffed by the years, to antique bathroom accessories. With items constantly coming (and going) through its doors, there's really no telling what you'll find here.

If you're staying the night, one of Portland's poshest options by far is the **Pomegranate Inn**, an eight-room bed-and-breakfast in the city's tony West End. The inn's exterior Italianate architecture is distinctive in this neighborhood of grand homes, while its interior is a quiet fantasy—part high Victorian, part pop art. Faux finishes, striking furniture, and surprising whimsical flourishes embellish its rooms—each uniquely decorated— making it at once both exotic and comfortable. Rates range from $159 to $409, depending on the room and the time of year; that price includes gourmet curated small plate breakfasts. The inn is located at 49 Neal St., and reservations can be made by visiting pomegranate inn.com or calling (207) 772-1006 between 8 a.m. and 10 p.m.

Baseball fan? Stick around to take in a **Portland Sea Dogs** game; the double-A team is affiliated with the Boston Red Sox, so you might even catch a Major Leaguer on a break from Fenway. Games are played at the frequently sold-out 7,350-plus seat **Hadlock Field**, an intimate stadium nested between railroad tracks and the brick Portland Expo building. Games here have the nostalgic feel of old-time baseball, and are intimate enough that you can actually hear players talking among themselves on the field. Come early if you have general admission seats so you don't end up way down the left field line.

Hadlock Field is located at 271 Park Ave., just off I-295. Parking can be a challenge during games; you can find overflow options at Fitzpatrick Stadium and the Maine Medical Center Garage on Forest Street. General admission tickets are $12, with reserved, box, and skyview seats going anywhere from $13 to $29. Order at seadogs.com.

Portland Is for (Art) Lovers

Portland is renowned for being an artist enclave; you can find galleries and art studios tucked away almost anywhere here. One great way to explore many of them is with the city's ever-growing and ever-popular First Friday Art Walk. The event is held the first Friday of every month from 5 to 8 p.m.—whatever the weather might bring—and the streets around Monument Square and the Old Port fill up with pedestrians. Many local bars and restaurants offer special deals on drinks and appetizers, and live music and street performers of all kinds aren't hard to find, either. Visit creative portland.com for details.

Greater Portland Area

While Portland is no doubt the hub of action in this region, you don't want to overlook its surrounding cities and towns—even for just a leisurely walk or drive on a sunny day. The Presumpscot River is literally the throbbing vein running through this area, particularly the once-thriving mill town of **Westbrook**. The roughly 28-mile-long river runs from Sebago Lake to Casco Bay and its name translates from Abenaki to "river of many rough places." (If you're a paddler, this gives you an idea of what it's like to navigate.)

One option for exploration is **Presumpscot River Preserve**. The 48-acre protected area features a 2.5-mile-long trail that traces the river on the Portland-Falmouth border and ends at Presumpscot Falls. The best way to access it is via Oat Nuts Park off Summit Street in Portland. **Riverton Trolley Park**, which crosses Westbrook and Falmouth, also makes a wonderful diversion for a walk, run, or bike ride. Opened in 1896 by the Portland Railroad Company, this large public green space once featured a croquet court, "casino" building, outdoor amphitheater and boat rides on a trout pond and the Presumpscot River; early 20th century city-dwellers were more than eager to pay the five cent trolley fare to make the day trip. Today, there are few of those diversions left, but the 2-mile riverside walk is nonetheless beautiful and historically fascinating, offering glimpses of ruins of the bygone era. The trailhead is located off Riverside Street in Portland; visit trails.org for maps and directions.

oldestlighthouse

Built in 1791, Portland Head Light is Maine's oldest lighthouse—and it is one of only four in the country to be commissioned by George Washington himself.

Just across the harbor from Portland, you'll find its subdued sister city of **South Portland**. This is home to the **Spring Point Ledge Lighthouse**, a still-working station built in 1897 in the "sparkplug" style (you'll understand the origin of the name once you see it). It's also the location of the adjacent former **Fort Preble** (1808–1950), where you can clamber around architectural ruins.

While you're in the area, you might as well pop in at **Portland Head Light** and the adjacent **Fort Williams Park**, located in the elegant, sleepy town of **Cape Elizabeth**. Although a tourist mecca, the side-by-side properties offer gorgeous views, sweeping hills, and the opportunity to explore imposing brick and stone military ruins, not to mention one of the country's oldest lighthouses. The Head Light, a venerable and handsome structure, stands on a rocky promontory at the edge of Fort Williams' grassy park. Completed in 1791 and occupied continuously until 1989, its house and grounds have a rich history, including frequent visits by Henry Wadsworth Longfellow, who befriended the keepers and often walked here from Portland. The *Museum at Portland Head Light* is located in the former keeper's quarters, and features a wealth of information on lighthouses and navigation going as far back as Egyptian times. The light tower itself is still owned and operated by the Coast Guard and is not open to the public, but visitors can walk around its base, crane their necks to examine its 80-foot-tall length, and enjoy the views looking out over Portland Harbor (and far beyond, when the visibility is right).

The grounds are open daily year-round from sunrise to sunset. The museum and gift shop are operated by the town of Cape Elizabeth and are open daily 10 a.m. to 4 p.m. from May through mid-Oct and weekends only in Nov. Admission is $2 for adults and $1 for children (ages 6-18). Visit portland headlight.com or call (207) 799-2661.

Nearby *Scarborough* is a bit more eclectic—in that among its attractions are two very different spectacles of speed, a giant chocolate moose, and an exclusive community that was home to one of Maine's great artists.

Let's start with speed. Just off I-95 is *Scarborough Downs*, a horse racing track that has been in operation going on 70 years. It's worth a visit just for the sheer spectacle of it; its sprawling clubhouse and grandstand sit in the midst of 500 acres, and overlook the fastest half-mile track in New England. Harness racing is the chief practice here (meaning horses race at a specific gate, pulling a driver in a two-wheel cart called a sulky). The building and benches outside are charmingly honkytonk and, beyond taking in the amazing skill and beauty of these thoroughbreds, it's a great opportunity to people-watch, too. It costs nothing to park or take in a race—betting is a whole different matter; that's up to you. Live racing is offered late Mar through Dec, Thurs, Fri and Sat in the summer and just weekends in the shoulder seasons. Visit scarboroughdowns .com for details.

Southern Comfort in Maine

The Pine Tree State isn't exactly heralded for its barbecue—lobster and shellfish rule around here). But Dennis Michael Sherman has set out to change that (if only a little bit). In 2006, he launched his DennyMike's line of sauces and seasonings, now crafted at a production facility in Westbrook. The Old Orchard Beach native—whose passion for barbecue was sparked during his college-time travels in Texas and Mexico, prime 'cueing territory—created products that are gluten free, nut free, without chemicals or artificial flavorings, and featuring fun names like "Chick Magnet," "Cow Bell Hell" and "Sublime Swine." You can find them at various independent markets throughout Maine or at dennymikes.com (which also features a store locator).

Is It Chocolate Mousse or Chocolate Moose?

While in Maine, you're no doubt hoping for a moose encounter (not involving your car, of course). Does a chocolate moose count? Whether it does or not, you can find one at Len Libby Candies in Scarborough. The shop boasts the world's only life-sized chocolate moose; weighing in at 1,700 pounds, it was hand-sculpted and unveiled on July 1, 1997. (Did the sculptor get to nibble on his/her mistakes, we wonder?) This chocolate version of the antlered symbol of Maine "wades" in a white chocolate pond in the candy shop's lobby. While you're there, you might as well pick up truffles, peanut butter cups, fudge, brittle, salt water taffy, little edible versions of Lenny, or (of course) lobster-shaped chocolates—or whatever else might satisfy your sugar tooth. The store was founded in the 1920s by its eponymous "Dean of Maine Candymakers," who was born in 1872 into the eighth generation of Libbys living in Scarborough. His great-grandfather once owned the Prouts Neck section of town in its entirety (read ahead for more on that), and young Len himself once worked as a houseboy for artist Winslow Homer. Located at 419 US-1, the store is open 7 days a week year-round, from 9 a.m. to 9 p.m. Visit lenlibby.com or call (207) 883-4897.

On the other side of I-95, meanwhile, is **Beech Ridge Motor Speedway**, which offers a variety of racing events on wheels, rather than hooves. These range from NASCAR-level races; to "Car Wars" featuring a good-old fashioned demolition derby; to a "Day of Destruction," described as a "a fender-bending free-for-all" with drag races, burn-outs, donut dashes and backward-driving stunts by amateur drivers in trucks, bombers, beetles, and classic cars. Events start at $7 per person, and are held from May to Sept. Visit beechridge.com or call (207) 885-5800.

Across town, things shift from the free-for-all to the exclusive: **Prouts Neck** is a rocky, old-moneyed peninsula dotted with a few dozen beautiful summer homes. This was the place painter Winslow Homer called home, and it inspired some of his later paintings depicting angry, churning surf. One of the best ways to enjoy this small seaside community is via the **Cliff Walk**, which is just as it sounds: Crossing low cliffs and salt marshes and alternating sandy and rocky beaches, set to the thrumming backdrop of waves and the cawing of birds.

Beyond the natural scenery, walkers will pass many unique, Shingle-style homes that were the signature of John Calvin Stevens. The Portland architect was also commissioned by Homer to convert a former carriage house into his residence and studio. Perched on a lookout with a distinctive second-story porch deck, the artist lived here from 1884 until his death in 1910. The historic 1,500-square-foot building (which is rather modest compared to the palatial standard on Prouts Neck and elsewhere around here) is now owned by the Portland Museum of Art (portlandmuseum.org/homer; 207-775-6148) which offers tours from late May through mid Oct. Cost is $65; students with a valid ID get a reduced rate at $25. This includes transportation to and from the museum in downtown Portland. There are also limited off-season rates in April and late Oct.

The cliff walk can be reached by following US 1 to Black Point Road to Ferry Road; park at the town beach (cost is $10) and the trailhead is back a little ways up the road from the beach. While you're out at Prouts Neck, be sure to check out **Black Point Inn** (blackpointinn.com; 207-883-2500), a mainstay since the late 1800s whose rooms and restaurant seem to lord over the tossing Atlantic. **Ferry Beach** is also a great spot for sunbathing and swimming. Another graceful beach option just north of Prouts Neck is **Higgins Beach**; it has the unique (and picturesque) feature of the decaying remnants of the shipwrecked *Middleton* protruding from of its sand like mossy, jagged bones.

Northern Casco Bay

About 12 miles north of Portland is the inviting seaside town of **Yarmouth**, settled in 1636 and observing the welcoming motto, "Our latchstring always out." This is instantly evident as you veer off I-95 at exit 17 and run into a huge and helpful tourist information center.

Head into town following US 1 to ME 115, where the village center and business district slope down to its sheltered harbor. Be sure to check out the adorably charming former Grand Trunk Railroad Depot building on Main Street. Built in 1906 and listed on the National Register of Historic Places, it once served the Canadian National Railway. On 118 East Elm St. is the Yarmouth History Center and headquarters of the Yarmouth Historical Society, whose museum displays a variety of photographs, archive materials, and antiques tracing the town's history. It also has rotating exhibits from local artists, and offers a lecture series featuring local historians and filmmakers. Hours are Tues through Sat, 10 a.m. to 5 p.m. For more info, visit yarmouthmehistory .org or call (207) 846-6259.

Just across the street is the entrance to **Royal River Park**, whose paved paths parallel the heart of the village, passing by three waterfalls and through open fields and 100-plus-year-old Hemlock stands. If you want a water-side view, there's a canoe launch behind the history center.

Continuing up the coast, the town of **Freeport** is probably best known as the home of **L.L.Bean**, the famous outdoor gear and clothing retailer. What started as a small shop specializing in leather-and-rubber boots for hunting has grown to the size of a regional shopping mall, with three levels of tents, hiking shoes, plaid shirts, khaki pants, winter jackets, and, of course, L.L.Bean hunting shoes. The flagship store marks the center of Freeport's retail district (you really can't miss it; just look for the giant boot outside). It's also open 24 hours a day, 7 days a week—for whenever you get that inkling for a fishing rod or a new sweater. Attracting thousands of shoppers annually, Freeport's brick-lined streets have become a certified outlet mecca, offering everything from Dansk dinnerware to Patagonia outerwear. To its credit, the town has retained much of its original architecture and flavor, and shoppers can leave their car and visit most shops on foot. In recent years, outlets have also started to crop up along US 1, where you can find massive parking lots and chain motels.

But there are a couple of spots in Freeport that have managed to escape the march of "progress." One is **Bessie's Farm Goods**, situated on 30 acres on Litchfield Road just 3 miles from L.L.Bean (leaving from the iconic store, head down Bow Street for a little over 2 miles, then take a left onto Litchfield). Its country store specializes in natural, Maine-made items: Anything from honey and maple syrup to clothing, beauty products and garden supplies. Bessie's also has extensive, year-round gardens and a menagerie of cute animals. Its owners Kathy Heye and Deede Montgomery, who opened the store in 2010, also harvest, spin and dye their own yarn and sell baked goods made from scratch. Bessie's is open Tues through Sat, 9 a.m. to 4 p.m. Visit bessiesfarmgoods.com.

Meanwhile, **Wolfe's Neck Center for Agriculture and the Environment** (wolfesneck.org; 207-865-4469) is easily one of the state's most scenic bits of agricultural land. Its 600-plus acres sit on the edge of northwest Casco Bay roughly four-and-a-half miles from Freeport center. Visitors approach on a dirt road with broad views across pastures toward the water and to the islands and peninsulas beyond. This alternative farm was initially purchased in 1947 by Lawrence MC and Eleanor Houston Smith, both vigorous advocates of no-pesticide agricultural methods. Relocating from Philadelphia, the Smiths pioneered ecologically sound methods of raising

freeport trivia

L.L.Bean is famous for its rubber-and-leather hunting boot—but it had a famous flaw: Wearers often found that their socks were sucked downward. If not tugged back up, the sock would undoubtedly end up half-off (requiring good-old moleskin to treat the resulting blisters and callouses). The boot was reengineered in 1999 with a narrower heel, ultimately solving the mystery of the sinking sock.

In 2018 the uniquely Maine retailer announced that it was ending its lifetime returns policy. Previously, this famous and popular selling point allowed customers to return the Bean's iconic products years (sometimes even decades) after they had been purchased.

beef, and the farm continues that practice today. The center is dedicated to regenerative farming and fighting climate change, and its vision is to create a model for net zero carbon farming. Its farmers grow year-round and use mobile greenhouses. Visitors are welcome to explore its nature trails, gardens, and barns, and to take part in its farm-to-table dinners, barn dances, hayrides, and educational workshops and talks.

The center also manages a campground (freeportcamping.com; 207-865-9307) which includes many sites along the tidal bay for overnight tenting and motor home use, as well as a handful of oceanfront cabins. There are ample opportunities for biking, kayaking, hiking, and fishing. Nearby is **Wolfe's Neck Woods State Park**, a 244-acre woodland park with a picnic area and several trails running through the forest and along the edge of the bay. (Be sure to keep an eye out for osprey.) It is open year-round, daily from 9 a.m. to sunset. Fees for day use are $6 for adult non-residents and $2 for senior non-residents.

To find the farm, head east on Bow Street from downtown Freeport for 2.4 miles, then make a right on Wolf Neck Road. After 1.7 miles, follow the signs and turn left onto a dirt road, then continue roughly a half-mile to the farmhouse. There's no charge to visit the farm or wander the grounds, which are open daily from dawn to dusk.

On the opposite side of I-95 from the outlets is one of the state's more unusual (and unexpected) attractions, the **Desert of Maine**. It initially formed when sand carried by glaciers flowed to the bottom of an ancient lake during the retreat of the last ice age. Then in the 18th century what started as a little patch of sand on a newly cleared farm grew and eventually spread to

Maine Mapped

If you bang around Maine enough, you'll hear many a reference to the "gazetteer"—and no doubt see more than one, rumpled and stained from years of love and use, laying across a backseat or tucked into the door pocket of a local's car or pickup. The DeLorme family introduced the original *Maine Atlas & Gazetteer* in 1976, and it quickly became a transportation Bible, renowned for its accuracy and inclusion of little-known roads and locales across the state's plethora of rural areas. The company eventually created the large-format detailed map books for all 50 states, and its DeLorme Map Store in Yarmouth became a tourist destination in and of itself, due largely to the massive revolving globe dubbed "Eartha" (at 1:1,000,000 scale) holding court in its glassed atrium. Alas, the company succumbed to today's GPS-guided culture; in 2016, it was bought out by Garmin. The tech giant still makes and sells the "paper maps," though, and you can find them at many a roadside store, rest stop or book store (and, of course, online). It's worth your while to pick one up—if only for the nostalgia factor.

OTHER ATTRACTIONS

Portland Museum of Art
7 Congress Sq., Portland
(207) 775-6148
portlandmuseum.org

Children's Museum and Theatre of Maine
142 Free St., Portland
(207) 828-1234
kitetails.org

D. L. Geary Brewing Co. (brewery tours)
38 Evergreen Dr., Portland
(207) 878-2337
gearybrewing.com

Maine Foodie Tours
(207) 233-7485
mainefoodietours.com

The Maine Brew Bus Old Port Spirits
79 Commercial St., Portland
(207) 200-9111
themainebrewbus.com

encompass around 200 acres. Becoming New England's long-lasting "dust bowl," its blowing, shifting sands engulfed trees and buildings over the years.

Like many unusual natural phenomena, this one attracted plenty of attention in the early days of the automobile, and it became a noted tourist trap in the finest sense of the word. (From a 1920s magazine article: "There are acres and acres of shifting sands which are fast obliterating grasses, bushes, trees and even buildings!") Today you can still tour the desert, take a narrated tour, participate in sand designing and gem stone hunts, visit a butterfly room, and explore a museum dedicated to the original 1797 Tuttle farm located in a 200-year-old barn. The Desert of Maine offers plenty of gee-whiz attractions for the average traveler, but it's especially appealing to those interested in geology.

Privately owned and operated, the Desert of Maine is open from mid-May to mid-Oct daily from 9 a.m. to 5 p.m., with guided tours departing roughly every half hour. Admission is $12.50 for adults, $7.75 for teens (ages 13-16), and $6.75 for children (ages 4-12). For more information call (207) 865-6962 or visit desertofmaine.com.

One of the more enduring and controversial historical figures in US history is **Admiral Robert E. Peary**, self-proclaimed discoverer of the North Pole and former resident of Casco Bay. Some hail him as one of America's greatest heroes; others dismiss him as an egomaniacal fraud. Photo analysis and exhaustive studies not-withstanding, no one seems to know for sure if Peary actually made it to the North Pole or perhaps erred in his calculations

Spend a Day in Brunswick

Brunswick's Maine Street (and no, that's not misspelled) features lots of restaurants, representing Thai, German, Indian, and American foods. Begin your day at **Broadway Deli** at 142 Maine St. It's not a deli at all, technically, but a small, family-owned and operated restaurant featuring a breakfast, comfort foods, and a comfy atmosphere. Luncheon menus often include local produce, with such seasonal niceties as fiddlehead soup. For more information call (207) 729-7781.

The Fort Andross Mill Complex at the north end of Maine Street is home to **Bangkok Garden Restaurant**. The venue serves authentic Thai meals with all fresh ingredients and levels of spice from "coward" to "native Thai." Menu items include pad Thai, pad prik king, stir fries, and lots of other traditional offerings. For more information call (207) 725-9708 or visit bangkokgardenrestaurant.com.

Fans of Indian food will revel in the entrees at **Bombay Mahal** at 99 Maine St. Curries come according to individual heat preferences, and all menu items are served with liberal helpings of soothing, Indian music. For more information call (207) 729-5260 or visit bombaymahalbrunswick.com.

Historic Fort Andross, a sprawling, brick building and former mill complex, has undergone a complete renovation, with an eye toward preserving the wonderfully rugged and rustic beams, timbers, and brickwork inside and out. Located on the site of a 17th-century fort, the 1857 structure was also known as Cabot Mill. Businesses here included cotton, synthetic and woolen cloth manufacturers, and shoe, brush, and fiberglass makers. Today, Fort Andross hosts not only modern offices, but a restaurant, a year-round indoor flea market, and in winter, an indoor farmers' market.

Leave Fort Andross and head for the **Swinging Bridge**, just off Mill Street. A classic example of suspension design, the bridge was designed and built in 1892 by John A. Roebling's Sons Co. for mill workers to cross the river from housing in Topsham to Cabot Mill. The old bridge was rehabilitated in 2006, and in 2009 Save Our Swinging Bridge.org, a tax-deductible organization, was created to maintain and protect the bridge and its environment. Unique and scenic, Swinging Bridge once again sways and bounces to the rhythmic tread of happy feet.

The **Androscoggin Riverwalk** crosses Swinging Bridge (parking is available at both ends) and winds along the **Androscoggin River**. The loop trail abounds with a variety of birds, trees, wildflowers, and plants. Heading back to Fort Andross, walkers in the mid-spring months might want to pause to see if alewives or other anadromous fish are running up the fishway at the hydroelectric dam. Across the Frank J. Woods Bridge be sure to visit the delightful riverside park. For more information on the Androscoggin Brunswick–Topsham Riverwalk, visit androscogginriverwalk.org. For details on Swinging Bridge, visit saveourbridge.org.

The **Bowdoin College Museum of Art** is a hidden gem home to one of the oldest collegiate art collections in the nation—and it is also widely regarded as one of the best. It comprises more than 20,000 artifacts, paintings, sculptures and works on paper from ancient to contemporary times, and its antiques include items from the Assyrian, Eyptian, Greek, Roman, and Byzantine eras. The museum is open to the public at no charge and offers a diverse range of changing exhibits. Visit bowdoin.edu/art-museum/ to see what's new.

(or doctored them). No matter where you stand on the debate, however, a couple of local attractions cast light on the explorer's personality and achievements.

Located in the far reaches of Casco Bay (technically in the town of Harpswell), **Eagle Island** (pearyeagleisland.org) was Peary's summer home for years when he was plotting and attempting his conquests of the Pole. As a teenager growing up in Portland, he vowed he would one day own the craggy 17-acre island. This he accomplished in 1879, purchasing it for $500. He built a home here in 1904, and then expanded it in 1912 with a pair of imposing circular stone rooms.

Peary's heirs donated the island to the state, along with much of the furniture from the years the explorer lived there prior to his death in 1920. Maintained and preserved by the state and the nonprofit Friends of Peary's Eagle Island, the main house and caretaker's cottage feature a large collection of photographs, papers and other items (including birds Peary collected as a young amateur taxidermist) that convey a sense of the late admiral's character. Be sure to leave time to wander the island; footpaths meander through forest and along rocky bluffs to its southern tip, which has been taken over as a rookery by hundreds of gulls.

Eagle Island is open seasonally from June to Labor Day, 10 a.m. to 5 p.m. Cost is $6 for adult nonresidents (ages 12-64), $4 for ME residents (ages 12-64), $2 for non-resident seniors (ages 65 and older), $1 for children (ages 5-11), and free for senior residents and children under 5. Because the island is a bird nesting sanctuary, its trails are only open after July 15. Moorings on the northwest side of the island are available to those traveling here on their own by power boat; kayakers and canoers can pull their vessels aground on a small beach also located on the north end. Others can hop a chartered boat; the Friends suggest Seacoast Tours of Freeport (seacoasttoursme.com) or Casco Bay Sights-N-Lights (cascobaysightseeing.com). Book reservations in advance and keep in mind that locations of departure and landing vary from day-to-day and are weather and tide dependent.

If your curiosity is piqued about Peary (say that three times fast), plan to visit the **Peary-MacMillan Arctic Museum and Arctic Studies Center**, located on the campus of Bowdoin College in **Brunswick**, a short drive north of Freeport. Housed on the first floor of distinguished Hubbard Hall, this thoroughly intriguing museum celebrates the Arctic accomplishments of Bowdoin alumni Peary and Donald MacMillan. Its exhibit rooms provide a good overview of their lives (MacMillan was on Peary's successful 1909 North Pole assault and subsequently became an able Arctic explorer in his own right) and see a number of the artifacts used during the attempts on the Pole, including

Chamberlain the Hero

One of the great heroes of the Civil War has long ties to Brunswick. **General Joshua Chamberlain** was a professor of rhetoric at Bowdoin College when the war broke out. He enlisted and was shipped south to fight with the 20th Maine Infantry Regiment. He soon proved his valor in a number of encounters (including the Siege of Petersburg), and was promoted to general. Chamberlain may be best known for his valiant stand at Gettysburg, which was well depicted in Michael Shaara's bestselling novel *The Killer Angels*.

After the war Chamberlain returned to Maine, where he served as four-term governor of the state, as well as president of Bowdoin College. Chamberlain's contributions are commemorated in two memorials in his hometown: A bronze statue of the general at the intersection of Maine Street and Bath Road; and the **General Joshua L. Chamberlain Museum**, operated by the Pejepscot Historical Society. Built sometime between 1824 and 1829 and once a dilapidated student apartment building, the house is slowly being renovated. Located at the corner of Maine and Potter Streets, the museum is open from May to Oct, Tues through Sat 10 a.m. to 4 p.m. and Sun 1 to 4 p.m. There are also select hours in the late fall. Guided tours are given. Admission is $12 for adults, $10 for seniors, students and military members, and $6 for children (ages 6-16). For more information call (207) 729-6606 or visit pejepscot historical.org.

dogsleds, snowshoes, and items toted along to ensure the explorers could enjoy afternoon tea.

Other rotating exhibits focus on Arctic clothing, contemporary Alaskan art, and tundra photography. Watch for the eerie tupilak carvings that the Angmagssalik Inuit created as effigies to bring harm to their enemies. And on your way out, note the Latin inscription carved in the lintel above the doorway: *Inveniam viam aut faciam*. According to Peary's biographer, the explorer penciled this motto above the bunk in his ship after losing most of his toes to frostbite during his unsuccessful 1899 expedition. From the Roman philosopher Seneca, it translates, "I shall find a way or make one." The museum is open year-round Tues through Sat from 10 a.m. to 5 p.m., Sun from 2 to 5 p.m. Admission is free. For information call (207) 725-3416 or visit bowdoin .edu/arctic-museum.

Sebago Lake Region

Sebago Lake has long been a popular destination with summer folks, who have ringed this massive lake with cabins and summer homes. The deepest lake in Maine, as well as its second-largest—it is 8 miles wide and 10 miles long, and its native name means "great stretch of water"— it touches the borders of the towns of its self-named Sebago, as well as Windham, Raymond, Naples, Casco, and Standish. While much of its beachfront is blocked off by private residences and campgrounds—or is accessible only to residents or their guests—there are public boat launches and beaches with access for the casual or out-of-town visitor. Those include **Nason's Beach** (875 Sebago Rd., Sebago), **Raymond Boat Launch,** and **Tassel Top Park**, both along Route 302 in Raymond (it costs a fee to use the latter); and the **Sebago Lake Station Landing** at Northeast Road Extension in Standish (costing $5 to park and $15 to launch and park).

Located at the north end of the water body, **Sebago Lake State Park** also features a boat launch and a handsome white sand beach. It is open year-round from 9 a.m. to sunset. Fees for entry are $8 for adult non-residents, $2 for senior non-residents, and $1 for children (ages 6-11). Those over 65 and under age 5 are free.

Heading in from the coast on ME 25 on Sebago's western side, you'll run into the bustling town of **Standish**. Here there's a mix of small businesses and residences, along with the requisite super markets, pharmacies, banks, and sub shops. It's easy to drive right past the 1789 **Marrett House**, tucked unassumingly along ME-25 (Ossipee Trail East) right before a busy set of lights. But don't make that mistake. Owned by Historic New England, the Federal-style home is classically New England with its white clapboards, contrasting black shutters and connected barn. It was once the home of the young Daniel Marrett, who moved here in 1796 as a new Harvard graduate taking the dignified post as the town's minister. The property remained in his family for 150 years and is remarkably unchanged; in fact, its parlor, with its Victorian wallpaper, carpet, and furnishings, is one of the most intact original rooms at any of the Historic New England properties. The three-story house is filled with pewter, ceramics, and textiles from the 18th and 19th centuries, and a "children's chamber" features a circa-1857 rocking horse. There is also an early 20th century perennial garden. The Marrett House is open from June 1 to Oct 15, the first and third Sat of the month only. Hours are 11 a.m. to 4 p.m., and tours are given on the hour. Cost is $8 for adults, $7 for seniors, $4 for students, and free for members of Historic New England. Visit historicnewengland.org/property/marrett-house or call (207) 882-7169.

For a dose of local entertainment, meanwhile, check out the **Schoolhouse Arts Center** (schoolhousearts.org; 207-642-3743) located in the picturesque and historic Old Standish High School in the middle of Sebago Lake Village. The unincorporated village is located within Standish, on the south side of the lake at the junctions of state routes 35 and 113. The nonprofit offers a variety of shows put on by locals, including anything from *Seussical*, to *And Then There*

Were None, to *A Charlie Brown Christmas*. It is community theater at its best. Tickets typically go for less than $20. And while you're right there, stop in at the **Sebago Lake Trading Company** (sebagolaketradingcompany.com), a true "trading company" in every sense of the phrase, offering a rotating variety of eclectic finds. You can't miss the handmade sign out front (often propped up with a patinaed wooden chair: "Vintage/Gifts/Home Decor." Hours are Sat 10 a.m. to 5 p.m. and Sun 12 to 5 p.m.

If you're coming in from the coast on RT 302, on the other hand—approaching on Sebago's eastern side—you'll quickly come across the twin towns of **Raymond** and **Casco**. The main drag cutting through them is a busy one, but you'll also find it lined with farmer's fields, farm stands, unique eateries and barns full of antiques. Keep an eye out for Hawthorne Road, located on the left as you're heading west on 302. The name isn't a coincidence: A little ways down the unassuming street is the boyhood home of Nathaniel Hawthorne (he was said to have lived there from 1813 to 1825). The simple white rectangular two-and-a-half story structure, with dual chimneys and a gabled roof, is owned and maintained by the Hawthorne Community Association. It is rarely open to the public, but its historical significance can just as easily be appreciated curbside. The celebrated author most known for his connections to Salem, Massachusetts, lived there before and during his years studying at nearby Bowdoin College. He wrote of it fondly in later years, saying "I have preferred and still prefer Raymond to Salem, through every change of fortune," and also lamented that, "I shall never again run wild in Raymond, and I shall never be so happy as when I did." Visit hawthorneassoc.com for more information on the author's time in town and association events.

If you're eager for more local history, not far away you'll find the museum and store operated by the Raymond-Casco Historical Society (it's on 302 in Casco just before you hit Naples; you can't miss the giant mural depicting a horse-and-buggy, sailboat and steam boat). It is open from Memorial Day through Labor Day, Sun and Wed, 1 to 3 p.m. Visit raymondmaine.org/community-resources/raymond-casco-hist-soc for more details.

Meanwhile, also relatively hidden away on Hawthorne Road is an enterprise of a completely different sort. **Sabre Yachts** (sabreyachts.com; 207-655-3831) has been building luxury boats here for more than 40 years; handcrafted, made on spec and encompassing both sailboats and motorboats ranging in length from 36 to 52 feet, they are world-renowned for their Made-in-Maine quality. The company manufactures its larger "Downeast-style" vessels out of its sister company Back Cove Yachts in Rockland. The Raymond shop is small and busy year-round, but staff are more than happy to give a tour of the elegant boats in various stages of production (the ones just ready to ship out are often dry-docked just outside the building). Be sure to call for an appointment.

Just down the road is **Naples**, whose small but busy causeway cuts across **Long Lake** and **Brandy Pond**. Along its length you'll find ice cream and T-shirt shops, mini golf, arcade games, small breweries and restaurants. The quaint **Naples Historical Society Museum** is also located just off the main throughway at 19 Village Green Lane. You'll see antique fire trucks and "snow rollers" (the precursor to the plow), as well as looms, clothing, and lots of archive photos. (This is also where you'll find one of the few public toilets in town.) Summer hours are Thurs, Fri, and Sat, 9 a.m. to 4 p.m.

The causeway was recently reinvigorated with new walkways, sidewalks, landscaping and infrastructure—and its former swing bridge, which proved a delight for boats but a headache for motorists, was replaced with a permanent structure. Paddleboats and canoes are available for rent; the adventurous type can go parasailing, while the more laid-back can opt for a leisurely ride on the **Songo River Queen II** (songoriverqueen.net; 207-693-6861) a pinstriped replica of Mississippi River paddle wheelers. From July through Labor Day, the boat trundles around the lake for one- and two-hour cruises. Also check the schedule for pre-season, post-season, and other special event tours. Prices of the daily excursions range from $15 to $25 for adults, and $8 to $13 for children (ages 4-12). All told, the causeway is a nice diversion on a summer day. If you're in town, check out its popular **Maine Blues Festival** (maineblues festival.com) always held on Father's Day weekend in June, as well as its glorious July 4 fireworks display (by far one of the best in southern Maine). Locals and tourists alike fill the shoreline and queue up in boats to watch the colorful starbursts light up the sky above the lake.

Bridgton

Nestled in the midst of five water bodies—Long Lake, Highland Lake, Moose Pond, Woods Pond, and Kezar Pond—at the foothills of the White Mountains, **Bridgton** can tend to be overlooked. But don't make that mistake; this mid-sized town has some great finds.

A note about the county lines in this area: They zigzag quite a bit, particularly between Cumberland and Oxford Counties; so don't be thrown or think you've gotten lost as you cross a "Welcome To" sign (because there'll likely be another one not far behind). Typically, this area identifies itself under the county-crossing umbrella of the Greater Bridgton Lakes Region.

The undeveloped land here was initially known by natives as "Pondicherry"; modern settlement began in 1770, and Bridgton was incorporated in 1794. Today, its population sits under 6,000, and the town has experienced a bit of revitalization in recent years, particularly in its downtown area—which features a diverse mix of historical, natural, cultural and commercial experiences within just a short walk of one another.

Along its compact strip you'll find the local Reny's department store, as well as several small boutiques, restaurants, cafes, and a barber shop. Your best bet is to park in the lot on Depot Street (just off Main Street behind Reny's) and explore by foot. Be sure to stop in at **Bridgton Books** on 140 Main St. This independent bookseller looks tiny from the outside, but it is deceivingly packed with volumes and ripe for browsing. It's also been put on the literary map: The small shop has hosted book signings by prolific horror master Stephen King, including for his *Finders, Keepers* and *Under the Dome*. King has ample landholdings and a vacation home in nearby Lovell, and (much like Bangor to the north), the area has provided inspiration and setting for many of his books and stories, most notably *The Mist*, *Under the Dome*, and *Cujo*.

Across the street you'll see the **Magic Lantern** pub and movie theater, whose interior mimics the Art Deco style of the great movie palaces of the golden era. Much like Bridgton Books, the first-run theater has had its spotlight moments: Stanley Kubrick's *The Shining* premiered here in 1980 (based on King's creepy novel of the same name, but openly panned by the outspoken author); the remake of *The Manchurian Candidate* also debuted here in 2004 (director Jonathan Demme in attendance). The Lantern was likewise the first in Maine to install state-of-the-art Dolby surround-sound. Visit magiclanternmovies.com or call (207) 647-5065 for more information. A little ways away (headed back toward Naples), you can enjoy an altogether different (and rare to find these days) cinematic experience at the **Bridgton Twin Drive-In**. One of the last remaining drive-ins in the state, its owners recently installed digital projectors enabling it to show first-run movies. It also holds a "Retro Tuesday" event weekly throughout the summer that showcases classic favorites such as *Grease*, *Dirty Dancing* and *The Rocky Horror Picture Show*.

Meanwhile, downtown Bridgton is where you'll find one the region's best historical gems. **The Rufus Porter Museum** (121 Main St.; 207-647-2828; rufusportermuseum.org) encompasses the restored John and Maria Webb House, which dates to the 1830s, and the Nathan Church House, which offers a fine example of Rufus Porter-style painted landscape murals. The Church house, for its part, has had a curious habit of not staying put in one place for too long. The red clapboard ca. 1790 building originally sat on High Street; in 1840, owner Augustus Perley thought it would be better suited at the foot of Highland Lake, so he had it tugged there by a team of oxen; in 1985 it was yet again relocated, this time up to North High Street, to save it from demolition. Finally, in 2016, it was (very delicately) hauled 3,500 feet to its current location (and hopefully its last? Only time and the history books will tell).

The parlor and front vestibule of the building are graced with sweeping murals depicting hills, lakes, islands and leafy trees; restored and re-created over the years, these are dated to 1828 and originally attributed to either Rufus Porter or his nephew Jonathan Poor. Porter, a Massachusetts native best known as an inventor and founder of *Scientific American* magazine, created these folk art style murals largely to pay for his room and board as he traveled throughout New England. The house and museum are open in the summer on Wed and Thurs, noon to 4 p.m., and Fri and Sat, 10 a.m. to 4 p.m. Admission is $8 for adults (15 and over).

Not far away is the **Bridgton Historical Society Museum** on Gibbs Road; its exhibits principally focus on the Bridgton and Saco River Railroad established in 1882 and decommissioned in 1941. It is open in July and Aug, Tues through Thurs, from 1 to 4 p.m. The society also offers summer tours of the **Peabody-Fitch Farm** (which is unique in that its "front" faces away from the road to the fields below) on 46 Narramissic Rd. Visit bridgtonhistory.org for more information.

Looking for a bit of natural respite? You don't have to go very far to find it. Located behind the Magic Lantern and the town parking lot is **Pondicherry Park**. Acquired by the town in 2012, its 66 acres with 2.3 miles of trails crossing woodlands and streams offer a nice change of pace. Even if you're not in a walking mood, take the time to check out the striking covered bridge that serves as its gateway. Featuring a unique curvature and sloping boardwalk, it was hand-set and hand-crafted of locally grown Hemlock. Park hours are 6 a.m. to 10 p.m.; there is no usage fee.

On the edge of town (headed toward Fryeburg), meanwhile, is **Shawnee Peak** (207-647-8444; shawneepeak.com), a small ski area on the side of Pleasant Mountain. When there's snow, it features 40 trails and three terrain parks and unique events like a downhill mattress race (which is really no more glamorous than it sounds, but certainly a blast for participants). In the warmer months, meanwhile, you can find hiking trails or rent canoes, cabins, or yurts.

Beaches are scattered around town, as well, including at **Highland Lake** just off Main St.; **Woods Pond** heading southwest toward Denmark; and **Salmon Point** (located within the town-owned Salmon Point Campground on Long Lake, and by far its most relaxing and scenic).

All told, recreational opportunities abound in Bridgton and beyond; be sure to pick up area guides available across town or at the chamber of commerce located next to Hannaford supermarket on 302. Also visit mainelakes.org or bridgtonmaine.org to check out the various options.

Looking to get a bite to eat? Check out **Black Horse Tavern** on 26 Portland Rd (ME-302), where you'll find burgers, steaks, chicken, and fish staples (207-647-5300; theblackhorsetavern.com). Near **Shawnee** is the laid-back **Campfire Grille** (207-803-2255; thecampfiregrille.com), whose fried calamari appetizer and margaritas are the rave of locals. A relatively new entry into the Bridgton culinary scene, meanwhile, is **Standard Gastropub** (207-647-4100; standardgastropub.com) set in a rehabbed gas station at 233 Main St. (you can't miss the funky painted gas pumps outside). It offers a limited menu that is "thoughtfully designed" and prepared from scratch, featuring burgers, BBQ, hand-cut Belgian fries and even a Korean-fried half chicken.

If you continue to head north on ME 117, you'll pass golf courses and sloping countryside before coming upon **Harrison** (the self-described "Friendly Village") with its busy downtown marina. The town offers numerous options for boating and swimming, and, although it can get cramped in the summer months, you'll find parking along side streets.

Harrison is also home to the venerated **Deertrees Theatre**. Now on the National Register of Historic Places, it was built in the early 1930s by Enrica Clay Dillon, a prominent opera singer who dreamed of creating a world-class theater in this idyllic setting. Selecting an old deer run outside of town and enlisting New York designer Harrison Wiseman, it took three years to bring her dream to fruition. The result was an "acoustically perfect" 350-seat theater built of rose hemlock that was harvested on-site and featuring hand-carved chandeliers, beams and doors. It quickly earned the reputation as "Maine's most enchanting theatre." Today, it continues to present an array of concerts and plays; tickets average around $20.

To find the venue, take a right onto Dawes Hill Road at the Congregational Church on 117, then hang your first left onto Deertrees Road; the theatre is about a half-mile down. During performances, volunteers are on-hand to help guide visitors to parking. The on-site box office is open in the summer from Wed through Sat, 1 to 5 p.m. Otherwise, call (207) 583-6747 or visit deertrees -theatre.org for tickets and information.

New Gloucester Region

In **Gray**, the **Maine Wildlife Park** is a sort of wild animal hospital, rehabilitation center, and nursing home for wildlife that are too vulnerable to return to the forests. The animals at this facility have either suffered from injuries or were orphaned before they could survive on their own. (Some others were raised illegally by humans and are now dependent on handlers to survive.) The center includes a picnic area, a short nature trail, and a wide range of local animals, including lynx, fox, woodchuck, moose, bald eagle, and bob-cat. There's also a fish hatchery. Located on ME 26 approximately 2.5 miles northwest of Gray, the center is operated by the Maine Department of Inland Fisheries and Wildlife. It's open daily year-round, from 9:30 a.m. to 4:30 p.m. The gate closes at 4:30 p.m., but visitors can remain until 6 p.m. Admission is $7.50 for adults (ages 13-59), $5.50 for seniors (ages 60 and older) and children (ages 4-12), and free for children under 3. For more information and details on special events, visit maine.gov/ifw/wildlife-park or call (207) 657-4977, ext. 0.

Getting back to truly wild nature, the 600 protected acres of **Pineland** crosses Gray and New Gloucester and is interlaced with more than 3 miles of hiking trails. You'll find a parking area on Gray's Depot Road. Be sure to also take the time to visit **Douglas Mountain**, a hilltop Nature Conservancy preserve that is a fine destination with a short hike on a clear day. It features four trails (each a mile or shorter) that lead to the 1,415-foot summit. On the top of the rocky hill is a 16-foot stone tower built in 1925 by the land's former owner, a surgeon who found relaxation in stonework. There are commanding views of the entire region, across Lake Sebago and Casco Bay to the east and westward to the Presidential Range of the White Mountains in New Hamp-shire. Look for a sizable boulder that has been carved with the phrase Non Sibi Sed Omnibus ("Not for one but for all"). Late-summer visitors will also be rewarded with ample crops of wild blueberries and blackberries along the trails near the ridge.

Continuing north on ME 26 (and before crossing the Oxford line), you'll pass a handsome assortment of brick and clapboard buildings on a gentle rise amid open meadows and orchards. This quaint little gem is the **Sabbathday Lake Shaker Community**, the last active Shaker community in the world. Fewer than a dozen Shakers now live in these venerable buildings on 1,800 acres of farm and forest land originally settled in 1793. The community carries on the traditions of Mother Ann Lee and her disciples, as expressed more than 230 years ago. These include an emphasis on simplicity in their lives and crafts, a commitment to industry ("Put your hands to work, and give your hearts to God"), and celibacy. The latter often gets the most attention from visitors, who raise the question of how the community has managed to propagate itself for nearly 200 years. The answer: For many years the Shakers adopted orphans, including one of the older Sisters still in residence today. After this practice was disallowed by the state, the community became dependent on converts to carry on their work.

The Shakers—not to be confused with the Quakers—received their name from the dances they once executed during their religious celebrations. The practice was discontinued around 1900 in deference to the older Shaker members. In addition to their religious ceremonies, the Shakers are best known for their furniture and baskets, which display an unmatched devotion to practicality and simplicity.

Learn more about the Shaker life and tradition through one of the village tours offered daily (except Sundays) throughout the summer. Six of the eighteen existing structures are open to the public. Nine of those were constructed before 1850, and all possess an unvarnished grace and refinement. Of particular note is the meetinghouse, built in 1794 and still used for Sunday services in the summer (the public is invited). The downstairs room is spare and open; the light streaming in through the windows seems part of the design. Examples of fine woodworking are displayed throughout several buildings, representing a variety of Shaker communities. You can identify every chair's provenance by the finials, which were unique to each community. The museum also has examples of later Shaker craftsmanship and design, some of which display a mild but startling flirtation with Victorian ornamentation. Be sure to stop at the gift shop, where you can buy herbs grown in the community's garden and sold here since 1799.

An introductory tour of the village (lasting about one hour) costs $10 for adults and $2 for children (ages 6 to 12). The first tour departs at 10:30 a.m. and the last at 3:15 p.m. Special tours also explore the community's expansive herb garden, and go more in depth into the village history. The museum is open and tours are offered Memorial Day weekend through Columbus Day (excluding Sundays). Hours are 10 a.m. to 4:30 p.m. For more information call (207) 926-4597 or visit maineshakers.com. (Yes, you read right: Even this simple community steeped in 18th-century values has embraced 21st-century technology.)

Places to Stay in Southern Maine

PORTLAND

The Danforth
163 Danforth St.
(207) 879-8755
danforthinn.com
Moderate
They call themselves
"swanky"—and they are.

The Westin Portland Harborview
157 High St.
(207) 775-5411
Moderate
Called "The Matriarch
of Hospitality," this hotel
in Portland's downtown
section offers amenities
galore.

Holiday Inn By the Bay
88 Spring St.
(207) 775-2311
innbythebay.com
Moderate

Inn at Park Spring
135 Spring St.
(207) 774-1059
innatparkspring.com
Moderate
Their gourmet breakfast
alone is worth the visit.

Portland Regency Hotel and Spa
20 Milk St.
(207) 774-4200
theregency.com
Expensive

CAPE ELIZABETH

Inn by the Sea
40 Bowery Beach Rd.
(207) 799-3134
innbythesea.com
Expensive
Set on Crescent Beach;
attentive staff

FREEPORT

Freeport Econo Lodge
537 US 1
(207) 865-3777
freeportmainehotel.com
Inexpensive
Great home base for
a Freeport shopping
expedition

SELECTED CHAMBERS OF COMMERCE

The Greater York Region Chamber of Commerce
1 Stonewall Ln
(207) 363-4422
gatewaytomaine.org

Ogunquit Chamber of Commerce
36 Main St.
(207) 646-2939
ogunquit.org

Wells Chamber of Commerce
136 Post Rd., Moody
(207) 646-2451
wellschamber.org

Kennebunk-Kennebunkport-Arundel Chamber of Commerce
16 Water St., Kennebunk
(207) 967-0857
visitthekennebunks.com

Old Orchard Beach Chamber of Commerce
11 First St.
(207) 934-2500
oldorchardbeachmaine.com

Greater Portland Convention and Visitor's Bureau
14 Ocean Gateway Pier
(207) 772-4994
visitportland.com

Harraseeket Inn
162 Main St.
(207) 865-9377
harraseeketinn.com
Expensive
A luxury inn located
within walking distance of
L.L.Bean

Maine Idyll Motor Court
1411 US 1
(207) 865-4201
maineidyll.com
Inexpensive
Cottages with modern
amenities, but a 1950s feel.
Hiking trails, some cottages
are wheelchair-accessible,
some with fireplaces, wood
provided. A real, down-
home getaway.

Places to Eat in Southern Maine

KITTERY

Bob's Clam Hut
315 US 1
(207) 439-4233
bobsclamhut.com
Inexpensive
Famous lobster rolls, a
roadside tradition

Chauncey Creek Lobster Pier
16 Chauncey Creek Rd.,
Kittery Point
(207) 439-1030
chaunceycreek.com
Inexpensive
A lobster pound where you
can sit down and eat and
even bring your own drinks

Warren's Lobster House
11 Water St.
(207) 439-1630
lobsterhouse.com
Moderate
Check out the beer batter
onion rings.

The Yorks

Dockside Restaurant on York Harbor
22 Harris Island Rd.
(207) 363-2722
dockside-restaurant.com
Expensive
Exceptional waterfront
view. Features local,
organic food and seasonal
specialties.

The Goldenrod
2 Railroad Ave.
(207) 363-2621
thegoldenrod.com
Inexpensive
Indulge in their homemade
ice cream and famous
saltwater taffy, dubbed
"Goldenrod Kisses."

Lobster Cove
756 York St.
(207) 351-1100
lobstercoverestaurant.com
Moderate
Everything from lobster
dinner to prime rib. Great
ocean views and indoor
and outdoor dining.

KENNEBUNKS

The Boathouse
21 Ocean Ave.
(207) 967-8225
boathouseme.com
Expensive
Fresh seafood with an
Asian influence

Federal Jack's Restaurant and Brewpub
8 Western Ave.
(207) 967-4322
federaljacks.com
Inexpensive
Good food, good service.
Try the summer ales.

The Burleigh at Kennebunkport Inn
1 Dock Sq.
(207) 967-2621
kennebunkportinn.com/
dining/
Moderate
Enjoy Maine produce,
including fresh blueberries
as well as diver-caught
scallops.

The White Barn Restaurant
37 Beach Ave.
(207) 967-2321
gracehotels.com/
whitebarninn/grace-dining
Expensive

PORTLAND

David's Restaurant
22 Monument Way, Ste
600
(207) 773-4340
davidsrestaurant.com
Moderate
Imaginative fish dishes
overlooking the hubbub of
Congress Square

DiMillo's On the Water
25 Long Wharf
(207) 772-2216
Dimillos.com
Moderate
A popular destination
serving in a large former
ferry car on the water

Duckfat
43 Middle St.
(207) 774-8080
duckfat.com
Moderate
"Alternative sandwich shop" known for its duck-fat Belgian fries

Fore Street
288 Fore St.
(207) 775-2717
Forestreet.biz
Expensive
Wood-fired oven cooks meats, veggies, seafood, and game within sight of diners. A special destination.

The Great Lost Bear
540 Forest Ave.
(207) 772-0300
greatlostbear.com
Moderate
Great beer bar with more than 70 taps, good food too. A fun destination, especially for those who love their brew.

Local 188
685 Congress St.
(207) 761-7909
local188.com
Spanish-inspired cuisine from fresh local ingredients

Street & Co.
33 Wharf St.
(207) 775-0887
streetandcompany.net
Expensive
Rustic charm, flame-prepared seafare with attention to delicate flavors

Three Dollar Dewey's
241 Commercial St.
(207) 772-3310
threedollardeweys.com
Inexpensive
Noisy, crowded, and great. Happy hour prices feature specials on mini-brews.

CAPE ELIZABETH

The Good Table Restaurant
527 Ocean House Rd.
(207) 799-4663
thegoodtablerestaurant.net
Moderate
Known for its "good honest food," especially seafood and beef

The Lobster Shack at Two Lights
225 Two Lights Rd.
(207) 799-1677
lobstershacktwolights.com
Expensive
Crashing surf, lighthouse, picnic tables overlooking the sea, and sumptuous seafood

FREEPORT

Azure
123 Main St.
(207) 865-1237
azurecafe.com
Moderate
Creative farm-to-table offerings; a local favorite regularly named "best restaurant"

Harraseeket Lunch and Lobster Co.
36 Main Street,
South Freeport
(207) 865-3535
harraseeketlunchandlobster.com
Moderate
Features seafood taken daily from their own boats

Jameson Tavern
115 Main St.
(207) 865-4196
jamesontavern.com
Moderate
Historic building, lots of charm, great mini-brews

Petrillo's Food and Drink
15 Depot St.
(207) 865-6055
petrillosfreeport.com
Moderate
Artisanal pizza and Italian entrées

YARMOUTH

Bistro 233
233 US-1
(207) 846-3633
Bistro233.com
Inexpensive
A great option for the whole family

Day's Crabmeat and Lobster Pound
1269 US 1
(207) 846-3436
dayscrabmeatandlobster.com
Famous lobster dinners attract local folks.

Muddy Rudder
1335 US-1
(207) 846-3082
muddy-rudder.com
Moderate
It's been around forever for a reason.

Woodhull Public House
30 Forest Falls Drive
(207) 847-0584
woodhullpublichouse.com
Moderate
Mexican food with a unique vibe

BRIDGTON

The Black Horse Tavern
26 Portland Rd.
(207) 647-5300
theblackhorsetavern.com
Moderate
Everything from blueberry salmon salad, to black angus meatloaf, to homemade cheese cake.

Campfire Grille
518 Portland Rd.
(207) 803-2255
thecampfiregrille.com
Inexpensive
Creative comfort food

Western Mountains

In their haste to visit the White Mountains of New Hampshire or the Green Mountains of Vermont, many visitors to New England tend to overlook the mountains of western Maine. These rolling, rugged hills haven't developed quite the popular mythology of the other mountains, nor do they offer as broad a range of services for travelers. But the region is well worth visiting for its dramatic landscapes, quiet byways, and vast lakes set amid forested hills. Those with a penchant for outdoor activities will find an abundance of walking, hiking, biking, canoeing and kayaking opportunities. Those whose inclinations take them indoors, on the other hand, will also find plenty to do, from historic homes to offbeat museums. Fine inns can be found throughout the area and there's excellent browsing at numerous unassuming antiques shops.

The Western Mountains aren't defined by a single monolithic mountain range, but rather, they consist of a series of hills and watersheds. Some 50,000 acres of the ***White Mountain National Forest*** slip over the border from New Hampshire into Maine, then unravel into the gentle Oxford Hills. The ***Mahoosuc Range*** passes near Bethel and is traversed by the Appalachian Trail; those who've hiked the entire 2,100-mile

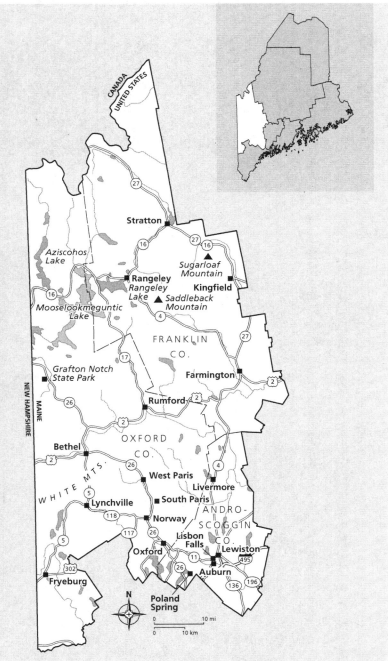

trail say the Mahoosucs contain some of the most difficult and dramatic segments along the entire route. From the summit of *Old Speck Mountain* on a clear day, you can see Mount Blue, an almost perfectly pyramidal hill 32 miles away in the heart of another range. There's also the Rangeley Lake region, with its network of lakes and mountains, and the impressive Carrabassett Valley, which is dominated by the Bigelow Range and offers some of the best Maine hiking opportunities outside of Baxter State Park.

Oxford County

Oxford County extends narrowly along Maine's western edge from the village of Porter to the Canadian border, far into timberland territory. The county tends to be rough-hewn in its geography and culture, with extraordinary gems—both literal and figurative—dispersed throughout.

White Mountains Region

Fryeburg sits on the far west end of Oxford County, nestled about halfway between the tourists hubs of Lake Sebago to the east and North Conway, New Hampshire to the west. A modest town of broad streets and open views, it is located on the well-traveled RT 302, and is home to the coed prep school *Fryeburg Academy*, founded in 1792 and one of the oldest private schools in the US. But it is perhaps best known for its self-named *Fryeburg Fair*—Maine's largest county fair, held annually at the end of September. The agricultural attraction, held at the fairgrounds just at the edge of town, started out as a county fair in the truest sense, and now attracts people from all over New England and the eastern seaboard. Some of the old-timey activities you'll find here include skillet and anvil throwing contests, tractor and horse pulling, pig and calf scrambles, harness racing, ox-yoking demonstrations, and livestock judging. There's also music, a flower show, wreath-making demos, and baking contests (including whoopie pies, blueberry desserts, and cheesecake). For more information and a show schedule, visit fryeburgfair.org.

Like many towns in this area, Fryeburg also lies on the Saco River, Maine's most popular canoeing route. The Saco is distinguished by many sandbars, which invite leisurely excursions with frequent stops. Be forewarned that the river is exceedingly busy on weekends, and some sandbars may offer all the remote wilderness character of *Old Orchard Beach* not far away on the coast (complete with the honkytonk feel, the rowdiness and the drinking; although recent efforts by the local police have attempted to curb that).

FAVORITE ATTRACTIONS

Rufus Porter Museum, Bridgton

Denmark Arts Center, Denmark

Evans Notch

Grafton Notch State Park, Bethel area

Maine Mineral and Gem Museum, Bethel

Norlands Living History Center, Livermore

Orgonon, Rangeley

Several canoe liveries can be found in and around the area, offering canoe rentals as well as shuttles up and down the river. Among the busiest and longest-running of these is **Saco Bound**, located just across the state line in Center Conway, New Hampshire. The outfit can help organize trips ranging from a 2-hour, 3-mile introductory paddle to a 3-day, 43-mile excursion. Prices vary, so call first (603) 447-2177 or visit sacobound.com. There's also **Saco River Canoe and Kayak** on Main St., Fryeburg (207-935-2369; sacoriver canoe.com), and **Saco Valley Canoe**, also in Center Conway (603-447-2444; sacovalleycanoe.com).

If you don't feel like paddling, there's easy access to a large sandbar on ME 113 north of town. Just park in the lot north of the bridge and walk down to the river.

For a quick and easy hike offering a rewarding view, try the **Jockey Cap Trail**. It's located just a half-mile east from the junction of ME 5 and ME 302; the trailhead and parking are behind **Quinns Jockey Cap Country Store.** The hike is less than a mile round-trip; at its bare rock top, you'll find a marker dedicated to Robert E. Peary, legendary for his North Pole excursions, who lived in town for a short period in 1877 and 1879. There's also a panoramic landscape compass identifying each visible summit in the distance.

Not far away you'll find more about the Peary story: On Elm Street in Fryeburg sits the **Admiral Peary House**, a pleasant bed-and-breakfast inn. As a recent college graduate, the Arctic explorer lived quietly here for two years while employed as a land surveyor. He later recalled his pleasant memories of Fryeburg, where he spent idle time practicing taxidermy. The exterior of the house retains its 19th-century farmhouse charm, but Peary certainly wouldn't recognize its interior (although he would likely appreciate it). The innkeepers maintain seven guest rooms that are furnished to represent world exploration destinations (Paris, Panama, the Orient, the Serengeti), as well as two rustic-style cabins and a loft apartment. Over the years amenities such as a clay tennis court, in-room jacuzzis and fireplaces, and a spacious country kitchen have been added. A comfortable deck overlooks the well-landscaped yard, and the guests' living room features a fireplace, big-screen TV and an antique billiards table. The guest rooms have more privacy than you'll find at many B&Bs, and guests are provided with a filling breakfast in the morning. Summer and fall rates run between $150 and $200, depending on the room (cabins are closer to $400). The inn is at 9 Elm St.; (207) 935-1269; admiralpearyinn.com.

Peary wasn't the only person of note to call Fryeburg (briefly) home. Author Clarence E. Mulford (1883–1956) lived here—not on a rugged butte in Utah—while writing his Hopalong Cassidy novels. A collection of his works and a sampling of memorabilia are housed in the *Clarence Mulford Room* at the *Fryeburg Public Library*. This reading room has a portrait of Mulford as well as displays of historic western guns (including a buffalo gun), model ships and stagecoaches, and a case of Mulford's collected works, including editions in Czech, Danish, and Finnish. The library is located in a former stone school-house built in 1832, one of only two known stone schoolhouses in the state. 515 Main St.; (207) 935-2731; fryeburgmaine.org/town-departments/library.

Heading northward from Fryeburg, you have a choice of two routes, both appealing. You can either drive north along ME 5 on the east side of Kezar Lake, or follow ever-narrowing ME 113 through scenic Evans Notch. The first route gives access to a venerable lakeside resort; the second offers a network of excellent hiking trails to the summits of open mountains.

The Last (and Most Notorious) Lumberjack

So the legend goes, he came out of his mother's womb already chewing tobacco, wearing caulk boots and holding a peavey and ax (if true, he most certainly marked his mother for life). Albert Lewis Johnson, more commonly known as "Jigger Johnson," is a folk hero around these parts—a notoriously hard-working, hard-partying, and seemingly indestructible legend. He was born in 1871 in Fryeburg and started out working at a young age as a "cookee" (cook's assistant) in logging camps, before becoming a logging foreman, trapper, and fire warden for the U.S. Forest Service. Stories of his exploits abound; he was said to have caught live bobcats barehanded, and kicked off the knots of frozen hemlock logs barefooted—then there were his drunken brawls, too numerous to mention. But he was of complex Yankee stock: A well-respected boss who was full of intuition and expected the very most out of his men—as well as a hothead who had an inhuman ability to consume massive quantities of any proof of bootlegged alcohol. He ultimately died in a car crash in March 1935, thus cementing his legend. The Forest Service named a campground in the White Mountains after the so-called "last lumberjack," and he is also immortalized in the writing of Stewart Holbrook and Robert Pike.

TOP ANNUAL EVENTS

FEBRUARY

Winterpaloozah!
Rangeley, mid-Feb
(207) 864-2771
rangeleymaine.com

JULY

Sebago–Long Lake Chamber Music Festival
Harrison, July & Aug
sllmf.org or deertreestheatre.org

Maine Gem, Mineral, & Jewelry Festival
Bethel, mid-July
(207) 665-2759
ocmgassoc.blogspot.com

Moxie Festival
Lisbon Falls, mid-July
moxiefestival.com

Founders Day
Paris Hill, mid-July
(207) 743-2980

AUGUST

Great Falls Balloon Festival
Lewiston–Auburn, late Aug
(207) 783-2249
greatfallsballoonfestival.org

SEPTEMBER–OCTOBER

Fryeburg Fair
Fryeburg, late Sept–early Oct
(207) 935-3268
fryeburgfair.org

Kezar Lake, bounded to the west by unspoiled mountains, is regarded by many as the state's most perfect. It's also one of its least accessible. (This is probably why it's considered nearly perfect; human influence unfortunately often brings its spoils.) Public roads touch upon the lake only at a crossing called "the Narrows," so the best views are reserved for those owning summer homes hereabouts—Stephen King among them. Fortunately there's an alternative.

Quisisana is a rustic lakeside resort set amid towering white pines. Here you're as liable to hear an aria emanating from the forest as the muffled call of a mourning dove. Since 1945 Quisisana has offered its guests both superb cuisine and a varied musical menu, with selections ranging from opera to popular show tunes. Owner Jane Orans recruits her summer staff from conservatories around the nation, and the students make beds, wait on tables, and perform nightly in the vintage wooden recital hall with dramatic views down the lake. Up to 150 guests reside in cozy white cabins scattered about the grounds and along the lakeshore, occupying their days with swimming, sunning, canoeing, and exploring the surrounding hills. Extra recitals are sometimes also scheduled for rainy-day diversions.

The musical repertory schedule is designed around a weeklong stay, but shorter visits can sometimes be accommodated early in the season. Quisisana is 3.5 miles north of Lovell; look for road signs as you approach. Plan on spending between $195 and $270 per couple per day and include three meals and entertainment. Rates are reduced in the off-season. For more information call (207) 925-3500 (in the summer) or (207) 833-0293 (in the winter), or visit quisisanaresort.com.

If you opt to head north on ME 113, meanwhile, you'll first drive through farmlands with open vistas of distant ridges. But soon enough these begin to converge at **Evans Notch**, and the valley becomes pinched and narrow, as does the road itself as you enter the national forest. As your car climbs north, views of the valley open up, with glimpses of scraggly peaks above. The forest is dense with birch, beech, and maple trees, which often overarch the road to create a shady canopy.

If you're so inclined, set out on one of the hiking trails to these ridges for sweeping views of western Maine and the taller peaks of the Carter and Presidential Ranges. A list of suggested hikes is available from the USDA Forest Service's office in Bethel (207-824-2134). One hike that may be accomplished in a couple of hours without a map or guide is to the summit of **East Royce Mountain**. This 1.3-mile trail ascends steadily through hardwoods and along an attractive brook, ending at open granite ledges with excellent views across rolling hills toward Kezar Lake. The trailhead, with parking for about twenty cars, is on the west side of ME 113 just north of where the road begins its descent toward the town of Gilead. The trail is moderately demanding and is well marked.

For a different method of climbing, consider signing up for llama or horse trekking offered through New England Horseback Riding and Carriage Driving at the **Telemark Inn Wilderness Lodge**. This distinguished inn, housed in a summer retreat built by a wealthy businessman in 1900, is located deep in the countryside near Bethel on the eastern edge of the White Mountains.

A Quiet Retreat for Campers

If you're equipped for camping, there are several USDA Forest Service campgrounds in the Evans Notch region, but none as quiet and remote as the **Crocker Pond Campground** located down a dirt road south of Bethel. With only seven campsites, it often fills on weekends but remains out-of-the-way enough that sites are generally available during the week. Several quiet ponds in the area are suitable for fishing, and a couple of hiking trails near the campground provide access to the backcountry. Site fees are $18 a night. For more information on Crocker or other recreational opportunities in the area, contact the Forest Service's Evans Notch Ranger Station in Bethel at (207) 824-2134.

Innkeeper Steve Crone, who has been working with horses, llamas, and sled dogs for more than two decades, was the first White Mountain entrepreneur to offer this pleasurable way of visiting the mountains. Crone offers trips by varied means and with different destinations, from open mountaintops to riverside glens. The inn also offers horse therapy, carriage driving, and dog sledding in the winter. The lodge has a handful of rooms, as well as authentic tipis where visitors can spend the night. Various packages are available depending on your interest. Call (207) 731-4747 or visit newenglandridinganddriving.com for more information.

Bethel Area

Heading northeast of the Evans Notch region, you'll soon arrive at the dignified town of **Bethel**, lined with yellow-and-white clapboard houses and abounding with evidence of a comfortable, prosperous history. A number of attractive early homes front the Bethel Common—an elongated greensward with benches and a fountain, rare for these parts of New England—as does the venerable **Bethel Inn Resort** (207-824-2175; bethelinn.com), a stately complex consisting of the original inn, built in 1913, and several outlying buildings. There is also a golf course and pro shop. Fairway town houses, a main dining room, a cozy tavern, and a lake house, sited 3 miles from the inn, round out its offerings. The tavern features reasonably priced entrees that are cooked to a turn. The braised pork shanks alone are worth the trip, and in warm weather, diners may sit in a screened-in porch and gaze out over the greens. The inn is also a favorite place in winter, when local ski areas do a box-office business. Nearby are the tasteful brick buildings of **Gould Academy**, a respected private secondary school founded in 1836.

In-town dining and lodging options include the **Sudbury Inn** and its "Suds" Pub (207-824-2174; thesudburyinn.com); **Brian's**, featuring upscale comfort food (207-824-1007; briansbethel.com); and the laid-back **Rooster's Roadhouse** (207-824-0309; roostersroadhouse.com). Fans of Chinese food will appreciate the fare at **Kowloon Village**, on Lower Main Street in Bethel. While the decor is anything but authentic, the food is the real deal. It offers an extensive and inexpensive menu featuring all the classic Chinese favorites, with most entrees running less than $10. Cocktails are equally good and fairly priced. Hours are Sun, Mon, Wed, and Thurs from 11:30 a.m. to 9:30 p.m., Tues from 4:30 to 9:30 p.m., and Fri and Sat from 11:30 a.m. to 10 p.m. Visit www.kowloonvillage.com or call (207) 824-3707.

Facing the common you'll also see the simple but distinguished Dr. Moses Mason House run by the **Bethel Historical Society**. This 1813 Federal-style house with the characteristic fan over its front door was built by Dr. Moses

Mason (1789–1866), one of Bethel's early civic leaders. The house is believed to be the first in the district to be painted white and the first built on a stone foundation; locals told Mason the wind would certainly blow it over (but as engineering would have it, it survived the centuries). Mason served not only as town doctor but also as postmaster and justice of the peace. The original contents of the house were auctioned off in the 1970s, but many of these items are finding their way back through local donations. The house and its intricate woodwork are meticulously maintained, with period furniture filling its rooms.

If you're interested in American primitive painting or the history of decorative arts, the front hallway alone is worth the price of admission. The walls of the entryway and the second-floor landing are covered with a sweeping paint-on-plaster mural attributed to well-known primitive painter Rufus Porter. A seascape with boat at anchor graces the first floor; along the stairs and on the second floor is a forest scene, dense with the delicately wrought boughs of white pines. The walls were first painted a century and a half ago, and they have never been papered or painted over, yielding one of the best examples of early decorative painting in the state. Be sure to also note the intriguing chair built by Mason: It is made of curly maple, crushed velvet, and moose horn.

The **Mason House** has nine period rooms, which are open July and Aug, Thurs through Sat from 1 to 4 p.m. or by appointment. Admission is $5 for adults and $3 for children (ages 6-12). There is also a special family rate of $10.

The historical society's **Robinson House**, featuring exhibit galleries, a museum shop, research library and archives, and administrative offices, sits right next door. It was built in 1821 for O'Neil W. Robinson and his wife Betsey H. Straw. Robinson was a successful businessman, state Senator, and Oxford County Sheriff, and also owned large tracts of timber land in several nearby New Hampshire towns. The Robinson house is open from Memorial Day weekend to the third Fri in Oct, Tues through Fri; from 1 to 4 p.m. on Sat and Sun from 1 to 4 p.m. (in July and Aug only). Admission is free. Call (207) 824-2908 or visit bethelhistorical.org.

Just northwest of Bethel is the booming **Sunday River Ski Resort**. For years Sunday River was a quiet family mountain that, like many small New England ski areas, was slowly succumbing to the times and headed for closure. However, after it was acquired by entrepreneur Les Otten, the resort

number, please?

Bryant Pond, a village just southeast of Bethel on ME 26, was the last town in the United States to give up the crank telephone. Until October 1983 anyone wishing to place a call told an operator the number he or she wanted to reach, and the call was patched through.

grew dramatically. The ski area was expanded along the ridge toward the New Hampshire border to include a vertical drop of 2,340 feet (the second largest in Maine and sixth in New England). The resort has become nationally famous for its snowmaking capacity—it sometimes produces enough snow to remain open into June.

As at most ski areas in the northeast, the pace tends to slacken in the summer, but the resort has bolstered that by developing a mountain-biking park with 60 miles of trails and access to the high rocky ridge via two chairlifts modified to carry bikes. It also offers scenic lift rides in the summer, as well as a disc golf course, zipline tours, a climbing wall, and bungee trampolines. The resort has also become host to the growing (and intensely amusing) *North American Wife Carrying Championship*, held in the fall. It is based on the 19th century Finnish legend of "Ronkainen the Robber," who made his men prove their worth by completing a difficult course with a heavy sack (or more likely a woman nabbed from a neighboring village) on their back.

To get to Sunday River, head north of Bethel on US 2, then look for signs indicating a left turn to the resort at about 2.5 miles. For more information call (800) 543-2754 or visit sundayriver.com.

You also can rent bikes at *Bethel Outdoor Adventures*, located on US 2 just north of Bethel. They have canoes, kayaks, tubes, and stand-up paddle boards, too, as well as a campground on the banks of the Androscoggin River. There are "short" day trips on the river (1-2 hours, 4 miles) and "long" ones (3-4 hours, 10 miles), and the company offers a shuttle service, as well. Visit betheloutdooradventure.com or call (207) 824-4224.

As you continue to head north on US 2, make a left onto ME 26. This will take you toward northern New Hampshire and into *Grafton Notch State Park*. This is one of western Maine's premier drives—rugged, rounded mountains rise up on either side of the winding road, and seem to catch wayward clouds on their summits. Clear, rushing streams and waterfalls cascade along the roadside, and the Appalachian Trail passes through here, as well. (Excellent day hikes can be launched along the trail in either direction.) Several roadside attractions feature engaging natural phenomena. At *Screw Auger Falls*, for instance, the river corkscrews down through a maze of granite scoured out by torrents during the thaw of the last ice age. *Mother Walker's Falls*, meanwhile, features a tiny waterfall underneath a massive slab of rock that crashed down from the cliffs above (but this one you really have to scramble around to find).

Oxford Hills

Oxford County is noted in certain circles for its deposits of rare minerals, including fine grades of tourmaline prized by gemologists (you'll see stores all across the state selling "fine Maine tourmaline"). To learn more about local minerals, be sure to check out the new *Maine Mineral and Gem Museum*, which had its grand opening in fall 2018. Located at 99 Main St. in downtown Bethel, the museum has stunning examples of hand-selected rock specimens from around the state, as well as a meteorite collection. Its research facility and laboratory are dedicated to the studies of mineralogy (the chemistry, structure, and physical properties of minerals), petrology (the conditions under which rocks are formed), and pegmatology (a coarse kind of granite or igneous rock). Hours are Mon through Sat, 10 a.m. to 5 p.m. (closed Sun). For details, visit mainemineralmuseum.org or call (207) 824-3036.

Those interested in a "field trip" to dig rocks can take one with *Maine Mineral Adventures*; based in Bryant Pond, the outfit brings rockhounds to Mt. Mica in *Woodstock*. Trips are offered every Sunday beginning at 9 a.m. Tickets cost $65 for adults and $35 for children (under 16), and prospectors can bring whatever they find back home. Minerals you're most likely to find include quartz, beryl, rose quartz, feldspar, smoky quartz, and mica. It's suggested you tote along two 5-gallon buckets; for the exceptionally prolific, additional buckets can be had for $10. Maine Mineral Adventures is open daily (that is, when the ground is soft enough to dig) from 10:30 a.m. to 3 p.m., and has sifting tables full of straight run mine material that is regularly brought in by dump truck. For $15, you get a "dig your own" bucket, or you can choose from prefilled specialty buckets in various levels of quality for $25, $50, or $100. Tourmaline is 100 percent guaranteed in every bucket. Visit digmainegems.com or call (207) 674-3440.

Another option is *Mt. Mann Jewelers* at 57 Main Street in Bethel. The shop carries examples of the minerals that collectors are likely to gather locally. Jim Mann, a professional jeweler and collector, has something for everyone, including children—he particularly hopes to get a new generation "hooked"

Elementary, Watson

Maine black bears are just as afraid of humans as we are of them, and encounters are usually rare. Nonetheless, bears are large, powerful carnivores and must be treated with respect. Never purposely approach a bear, especially a sow with cubs. Stand still, and if a bear approaches too close, back away to safety. As a last resort, never run, but wave your hands, holler, and present a big profile. And never climb a tree because black bears can climb, too. For all that, though, black bears are reclusive, retiring animals, and a bear sighting (at a safe distance, of course) is a rare treat. So when the opportunity presents itself, enjoy it!

on mineral collecting. Mt. Mann Jewelers is open year-round, Tues through Sat, from 10 a.m. to 5 p.m. For more information call (207) 824-3030.

Bethel Outdoor Adventures also offers guided tours of mine excavations. This includes a visit to two different tunnels, where area minerals and the techniques used to mine them are dramatically presented.

In nearby *Rumford*, whose downtown is located on a river island in the shadow of a Boise Cascade paper mill, you'll find a "gem" of a different sort. The former industrial town retains the vestiges of a unique and enlightened experiment in corporate paternalism dating from the early 20th century. The *Strathglass Park Historic District* consists of fifty-one elegant brick buildings located in a park-like setting amid pines and silver maples located on a hillside across from the mill. The neighborhood's character is sort of Birmingham, England—by way of Boston's Beacon Hill.

The homes were built in 1901–02 by Hugh Chisholm, a principal in the Oxford Paper Company. Appalled by the living conditions of many company workers and hoping to attract a more qualified workforce, Chisholm commissioned a New York architect to design these spacious duplexes surrounded by broad lawns. Workers nominated by their foremen were given first crack at renting the new homes at reasonable rates, for which all services were provided. The company sold off the buildings in the late 1940s, and today they are all privately owned. For the most part, they remain in fair to good condition. To reach Strathglass Park, turn off US 2 uphill on Main Street, then make the next right between the tall stone columns.

Another intriguing historic setting, albeit from an earlier age, may be found in southern Oxford County, not far from ME 26. *Paris Hill* is notable both for its assortment of handsome Federal-style homes and as the birthplace of Hannibal Hamlin, a Maine political icon and vice president under Abraham Lincoln in his first term. This ridgetop setting, with views toward the White Mountains, serves as a fine backdrop for an uncommonly well-preserved village of 19th-century houses. With the highway some distance away, it also has a dignified country feel.

The *Hamlin Memorial* (207-743-2980; hamlin.lib.me.us) in Paris Hill is located adjacent to Hannibal Hamlin's grand estate on the village green and is the only building open to the public. This stout granite building served as a local jail between 1822 and 1896. In 1901 it was purchased by one of Hamlin's descendants and converted into a library and museum, which it remains to this day. The museum displays examples of early American primitive art, local minerals, and items related to Hamlin's life such as portraits and campaign artifacts. It is open year-round, Tues from 11 a.m. to 5 p.m., Thurs from 1 to 6 p.m., and Sat from 10 a.m. to 2 p.m.

Gilded Hills

Ever hear of the Maine gold rush? Didn't think so. But the nation's first gold strike was in **Byron**, a small town on ME 17 north of Rumford. That find—a legitimate if small one—triggered a whole series of later gold rushes following the 1849 California gold rush. The fortunes made out West made it easy to dupe investors into believing that they should act quickly if they didn't want to get left behind. Under such mass delusion, a number of "paper mines" and fraudulent corporations were created to tap Maine's untold gold wealth—subsequently enriching the unscrupulous and impoverishing the gullible.

Like many scams, this one was made all the more believable because gold does exist naturally in parts of Maine. Even today the land around the Swift River in Roxbury and Byron grudgingly yields up gold flakes and the infrequent tiny nugget. You can try your hand at gold panning anywhere along the stream. A good place to begin is the Maine Mineral and Gem Museum, where you can ask for advice on where to go and the best techniques.

At any rate, panning is a good excuse to poke around on quiet streams. You may even run into an old-timer panning along the stream, who may proffer some suggestions and stories.

In nearby South Paris is the ***McLaughlin Garden and Horticultural Center***, a scenic, unassuming find in an otherwise busy concrete jungle lined with gas stations, fast food restaurants, small markets and vintage motels. Bernard McLaughlin, an amateur gardener who worked in a local grocery store, started planting and cultivating the gardens in 1936. When he retired in 1967, he devoted himself to them full-time, collecting plants from the world over. After McLaughlin's death, the home and gardens were acquired by a nonprofit foundation, which now maintains the grounds and is striving to restore them to their former grandeur with the help of various other groups, including the Maine State Historic Preservation Commission and the national Garden Conservancy. There are also a store and a gracious cafe on the grounds, where visitors can enjoy light lunches or a nice cup of tea and pick up a variety of seeds, plants, and garden tools. From Mother's Day weekend through Oct, the cafe and store are open Tues through Sun, 10 a.m. to 4 p.m.

The gardens are located at 97 Main St. (ME 26) in South Paris (just before the county court house and the old brick railroad station). They are open from dawn to dusk during the growing season. Admission is free (donations accepted). For more information call (207) 743-8820 or visit mclaughlingarden .org. Check out the website for special events, such as wildflower celebrations, lilac festivals. and various workshops and lectures held throughout the year.

Road to Whimsville

It's a good bet that you won't find a more international collection of place names than in western Maine (except of course, in Europe itself). Perhaps the most famous signpost is in **Lynchville** (near North Waterford), at the intersection of ME 5 and ME 35. Here you'll see the mileage to nearby Maine towns with names like Denmark, China, Poland, Paris, and Norway. The famous sign has appeared in postcards and countless snapshots. It's also been cut down and stolen dozens of times. So today, it's now mounted on steel I-beams, cleverly planked with wood to preserve the old-fashioned effect.

Another riff on the same theme can be found at a lesser-known signpost in the village of **Casco**, over near Lake Sebago. That signpost offers direction and mileage to these familiar-sounding Maine towns: Washington, Jefferson, Madison, Monroe, Jackson, Van Buren, Harrison, Lincoln, Garfield, and Clinton. It was put up in the mid-1990s by a local Boy Scout troop.

Another unique find is the ***Celebration Barn Theater***, located on 190 Stock Farm Rd (just off ME 117). The nonprofit offers "immersive physical theater training," where artists live, rehearse, and perform on-site. The off-beat locale features an eclectic range of shows throughout the summer, including small concerts and contemporary dance recitals, as well as storytelling events and the spectacle of clown duos and circus performers. A longtime mainstay is Mike Miclon's "The Early Evening Show," a spoof of late night talk shows featuring special guests, improvisation, sketches, and audience participation. The show is held the first Sat of every month at 7:30 p.m. Tickets are $16 for adults, $14 for seniors, and $10 for kids. For details, visit celebrationbarn.com or call (207) 743-8452.

Androscoggin County

Androscoggin County tends to fall between the cracks. It's not the Casco Bay region, but neither is it the Oxford Hills or the Kennebec Valley. We've included it in the Western Mountains section because many people travel through the county en route to the mountains from the coast. Don't rush the trip; this small county is best appreciated at a slower pace.

Poland Spring Area

Just north of the Sabbathday Lake Shaker Community (see Southern Maine/ New Gloucester Region) in Cumberland County, you'll cross the county line and come to ***Poland Spring***. Actually, there's a good chance you'll drive right through it without noticing it. History is strong here, but as with many off-the-beat Maine locales, a town center is not. Maine, although initially part of Massachusetts, is not known for the lush town commons so prevalent in its neighbor to the south.

Poland Spring gained worldwide fame in the 19th century for its waters. In 1794 Jabez Ricker of Alfred, Maine, purchased the land here with its fine spring from the Shakers and established a farm and an inn for travelers. Business was steady, if not spectacular, for half a century, until Jabez's son, Hiram, became convinced that the waters from the spring had cured him of chronic dyspepsia. The spring soon became well known for its healing abilities, and by 1876 the Rickers advertised their water as "a sure cure for Bright's Disease of the kidneys, stone in the bladder and kidneys, liver complaint, dropsy, salt, rheum, scrofula, humors, and all diseases of the urinary organs." A sprawling grand hotel with sweeping views of the Oxford Hills was built in 1875, with the famous waters brought into the hotel via steam pump. At its pinnacle the resort boasted a 200-foot-long dining room and a fireplace that consumed 6-foot logs. The complex also included a number of spacious annexes and outbuildings for guests and staff.

Much of the resort's history may be seen in exhibits in the **State of Maine Building**, located off ME 26 on the grounds of the former **Poland Spring Hotel** (you can't miss the signs). This turreted stone building was constructed for the 1893 Chicago World's Fair, where it was used to display Maine's products. After the exposition the Rickers dismantled the building, shipped it to Maine by train and ox cart, and rebuilt it on their grounds as the resort library.

Managed by the Poland Spring Preservation Society founded in 1976, the building contains fascinating memorabilia of the Poland Spring Hotel, including a model of the magnificent resort itself (which was decimated by fire in 1975), early photographs, and examples of dinnerware and other accoutrements of resort life. There are also detailed cardboard models of architecturally significant buildings of Maine, constructed by Larry Smith. Here you can find the **Maine Gold Hall of Fame**, as well.

The State of Maine Building is an architectural gem, with an open, courtyard-like interior and a lacy skylight brightening the dark woodwork. The building and gift shop are open from mid-May through mid Oct, Mon, Thurs, Fri and Sat from 9 a.m. to 4 p.m., and Sun from 9 a.m. to 1 p.m. For more information call (207) 998-4142 or visit polandspringps.org.

Next to it is early 20th century **All-Souls Chapel**, which began with a simple effort in 1885 by Julius Gassauer to provide religious services to resort employees. The structure and its tower were crafted of Maine-quarried granite, and the chapel is graced with elegant stained glass windows. You'll also see the Poland Spring Resort nearby, where in addition to spending a swanky night or weekend, you can golf an 18-hole course or explore a network of groomed, on-site trails. Visit polandspringinns.com or call (207) 998-4351.

Poland Spring bottled water is still sold in stores all along the eastern seaboard and beyond, although the claims of its healing powers have been tempered somewhat. (It cures thirst, but little else.) Over the years, also, there have been questions about the validity of its "source"—but the company claims its product is 100 percent natural spring water derived from eight springs across Maine. You'll find its bottles in virtually all state grocery and convenience stores (and you might even hear or see commercials with the catchy ditty, "Poland Spring: What it Means to be from Maine"). The Nestle conglomerate now owns the company and pumps water up from the Poland aquifer and other springs for bottling and reshipping.

While in town, check out the recreation options at **Range Pond State Park**, whose entrance is off Empire Road. It features a network of easy trails crossing old logging roads and railroad beds, as well as a white sandy beach with an adjacent 1,000-foot-long promenade. For mountain bikers, there are 8 miles of beginner-level trails that have recently been added and updated by the park working with the Maine chapter of the New England Mountain Bike Association; in addition to blazing trails and keeping the woods trimmed back, they have installed bog bridges and signs. The park is open year-round, 9 a.m. to sunset. Entry fee is $8 for adult non-residents, $2 for senior non-residents, $1 for children (ages 5-11), and free for children under five and seniors (over 65).

Lewiston–Auburn and Vicinity

Not far from Poland Spring is the unassuming town of **Lisbon Falls**, dominated by formidable brick factory buildings along the Androscoggin River. Here in the center of town, you'll find a small restaurant paying homage to another beverage that claimed to be its own curative elixir.

In 1885 Dr. Augustin Thompson, a native of Union, Maine, patented and began producing a bitter, non-alcoholic drink he called Moxie Nerve Food. A master of marketing, he claimed that the secret to the beverage had been obtained by one "Lieutenant Moxie." Adventurer Moxie had witnessed South American Indians consuming the juice of a certain plant, which infused them with preternatural strength. So the story went, the miraculous plant was brought back from overseas and given to Dr. Thompson, who distilled his beverage and named it after its discoverer (whose true identity has been lost to history). Thompson claimed that **Moxie** would "cure brain and nervous exhaustion, paralysis, loss of manhood, softening of the brain and mental imbecility." And bet you didn't know that the name was so popular that it became the derivation of the English word synonymous with pluck and courage. Moxie was one of the first mass-produced soft drinks in the country, and the caramel-colored, distinctly-flavored liquid was the drink of choice throughout New England in the early 20th century until being eclipsed by Coca-Cola. Known for its bright orange cans and bottles, it was named the official state soft drink in 2005. Many a long-time Mainer will continue to claim that the distinct beverage is their all-time favorite; it is an acquired taste, for sure, defying explanation—while visiting Maine, there's no better time to try it for yourself.

So exactly where does Lisbon Falls come into this tale? Through the doors of Frank's Restaurant and Pub, named for the late Frank Anicetti, "Mr. Moxie," or "Moxie man." For decades, his Kennebec Fruit Store was known as the *Moxie Capital of the World*. Opened by his grandfather in 1914, it became a virtual Moxie museum over the years, housing a wide selection of Moxie paraphernalia (T-shirts, books, signs, and much more) and other items of interest to Moxie aficionados, history buffs and antiquers. Anicetti also sold his own Moxie ice cream (an acquired taste in and of itself), and became well-known for his love of the soda and his willingness to talk about Moxie and its history longer than probably any other living human being. Anicetti passed away in 2017, and his former store has been transformed into Frank's, named in his honor and featuring some of his beloved memorabilia, as well as an assortment of burgers and salads, "Moxie BBQ" sauce, and of course, a Moxie float. You can find it at the corner of ME 196 and Main Street in downtown Lisbon Falls. Visit franksrestaurantpub.com or call (207) 407-4606 for more information.

Lisbon also hosts the celebrated *Moxie Festival* every year in July (which, too, was begun by the Moxie-fervent Anicetti). The three-day event is held across town, and features a 5K run, block party, parade, fireworks, talent contest, recipe contest (you won't believe what people come up with, from taffy and shortbread to sliders and wings), and a chugging challenge that is "not for the faint of heart of the esophagus." Winners, including several-time champion Beau Bradstreet of Bridgewater, Maine, can consume at least seven cans in 2

notonasunday

Up until recently, Maine had some of the most far-reaching blue laws on the books—those legal strictures against selling on Sunday. They were repealed in 1990 for all shops and retailers (although alcohol is prohibited for sale in stores from 1 to 6 a.m. daily, and from 1 to 9 a.m. on Sun)—except for one group. Automobile dealers are still required by state law to close on Sunday. That exception came at the request of both the dealers (who wanted rest) and customers (who liked to window-shop without having salespeople hovering). Hunting on Sunday is also prohibited in Maine.

minutes. Visit moxiefestival.com. Still craving more Moxie? Check out the New England Moxie Congress at moxiecongress.org, and the company's website at drinkmoxie.com.

Down the road, the twin cities of **Lewiston–Auburn** form the commercial center of Androscoggin County, making up Maine's second-largest urban area (after Portland). The twin cities were widely known in the 19th century as one of the shoemaking capitals of New England. During World War I, 75 percent of all canvas shoes in the world were made in Lewiston.

The city's luster was lost with the shuttering of the factories, however—and as is the case with many former mill cities, the area is working to redefine their image and downtowns. Vestiges of its boom times are clearly seen in the vast Dickensian factory buildings lining the river's edge. Between the two cities the Androscoggin River tumbles over a series of falls, and during spring, the runoff presents a gloriously tumultuous display. West Pitch Park on the Auburn side of the river is a fine place to view both the cataracts and Lewiston's historic skyline of square factories punctuated with soaring spires. You can further explore its history at the **Museum Lewiston-Auburn** (museumla.org) on Canal St.

You might find it worthwhile to visit the spires at the **Basilica of Saints Peter and Paul**, an imposing Gothic edifice that looms over Lewiston and lends it a distinctly European flavor. Built during the Great Depression, the church is a proud testament to the city's fiercely Catholic French–Canadian population, which settled here in great numbers during Lewiston's glory days as an international manufacturing hub. It is notable for a pair of 168-foot towers made of Maine granite, as well as a magnificent, lofty nave with a lovely rose window. After years of deterioration, an extensive $2 million restoration brought back much of its former luster.

Also in Lewiston is the campus of **Bates College**, a distinguished four-year liberal arts school that can claim Edmund Muskie and Bryant Gumbel among its alumni. Bates began more than a century ago as a Baptist seminary; it subsequently expanded both its academic mission and its campus. Many distinctive buildings grace the attractive grounds, which are overarched with an abundance of trees. Worth visiting is the modern **Olin Arts Center**, which stages community performances and displays the college's permanent collection. Paintings in the college's airy art museum include rotating exhibits from students and locals, as well as works from the noted **Marsden Hartley Memorial Collection**. Hartley was a Lewiston native who went on to international acclaim as one of the most important modernist American painters. He is known for his bold, colorful landscapes, many of which portray the hills and coastlines of Maine.

One of the best antiques shops in the state is across the river in *Auburn*. Don't come to *Orphan Annie's* looking for Empire furniture or moose heads. Marketing itself as three floors of "stuff" at 96 Court St., the focus here is on collectibles you can carry with you, many dating from the art deco and art nouveau periods. Look for old toys, hats, Depression glass, cigarette cases, and advertising pieces, along with their superb collection of early stained glass. It's a great place to lapse into nostalgic reveries, and an easy spot to lose track of time. (But you can always buy an antique watch here to solve that problem.) It's open Mon through Sat from 10 a.m. to 5 p.m., and noon to 5 p.m. on Sun. Annie's also features a furniture warehouse sale every Mon from 10 a.m. to 1 p.m. For more information call (207) 782-0638 or visit orphananniesme.net.

If you're in town at the time, you also don't want to miss the *Great Falls Balloon Festival*, (207-240-5931; greatfallsballoonfestival.org) held annually in August. Established in 1992, the nonprofit fundraiser is based out of Simard-Payne Memorial Park in Lewiston, and features a parade, carnival, balloon rides, and a special "moonglow" event where visiting balloons inflate and light their burners to create a ground-level light show.

A Real Maine Knockout

It's an iconic sports image: Boxing great Muhammad Ali standing over knocked-out opponent Sonny Liston, goading him on with a gloved hand. It is arguably one of the greatest moments in modern sports history—but did you know it took place in (of all places) Lewiston? It nearly didn't. The second of two fights between the feuding boxers was scheduled for May 25, 1965 in Boston. The first bout was held on Feb 25, 1964 in Miami; Ali, who had recently changed his name from Cassius Clay and announced himself as a black Muslim and member of the Nation of Islam, had won by technical knockout (ultimately a controversial decision). Leading up to the rematch, Liston, who had a long criminal history and had in fact learned to box while at the Missouri State Penitentiary while doing a stint for armed robbery, was once again arrested. Reactionary Boston officials feared that promoters Inter-Continental were somehow tied to organized crime, and, just 18 days before the fight, the company decided to pull out of the city and go elsewhere. Organizers were in a hectic scramble; Maine Governor John H. Reed stepped forward and the fight was quickly relocated to the Central Maine Youth Center (today the Androscoggin Bank Colisee). Due to the location as well as the controversial nature of its two headliners (people feared an outbreak of violence), the arena was only about half-full. But the fight went down in history, with the famously bombastic floating-like-a-butterfly-stinging-like-a-bee Ali knocking Liston out in the first round. Lewiston, for its part, went down in history as one of the smallest cities in the U.S. to host a heavyweight title bout, and the fight remains the only heavyweight title event held in Maine.

Livermore Area

Maine's numerous historic homes and buildings—from Kittery to Madawaska—provide good vantage points for viewing the state's past. But one destination near the town of *Livermore* offers much more than just a view. Here, visitors can travel back in time; more precisely, they can experience life on a Maine farm ca. 1870.

Washburn-Norlands Living History Center, set on 445 acres of forest and farmland, literally keeps old-time traditions alive. The site is the ancestral home of the political dynasty the Washburns, whose ancestors went on to become US senators, Secretaries of State, foreign ministers, governors, and prominent war generals and captains. It was named by Charles Ames Washburn after a line in a Tennyson poem that describes winds howling across rolling fields: "When the long dun wolds are ribb'd with snow / And loud the Norland whirlwinds blow."

And while other living history museums give you a view into the past, Norlands actually lets some visitors live it; the site offers 24-hour live-in programs, where participants (ages 9 and up) take on the habits, duties, and chores of a resident in the 1870s (this is down to the clothing and the facilities—chamber pots and privies). There's a minimum of eight participants, and cost is $125 for adults and $95 for children (ages 12 and younger). Norlands is located on Norlands Road (off ME 108) northeast of Livermore and south of Livermore Falls. For more information visit norlands.org or call (207) 897-4366.

Not looking for that much of an immersive experience? Norlands offers daily living history tours for the modern 21st century traveler, complete with reenactors. These run in July and Aug on Tues, Thurs and Sat, from 11 a.m. to 4 p.m. The tours bring alive the wilds of Maine as they were in the early 19th century. There's a full site tour, a tea party, and lots of storytelling: In the Gothic library you'll hear stories about the fantastically successful Washburn sons, who built the room lined with impressive antique volumes as a memorial to their parents. Three of the brothers served in the US Congress simultaneously (representing three different states), a feat that has not been duplicated by any family since.

Franklin County

Rugged *Franklin County* includes Mount Blue, Rangeley Lake, the Carrabassett Valley, and a host of remote villages. Accommodations range from high luxury to basic necessities, but the landscapes and bountiful wildlife are uniformly enchanting.

Rangeley Lakes Region

As you head north, a "must-drive" is the **Rangeley Lakes National Scenic Byway**. Crossing through a region with more than 40,000 acres of conserved public lands and taking you through forests and across fields, streams and chains of lakes and ponds, it begins at Smalls Falls on ME 4. One of the highlights is known locally and simply as **Height of Land**. Located on the top of Spruce Mountain in Rangeley, it offers a classically Maine view that cascades down to Rangeley Lake; you'll know it when you've arrived. After following the twisting road as it ascends the rolling hills, you'll suddenly come upon **Mooselookmeguntic Lake**—massive, indomitable, and (most likely, no matter the time of year) stippled with whitecaps. The view is perhaps the most spectacular in Maine, made all the more so because it comes so unexpectedly.

The far lakeshore and two of the largest islands clearly visible at the southern end of the lake—Toothaker and Students—are part of a 6,000-acre wilderness preserve that is private but open to the public. The **Stephen Phillips Memorial Preserve** was set aside three decades ago by Phillips (since deceased), who feared the twin threats of commercial development and state management. His concerns about development proved well founded: Much

Snowmobile Boom

Winter is often considered the slow season in Maine, when residents seem to slip into a sort of quasi-hibernation along with the bears and other wildlife. The booming popularity of the snowmobile has helped to change that, however, with many mountain communities experiencing more business on winter weekends than they do in the summer.

Maine has some 12,000 miles of groomed snowmobile trails lacing its interior, and services aren't hard to find along the way. It's rare to go more than 30 miles between fuel or food stops; look for the informal signs tacked up to trees at intersections pointing you to these outposts of civilization.

Those with their own snowmobiles undoubtedly have a long list of favorite destinations. If you don't own a snowmobile and you're interested in sampling some time on the trail, a growing number of outfitters are now offering rentals, lowering the threshold to motorized winter adventure.

In the Rangeley Lakes region, you can try Dockside Sports Center (samosetfour seasons.com; 207-864-2424) or Rev-It-Up Sports Shop (revitupsports.com; 207-864-2452), both of which offer rentals and can provide tips on destinations. Try Flagstaff Rentals Maine (flagstaffrentalsmaine.com; 207-246-4276) in Stratton (near Sugarloaf). For a wealth of information on laws, trail conditions, events, or clubs, check the Maine Snowmobile Association (mesnow.com; 207-622-6983).

of Mooselookmeguntic's shoreline was subdivided and developed for second homes during the real estate frenzy of the 1980s. The dozens of miles of lakeshore and island property in the preserve are maintained in a natural state and offer some of the more scenic and wild landscapes in Maine. A handful of its lakeside campsites are within a short walking distance from a car, but the majority of the 67 maintained campsites are accessible only by boat. And they're rustic, true "wilderness camping" with no electricity or showers.

True to its out-of-the-way quality, reservations are accepted by mail (P.O. Box 21, Oquossoc, ME 04964) or phone (207-864-2003 from May to Sept). The preserve has a website featuring basic information: stephenphillipswilderness camping.com. If you don't have a reservation, a wooden board near the preserve headquarters is adorned with color-coded washers indicating "available," "occupied," and "reserved" sites.

If you'd rather travel by foot than canoe, a number of excellent hikes are available in the Rangeley region. For starters, you might hike the mile-long trail to the summit of **Bald Mountain**, located on Mooselookmeguntic's lakeshore near Oquossoc; look for trail signs on the lakeshore road 0.8 mile south of Haines Landing. For the more ambitious, a hike along the Appalachian Trail to the top of **Saddleback Mountain** offers rewarding views and a chance to explore a distinctive alpine ecosystem along the barren, windswept ridge. The rugged hike is just over 10 miles round-trip, starting where the Appalachian Trail crosses ME 4 between Rangeley and Madrid. Be sure to bring warm clothing; the weather can deteriorate rapidly above timberline, proving unpleasant for the ill prepared.

The sleepy town of **Rangeley**, on the east shore of sparkling Rangeley Lake, has been a favorite destination for outdoorspeople for more than a century. The town's elevation is 1,546 feet, and the evening temperature often has a bit of a bite even in the middle of summer. Outdoor activities like hunting, fishing, and canoeing are the main allure during the warmer months, and in the winter, both downhill and cross-country skiing, as well as snowmobiling and ice-fishing, serve as the main entertainment. Travelers find a number of options for lodging and restaurants in the area, from modern to rustic. The chamber of commerce (207-864-5571; rangeleymaine.com) can offer plenty of information on what's available.

One person smitten with the Rangeley region was **Wilhelm Reich**, a controversial scientist who worked with Sigmund Freud. While working with the founder of psychoanalysis in Austria, Reich came to believe that Freud's theories of sexual behavior not only had academic usefulness but also could be applied clinically. At the time, it was difficult to one-up Freud and his theories on human repressed sexual urges, but Reich did; he authored *The Function of* *the Orgasm* and attempted to cure neuroses by releasing sexual energy. This was scandalous enough, but his theories about "orgone"—a sort of life force that he claimed could be detected, measured, and manipulated—led to a final break with Freud.

Following Hitler's rise to power, Reich departed Austria and lived in four countries before finally settling at Rangeley in 1942 to further his study of "orgonomy." He designed and built an angular stone house, high upon a hill overlooking the lakes, which he called **Orgonon**. With an array of peculiar-looking devices, he set about furthering his studies but failed to convince many mainstream scientists of orgonomy's validity. He also constructed something called a "cloud buster," a creation that looks like an alien death ray fit for celluloid. He claimed that it removed orgone from the atmosphere, thereby shifting the atmospheric balance and producing rain.

In 1947 the *New Republic* published an article entitled "The Strange Case of Wilhelm Reich," drawing attention to the scientist's claims. The article brought unwelcome attention from the Food and Drug Administration, particularly the "orgone energy accumulators" he built at Orgonon. Patients would sit in these boxlike accumulators, which were designed to absorb orgone and infuse the inhabitants with a renewed energy. The FDA accused Reich of fraud and took him to court. Reich paid no attention to the courts, which he maintained lacked the authority to pass judgment on scientific matters. But he was finally arrested in 1957 after one of his students crossed state lines with an accumulator. The strange case of Wilhelm Reich ended at a federal penitentiary, where shortly after incarceration he died of heart failure at the age of 60.

Orgonon was bequeathed to a private trust and today its 175 acres is managed as a memorial to Reich. The building and views are visually stunning, and the slide show about Reich's life offers a fascinating look at a complex mind. Many of Reich's esoteric devices are on display inside the house, as is his office, library and art studio where he created many of his Edvard Munch–like works after taking up oil painting in 1952. There's even a cloud buster exhibited near a bust of its creator, located at an overlook just a short walk from the house (which also boasts a magnificent view of Rangeley Lake).

Orgonon's museum and energy observatory is open in July and Aug, Wed through Sun from 1 to 5 p.m. In Sept, it is open only on Sat from 1 to 5 p.m. Private tours are offered at other times of the year. Admission is $8 for adults, and children (under 12) are admitted free. The grounds are 3.5 miles west of the town of Rangeley on ME 4. Visit wilhelmreichtrust.org or call (207) 864-3443 for more information.

Just a mile east of Rangeley on ME 16 is the **Maine Forestry Museum at Rangeley**, which started as the Rangeley Lakes Region Logging Museum in 1979. It took seed about ten years earlier, when longtime woodsman and resident Rodney Richard saw a timber foreman about to dump an antiquated piece of logging equipment down an embankment. "I'll take that," he said, and so the collection began.

The museum is a good spot to learn more than a little about the history of the timber industry in the region, which was home to the state's last stands of virgin timber (not surprisingly, they didn't survive the late-19th-century logging boom). Exhibits include hundreds of burly and rusted artifacts from the golden days of timbering, along with more contemporary chainsaw carvings and the wonderful faux primitive oil paintings of Alden Grant.

The museum is open Wed through Sun from 10 a.m. to 4 p.m., June to Sept. The site also offers craft and apple harvest festivals, as well as a popular annual logging festival encompassing numerous competitions, a parade and a "bean hole" dinner. For more information, visit maineforestrymuseum.org or call (207) 864-3939.

While you're in town, you don't want to miss out on the **Rangeley History Museum** or the **Outdoor Sporting Heritage Museum**. The two points of interest are situated on opposite ends of Rangeley Lake: The history museum inside an adorably tiny red square building; the sporting museum in a fittingly rustic-looking A-frame cabin. The historical society (rangeleyhistoricalsociety .org) is open in July and Aug, Tues to Sat, from 11 a.m. to 2 p.m. The sporting museum enjoys more expanded hours, open in May, June, Sept and Oct, Wed to Sun from 10 a.m. to 4 p.m., and seven days a week during those same hours in July and Aug.

Classic lakeside lodging can be found at **Grant's Kennebago Camps**, located 9 miles up a dirt road west of town. At the end of the 19th century, Kennebago Lake was renowned for its king-size brook trout, and eager "sports" ventured here to try catching them. Today the camp features a cluster of updated cabins around a main lodge, many of which feature remarkable lake views and have names such as "Bago," "Skeet" and "Royal Blue." Meals are served in a dining room whose walls are chock-full of bits of angling history. For reservations or information call (800) 633-4815 or visit grantscamps.com.

About 30 miles from Rangeley on Lake Webb near the town of **Weld** is another wonderful place to spend a night. The **Kawanhee Inn** was built in 1929 by a camp shop instructor as a place for parents to stay when visiting their kids at the adjacent summer camp of the same name. It's classic Maine, built with yellow birch and a cobblestone fireplace, the whole affair seemingly held together by the creaks of the lustrous pine boards. The guest rooms in the lodge are fairly small, with most sharing hallway baths, but they offer a charmingly rustic interior. A dozen cabins along the lake also are available for rent, although these are usually reserved by the week. The whole place is Maine peace and tranquility at is best, and there's no shortage of activities to keep you and your family busy, from boating, to hiking, to golfing. Inn rates are $110 to $165 daily for lodge rooms and from $200 to $300 for one-to-three-bedroom cabins. Weekly rates start around $1,300. The Inn is open from June through the end of Sept. Visit kawanheeinn.com or call (207) 585-2000.

You can even pan for gold along the Swift River not far away at **Coos Canyon Rock and Gift** (207-364-4900; cooscanyonrockandgift.com). The family has been prospecting here since the 1950s.

Carrabassett Valley

It's inevitable: If you're in Maine, you're going to want to see a moose (what's not inevitable is actually seeing one). One opportunity is taking a drive from Rangeley to Stratton and onward up to **Eustis**. This remote 25-mile trip up ME 16 and continuing on ME 27 passes through prime moose habitat, with low-growing shrubs offering a tasty banquet for these herbivores. Your best bet is to head out shortly before sunset and enjoy the drive. Remember, though, that moose are huge animals, with little fear of motor vehicles. Moose/car collisions are all too common, so exercise extreme caution.

In Eustis look for the roadside historical marker overlooking the Dead River, along the route of Benedict Arnold's 1775 march toward Quebec. (For background, see information on the Arnold Historical Society Museum, Lower Kennebec Valley/Gardiner and Hallowell.) At this bend in the river, the ill-starred expedition faced hurricane-force winds that toppled trees, thus creating yet another obstacle. In the distance you can see **Bigelow Mountain**, named after Colonel Timothy Bigelow of Arnold's crew, who scaled the 4,150-foot peak in a vain attempt to see the lights of Quebec.

The towns along this part of ME 27 fall within the orbit of **Sugarloaf USA**, a modern, active ski area offering more than 2,800 feet of vertical drop, the largest in Maine. Sixteen percent of those are expert-only. In the summer months attention shifts to golf and Sugarloaf's well-respected 18-hole golf course, designed by noted golf course architect Robert Trent Jones II. There's also mountain biking on an expanse of local trails. The resort itself is concentrated around the base of the mountain and features a seven-story brick hotel and a number of condominium clusters; condos may be rented by the night or the week. For more information call (800) 843-5623 or visit sugarloaf.com.

Kingfield is the gateway to Sugarloaf and the Carrabassett Valley. Named after William King, Maine's first governor, Kingfield is a handsome

Porches for Rocking

In the transitional period between the weeklong vacation at the sprawling summer resort and the overnight stop at a simple motel, visiting Maine more often than not can mean renting a lakeside cabin for a week or two. (In Maine these are often called "camps," which are not to be confused with the rustic sort you find in the wilderness or the kind that urbanites deport their kids to in the summer.) Spend your days fishing, canoeing, or biking—gentle exploration where the chief quest is to fill an idle day.

There's still much to be said for this sort of vacation, and Maine is an excellent destination for this brand of advanced idleness. How to find the perfect place? There are a variety of rentals showcased online; another alternative is the Maine Tourism Association, whose site is plentiful and well-updated (800-767-8709; mainetourism.com). You can download a PDF or request a paper version of its free *Maine Guide to Inns and Bed & Breakfasts* and *Maine Guide to Camps & Cottages*. Updated annually, these handy brochures offer brief descriptions and photos of available spots around the state.

and dignified town with a vaguely Old West feel to it, a world apart from the modern chalets of Sugarloaf. Travelers are often attracted here for more than just the skiing.

Before leaving Kingfield be sure to visit the **Stanley Museum** on School Street. You've no doubt heard about the Stanley twins, F. O. and F. E., inventors of the Stanley Steamer. The twins and their five brothers and sisters were born and raised in Kingfield, and this intriguing museum is a well-designed memorial to their many talents. Even before the twins launched their automobile enterprise, they had made their fortune with inventions in the dry-plate photographic process, creating a company that was eventually purchased by George Eastman, Kodak's founder. Funds from their photographic enterprise enabled the brothers to launch their steam car company.

The museum, housed in a Georgian-style schoolhouse built with Stanley family donations in 1903, includes an informative exhibit on the family's history as well as three restored steamers. These aren't simply static museum pieces; the staff periodically takes them out for parades and other events. (The oil pans on the maple floor beneath the cars attest to their operational capabilities.) These exquisite automobiles, which had more in common with steam locomotives than with today's internal combustion engines, were first constructed as a hobby. When the Stanleys brought their car to the first New England auto show in 1898, they won both the time trials and the hill-climbing contest and received one hundred orders within a week. The autos were manufactured between 1897 and 1925, reaching their pinnacle in 1906, when they set a land speed record of 127 miles per hour.

Founded in 1981, the museum, located in an elegantly pillared, pale yellow mansion, also celebrates the achievements of the other Stanleys, most notably Chansonetta, the twins' younger sister, who proved herself an accomplished photographer. Her haunting portraits of rural and urban New England in the late 19th century are exceptional and have recently attracted respect and attention in the fine-arts world.

The Stanley Museum is open May through Oct, Tues through Sun from 11 a.m. to 4 p.m., and Nov through Apr, Tues to Fri, 11 a.m. to 4 p.m. Admission is $4 for adults, $3 for seniors, and $2 for children (ages 12-18). For more information call (207) 265-2729 or visit stanleymuseum.org.

At the northern end of the Sugarloaf universe is the town of **Stratton,** which offers several low-key hotels and restaurants. Among the more interesting is the delightful **White Wolf Inn**, a restaurant/inn on Main St./Rte. 27 dating to 1935. The chef/owner prepares all menu items fresh from scratch, so don't miss a meal here. Offerings include everything from prime rib and barbecued beef to duck, quail, and smoked trout, as well as giant "wolf" burgers and "down home" turkey pot pie. Specials always change according to chef whims and availability of ingredients. Then there are the homemade desserts, which are sumptuous and vary with the seasons.

The inn offers air-conditioned rooms, and it is also pet-friendly, so don't hesitate to bring your four-legged companion. Room rates during the week are $69 for two, increasing to $79 on the weekend. For more information visit thewhitewolfinn.com or call (207) 246-2922.

Farmington and Vicinity

Another bit of local celebrity may be found on the eastern edge of the county, in the prosperous town of **Farmington**. A branch of the **University of Maine** is located here, as is the nearby **Nordica Homestead**, birthplace of one of opera's glamorous stars. Lillian Norton was born at this modest farmhouse in 1857, then at age 7 moved with her family to Boston. In Beantown she studied at the conservatory under John O'Neil, who rightly marked her as someone with significant talent. Following her studies, she changed her name to Nordica to reflect her northern roots, and was soon off to Europe. There she took the concert halls by storm. She became widely renowned as one of the few sopranos who could sing Wagnerian roles in tune, and she was feted by kings and presidents alike.

Well after her fame blossomed, Nordica's sisters purchased her birthplace as a birthday present for the star. Following the diva's death in 1914 (she succumbed to pneumonia while on a tour of the South Pacific), the 1840 home situated on 108 acres became a memorial to the legendary singer, and many of

Unassuming Wilton

Southwest of Farmington is the unassuming lakeside town of **Wilton**. There's not much here to attract the attention of tourists, but it is home to some intriguing historical footnotes. In 1823 **Sylvia Hardy** was born here. At just shy of 8 feet tall and weighing 400 pounds, Hardy became known as the "Maine Giantess." As with many unusually tall and short people of the era, she was recruited by P. T. Barnum, who billed her as the "tallest woman in the world." She died in 1888 and is buried in the Wilton cemetery.

Wilton was also home to **Henry Bass**, inventor of the loafer and founder of a successful shoe manufacturing empire. A bit of trivia: The famed Bass "Weejun"—a sort of fancy moccasin—gets its name from the last two syllables of "Norwegian."

Wilton was likewise the site of the first (and last known) fiddlehead cannery, W.S. Wells & Son, still in operation today. Fiddleheads are those springtime New England delicacies that go so well with scrambled eggs and served as a side dish. You can usually find canned fiddleheads in supermarkets around Maine.

her possessions were shipped here. Among the interesting items in the collections are the diva's opera gowns (including a Viking-helmeted Brunhilde outfit), stage models, and numerous portraits and photos chronicling her career. A number of gifts presented to Nordica by admirers are also on display; they include a lacquered teakwood table from the empress of China and a garish velvet-and-gilded chair from Diamond Jim Brady.

The Nordica Homestead is located off ME 4 and ME 27, 2 miles north of Farmington. Turn right on Holley Road and continue for 0.5 mile; the homestead is on the right, marked with a large wooden sign graced by the prima donna's face. The museum is open June 1 through Labor Day, Tues through Sun from 1 to 5 p.m. Cost of admission is $5 for adults and $2 for children. For more information visit lilliannordica.com, or call (207) 778-2042.

We can't leave Farmington without mentioning that it was also the home of Chester Greenwood, who in 1872 invented that humble but eminently useful bit of winter outerwear, the earmuff—or "ear protector," as he called it. The town has celebrated his accomplishment for decades, particularly each Dec on **Chester Greenwood Day**, when the earmuff-adorned citizenry assembles for considerable mirth and frivolity. A parade through the downtown area even features earmuff-clad cars, tractors, and animals—and keep your eye out for the giant earmuffs that pop up to adorn local homes and businesses. Visit downtownfarmington.com.

Places to Stay in the Western Mountains

BETHEL

The Bethel Inn Resort
21 Broad St.
(207) 824-2175
bethelinn.com
Moderate
See main entry (p. 66)
for full description

Sunday River Ski Resort
15 South Ridge Rd., Newry
(207) 824-3000
sundayriver.com
Moderate
Favorite place to ski and
stay, with snow lasting for
a long season here (even
into spring)

CARRABASSETT VALLEY

The Herbert Grand Hotel
Main St., Kingfield
(207) 265-2000
herbertgrandhotel.com
Inexpensive
Historic hotel. Owners cater
to guests. Comfortable and
affordable.

Sugarloaf Inn
Sugarloaf Mountain
(800) THE–LOAF or
(207) 237-2000
sugarloaf.com
Inexpensive
Convenient location; cozy
and affordable

FARMINGTON

Farmington Motel
489 Farmington Falls Rd.
(800) 654-1133 or
(207) 778-4680
farmingtonmotel.com
Inexpensive
Great home base for fishing
and ski vacations

Mount Blue Motel
454 Wilton Rd.
(207) 778-6004
colonialvalleymotel.com/
mount-blue-hotel
Inexpensive
Offers free coffee and
continental breakfast

SELECTED CHAMBERS OF COMMERCE

Androscoggin County Chamber of Commerce
415 Lisbon St., Lewiston
androscoggincounty.com
(207) 783-2249

Bethel Area Chamber of Commerce
8 Station Pl
bethelmaine.com
(207) 824-2282

Franklin County Chamber of Commerce
franklincountymaine.org
(207) 778-4215

Greater Bridgton Lakes Region Chamber of Commerce
101 Portland Rd, Bridgton
mainelakeschamber.com
(207) 647-3472

Oxford Hills Chamber of Commerce
4 Western Ave., South Paris
oxfordhillsmaine.com
(207) 743-2281

Rangeley Lakes Region Chamber of Commerce
6 Park Rd., Rangeley
rangeleymaine.com
(207) 864-5364

FREYBURG/LOVELL

Center Lovell Inn and Restaurant
ME 5, Main St.
(207) 925-1575
centerlovellinn.com
Inexpensive
Martha Stewart and Rachael Ray both rate the inn and restaurant highly. Great mountain views.

The Oxford House Inn and Restaurant
ME 302
(207) 935-3442
oxfordhouseinn.com
Moderate
Built in 1913 by John Calvin Stevens, and featuring the granite-walled pub Jonathan's

Pleasant Point Inn and Resort
159 Pleasant Point Rd.
(207) 925-3008
pleasantpointinn.com
Moderate
Offers come complete with continental breakfast

RANGELEY

Country Club Inn
56 Country Club Rd.
(207) 864-3831
countryclubinnrangeley.com
Inexpensive
A comfortable stay for a Rangeley Region salmon-fishing trip.

The Rangeley Inn
2443 Main St.
(207) 864-3341
therangeleyinn.com
Moderate
The restored landmark property dates to the late 19th century.

WATERFORD

Bear Mountain Inn
364 Waterford Rd.
(207) 583-4404
bearmtninn.com
Moderate
Rustic, serene and cozy

The Waterford Inne
258 Chadbourne Rd.
(207) 583-4037
waterfordinne.com
Moderate
Classic country setting includes red barn, rolling hills, and small pond. Feel free to bring your pet.

Places to Eat in the Western Mountains

BETHEL

Kowloon Village
Mountain View Mall, Lower Main St.
(207) 824-3707
kowloonvillage.com
Inexpensive
See main entry (p. 66) for full description.

Sudbury Inn
151 Main St.
(207) 824-2174
thesudburyinn.com
Moderate
Built in 1783, old-time elegance. Try its rack of lamb or roast duckling.

Sunday River Brewing Company
29 Sunday River Rd.
(207) 824-4253
sundayriverbrewing
company.com
Moderate
Good deals on draughts and wings

FRYEBURG

302 West Smokehouse and Tavern
636 Main St.
(207) 935-3021
302west.com
Inexpensive
A boisterous local hangout full of personality

Oxford House Inn
548 Main St.
(800) 261-7206 or
(207) 935-3442
oxfordhouseinn.com
Expensive
Package deals include food, wine, and canoeing.

Two Black Dogs Country Pub
2 Jockey Cap Ln
(207) 256-3036
twoblackdogspub.com
Moderate
Comfort food aplenty, including pigs in a blanket and mac-n-cheese

**KINGFIELD &
CARRABASSETT VALLEY**

The Herbert
246 Main St., Kingfield
(207) 265-2000
Moderate
See main entry (p. 87)
for full details.

One Stanley Avenue
1 Stanley Ave., Kingfield
(207) 265-5541
stanleyavenue.com
Expensive
Features regional
delicacies. Classic Maine
cuisine.

Tufulio's
Valley Crossing, on ME 27
(207) 235-2010
Moderate

RANGELEY

Country Club Inn
56 Country Club Rd.
(207) 864-3831
countryclubinnrangeley
.com
Moderate
Seafood fans will
appreciate pan-seared
Alaska salmon served on
black bean relish. Or try
the seafood Newburg with
lobster, shrimp, scallops,
and haddock.

**The Rangeley Inn Dining
Room**
2443 Main St.
(207) 864-3341
therangeleyinn.com
Moderate
Savor a sample from their
extensive wine collection—
or just enjoy one of the
many Maine micro-brews.

Lower Kennebec Valley

The **Kennebec River** flows from Moosehead Lake in northern Maine some 150 miles to the Atlantic Ocean at Phippsburg. The rushing water body is famed for the excellent fishing and challenging white water along its northern stretches (see the North Woods section). As it descends toward the sea, the river slows and broadens, meandering through farm country and past former mill towns, trading posts, forts, and other vestiges of a varied history. The Kennebec was one of the first rivers in Maine to be explored by Europeans, who established trading routes along its length. In fact, Massachusetts's Plymouth Colony built a fur-trading post at what is present-day Augusta as early as 1628. Some historians say that business was so profitable that settlers were soon able to pay off the lofty debts incurred by the *Mayflower* expedition.

Kennebec County

Kennebec County is a rough triangle right in the middle of the state's southern tier. While it is some distance inland from the coast, it can trace its history to seafaring days when lumber ships sailed up the broad river valley, providing a vital link to

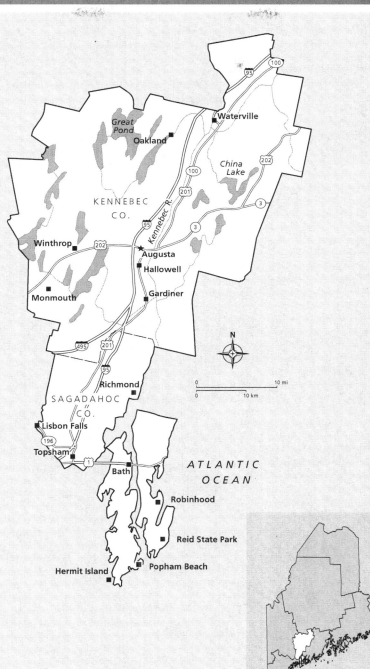

Great
Pond

Waterville

Oakland

China
Lake

KENNEBEC
CO.

Kennebec R.

Winthrop

Augusta

Hallowell

Monmouth

Gardiner

N

SAGADAHOC
CO.

Richmond

Lisbon Falls

Topsham

Bath

ATLANTIC
OCEAN

Robinhood

Reid State Park

Hermit Island

Popham Beach

0   10 mi
0   10 km

the world beyond. Today this gentle region offers inviting pastoral landscapes and historic riverside communities, including within the state capital of Augusta.

Waterville Region

Starting upriver from *Waterville*, you'll find the *L. C. Bates Museum*, on the campus of the *Hinckley School* just off US 201 south of the intersection with ME 23. It was founded by L. C. Bates, a successful entrepreneur from West Paris, Maine, who financed the conversion of this industrial arts building to a museum in 1924. The conversion produced eight galleries full of exhibits on natural history. The museum operated until the late 1960s, but then fell into disuse and closed for nearly three decades. In 1990 a group of local citizens banded together to reopen the museum, which had been largely undisturbed over the years save for an impressive accumulation of dust and cobwebs.

Thanks to this benign neglect, the museum was preserved in a wonderfully archaic state. Located in a sprawling turreted brick manor, it boasts a copious collection of minerals; baskets by the Penobscot Indians; cases featuring stuffed bear, caribou, and the peculiar calico deer; and no fewer than seven magnificent moose heads. Among the best elements of the collection are its stuffed birds—including exotic birds of paradise and the rare quetzal from Central America—which are displayed against outstanding impressionistic backgrounds painted by nationally known illustrator Charles D. Hubbard. Be sure also to note the massive stuffed marlin caught off Bimini in the Bahamas by novelist Ernest Hemingway in 1935. No one seems to be able to explain quite how it got here (in fitting with the globetrotting writer's peculiar ways). There are several walking trails on the grounds; they pass quite a few handsome stone edifices and memorials. These trails are open to the public during museum hours; ask for a trail brochure at the front desk.

birdtrivia

Ospreys (also called sea hawks) are large, handsome silvery-white raptors that all but disappeared from Maine in the 1950s and 1960s due to DDT poisoning. They've bounced back with vigor in the late 20th and early 21st century, and nesting pairs now number in the thousands. Living exclusively on fish, they mate for life, and are distinguished by their fishing style—they basically dive bomb the water from as high as 100 feet before swooping back in the air with their prey. Look for the unkempt nests on piers and telephone poles, particularly on power towers along I-95 between Augusta and Bangor.

The Bates Museum is open from Apr 1 until the middle of Nov, Wed through Sat from 10 a.m. to 4:30 p.m. and Sun from 1 to 4:30 p.m.; other times

Getting Your Two Cents' Worth

Waterville is—or was—home to the world's only pedestrian toll bridge. Look for the **Ticonic Foot Bridge** crossing the Kennebec River in the downtown area. Spanning 400 feet, it was built in 1903 for workers who had to cross from their homes on the far side of the waterway to the Scott Paper Company. From the time it opened until 1962, every person who crossed it was charged two cents, gaining it the more enduring local name, the **Two-Cent Bridge** (Ticonic was derived from the native "Teconnet," named for a local Wabanaki tribe leader). It was closed to foot traffic in 1990 after a rowdy group decided it would be fun to jump up and down in unison, knocking it out of alignment. It underwent significant repairs paid through city bond funds in 2010 and 2011.

are available by appointment. Admission is $3 for adults and $1 for children (18 and younger). For more information call (207) 238-4250 or visit gwh.org/lcbates.

Waterville is perhaps best known for being home to *Colby College*, located just outside town on gentle Mayflower Hill and offering a sweeping view of the rural countryside. The campus has a staid, brick-and-ivy appearance typical to universities across New England, and the college can trace its ancestry to 1813, when it was founded as the Maine Literary and Theological Institution. Following the Civil War it was renamed for Gardiner Colby, a Boston merchant and philanthropist, and in 1871 the college began admitting women. Although the campus has a historic and settled character, that can be a bit misleading. The college moved from its original downtown site in the early 1950s, and today's classically styled buildings date from that era.

Well worth visiting when you're on campus is the *Colby College Museum of Art*. Focusing on American and contemporary art, its impressive collection ranges from the works of such Maine luminaries as Winslow Homer, John Marin, and Andrew Wyeth, to legendary masters like Whistler, O'Keeffe, Picasso, van Gogh, Renoir, and Degas. It is particularly known for its collection of paintings by contemporary artist Alex Katz. A recent gift worth more than $100 million from longtime benefactors Peter and Paula Lunder—who have provided hundreds of pieces of art to Colby and other institutions over the years—will allow the museum to expand its emphasis on American art with a dedicated research institute on the subject. Hours are Tues through Sat from 10 a.m. to 5 p.m. and Sun from noon to 5 p.m.; during the academic year it is open on Thurs until 9 p.m. Closed Mon and on major holidays. Admission is free. For more information call (207) 859-5600 or visit colby.edu/museum.

In downtown Waterville you'll find the *Railroad Square Cinema*. It is a rare treat this day and age: A small local theater that screens a variety of independent and art-house films. Its owners originally took two good ideas—fine movies and fine foods—and combined them into a locale with a funky lobby restaurant. However, a fire in 1994 forced the theater into new quarters; today, the three-screen theater located on 76 Main St. is owned by the nonprofit Maine Film Center (mainefilmcenter.org). It is renowned for hosting the annual *Maine International Film Festival* (miff.org) in July, which attracts hundreds of movie-lovers to Waterville's compact downtown area. For more information visit railroadsquarecinema.com.

Just a few storefronts down at 93 Main St. is the historic *Waterville Opera House*; opened in 1902, its classic, 810-seat auditorium offers performances spanning the cultural spectrum: from ballet to country bands, children's productions to marching band reveries. Visit operahouse.org to find out more about its events.

Now for something completely different: Not far from the bustle of the city in *Unity* is a small (and relatively recently settled) enclave of Amish families. Looking for large, relatively inexpensive tracts of land (and finding them), they relocated to the area from long-established settlements in Aroostook County. Others have since joined them—those not raised in the Amish tradition but looking to escape the confines of contemporary life. Today, the community runs a market on 368 Thorndike Road that is particularly beloved for its donuts, which come in flavors like maple cream, pumpkin cake, and good-old fashioned jelly (but show up early; they're only available on Wed and Sat mornings and they sell out fast). Not far away on Leelyn Road there's also a charcuterie run by big-city-chef-turned-Amish-convert Matthew Secich. That 180-degree turn in values and lifestyle earned the cook and his family a spot in the limelight for a time; but now with things settled down, they focus on making a variety of exemplary cured and smoked meats and cheeses, as well as fresh bread and specialties such as marinated and smoked olives. The rustic little store is only open certain days of the week (typically Wed, Fri, and Sat), so don't miss the opportunity to pop in.

While you're in town you're bound to see the local Amish walking, riding one-speed bikes, or leading carriages along blacktop roads. They're friendly and happy to talk, but please respect their values—one specific no-no is taking pictures of their faces (following the Biblical commandment against graven images and pride).

An equally unexpected find here is the *Savage Oakes Vineyard and Winery*—not necessarily for its 100-percent locally harvested wine (although its award-winning blueberry variety is not to be missed) but for its growing eminence as an outdoor venue. Hundreds of guests have gathered on its lush and rolling grounds for its limited summer concert series, which have included such headliners as Graham Nash, Chris Isaak, and the Indigo Girls. Visit savage oakes.com to find out more. Also check out **Sweetgrass Winery and Distillery** (207-785-3024; sweetgrasswinery.com), which boasts unique offerings such as wild Maine blueberry sangria, Back River gin, and rhubarb smash. The location also hosts the annual Maine Outdoor Film Festival.

Union is perhaps best known, however, for its lively **Common Ground Fair**, sponsored by the **Maine Organic Farmers and Gardeners Association**. An annual tradition held over three days in late September, the event has grown steadily over the years, now attracting upward of 60,000 visitors. It features agricultural demonstrations, as well as examples of traditional New England crafts and activities, such as blacksmithing, stone cutting and carving, and horse-powered logging. Crafters and food vendors also hawk their wares, and there are presentations related to social and political action, environmental concerns and health and healing. (And of course, entertainment, too.)

Between 1976 and 1997 the fair was held in Windsor at the community fairgrounds; in 1998 it moved to its own 220-acre grounds between Unity and Thorndike. The fairgrounds are located on Crosby Brook Rd. off ME 220; keep an eye out for signs. Daily admission is $15 for adults ($10 if bought in advance); $10 for seniors ($8 if bought in advance); children (under 12) and seniors (over 65) are free. For more information call (207) 568-4142 or visit mofga.org.

Makin' Whoopie

Maine is no doubt renowned for its moose, its lobster, its wild blueberries, and its potatoes (grown on vast swaths of farmland up north). And you can add a delightful culinary confection to that list: The whoopie pie. The frosting-filled cake sandwich can be found in stores all over the state, as well as in gourmet bakeries and snack shops. Maine vies with other states (most notably Pennsylvania) as having invented the delicious snack, and locals also once lobbied to have it named the official "state dessert" (but blueberry pie made with wild Maine blueberries reigns supreme in that category). Its sumptuous existence is celebrated at the annual **Maine Whoopie Pie Festival**, held in Dover-Foxcroft in June (mainewhoopiepiefestival.com); and the state holds the title for the largest whoopie pie ever made, weighing in at 1,062-pounds. Check out **Wicked Whoopies** (wickedwhoopies.com), with bake shops in Freeport and Farmingdale; **Steve's Snacks** based out of Skowhegan (stevessnacks.com); or **Cape Whoopies** in South Portland (capewhoopies.com). Gourmet varieties sold by the latter go for (gulp!) $59 a dozen and include a classic variety, as well as such originals as "code red" (red velvet with strawberry cream), "crazy nut job" (walnut cakes with Frangelico cream), and others styled after Boston cream pie or incorporating egg nog, mint, apple spice cake, ginger or pumpkin. There's a reason for that name: You can't help but see the delectable treats and say, "Whoopie!"

Augusta and Environs

The state capital and its surrounding area is small and unassuming (people often overlook it entirely, mistaking the hipper Portland to the south or the synonymous-with-Stephen-King Bangor up north as the state political seat). But it has many nooks and crannies to explore, too.

Classic plays are performed throughout the summer by the **Theater at Monmouth**, a professional repertory company founded in 1970 some 13 miles west of Augusta. Several plays are staged each season, and the series usually includes a work or two by Shakespeare. Shows rotate throughout the week, offering theatergoers the option of coming back a second night for something different. Reservations are recommended. For more information on performances, call (207) 933-9999 or visit theateratmonmouth.org.

Even if you're not much of a theater aficionado, it's still worth a trip to **Monmouth** to view **Cumston Hall**, the historic grandiose building where plays are staged. Built in 1899–1900, this architectural flight of fancy incorporates minarets from the Middle East, Palladian windows, classical pediments, Romanesque arches and flourishes, and Victorian stained glass. Its interiors are lavishly painted with elaborate murals featuring Renaissance-style draped figures and hovering putti. In addition to the opera house, the building is home to the town library, and it also serves as a performance space for numerous other community and school groups.

The building was designed by Harry H. Cochrane, a Monmouth resident of multiple talents. Sometimes called the "Maine Leonardo," he was an artist and muralist by training. While he lacked formal education in architecture, (so he told an interviewer) he studied the building arts to aid his career in decorating public spaces. Cochrane went on to paint the murals in the building, design the stained glass, create the plaster ornamentation, and compose the music and conduct the orchestra for the building's opening night. He later designed six other houses scattered about Monmouth, a town that displays an architecturally eclectic style. Monmouth is also home to the eponymous **Monmouth**

FAVORITE ATTRACTIONS

The Colburn House, Gardiner

L. C. Bates Museum, Waterville region

Maine Maritime Museum, Bath

Maine State Museum, Augusta

Town of Richmond

Town of Unity (Amish settlement and store)

TOP ANNUAL EVENTS

MARCH

The State of Maine Sportsman Show
Augusta, late Mar
(207) 622-4242
mainesportsman.com/sportsmans-show

MAY

Maine Mineral Symposium
Augusta, early May
nemineralconference.org

JUNE

Whatever Week Family Festival
Augusta to Hallowell, late June–early July
(207) 623-4559
augustamaine.com

JULY

Heritage Days
Bath, late June-early July
bathheritagedays.com

SEPTEMBER

Common Ground Fair
Unity, third weekend after Labor Day
(207) 568-4142
mofga.org

The Maine Storytelling Muster
Waterville, mid-Sept
blackstonestoryteller.com/
maine-storytelling-muster

Museum, a small but engaging historical museum open Wed through Sun from 1 to 4 p.m. For more information call (207) 933-2287.

The *Maine State Museum* in Augusta should, by all accounts, be on the beaten path. Surprisingly, it isn't. Few Maine residents—and even fewer out-of-staters—seem to be aware of this jewel of a museum. Evidently its administrators have done a far better job in designing the thoroughly modern, informative, and appealing venue than in getting the word out about it.

Housed in one of those nondescript gray buildings that seem to characterize government complexes everywhere (the museum shares a roof with the Maine State Library and Archives), the collections are aesthetically arranged and neatly presented. There's a sense of discovery and exploration around each corner, from grainy film clips of early loggers working the river drives to a convincing replica of a water-driven woodworking shop. Extensive exhibits provide an overview of both the cultural and the natural history of the state—from the craft of boatbuilding to the extinction of the eastern caribou.

One exhibit of particular interest, "12,000 Years in Maine," covers the broad sweep of the state's earliest inhabitants. A dozen millennia ago, the state's terrain resembled an open Arctic tundra more than the dense woodlands of today, and migratory Native tribes passed through the region hunting caribou. This is reflected in artifacts found near Aziscohos Lake (near Rangeley) and a full-scale diorama of a prehistoric meat cache. Take the time to see the unique artifacts

Hate/Love Relationship

Maine people are big on wood-burning stoves. In late summer, when the first tinge of fall arrives, everyone is keen to fire up the woodstove to "take the chill off." A drive through any Maine village, town, or city at this time will reveal smoke lazily curling from dozens of chimneys. The air acquires the near-cloying scent of smoldering maple. It's a time to reminisce and revel in the change of the seasons. The cozy warmth of the woodstove feels good, like the embrace of a dear, old friend. By late March, however, the woodstove wears out its welcome. People complain about the mess from the wood, the ashes, the nuisance aspect of going to the woodshed in inclement weather. Instead, locals concentrate on the coming spring, when wood-stoves are (usually) no longer needed. It's a long game of waiting, wishing, and mark-ing the time. But, many say, that's part of the adventure of living in a land with four distinct seasons (well, some would argue two—winter and summer). Come fall, the woodstove will be a close and comfy friend once again.

from the so-called Moorehead phase of Native American development (4,800 to 3,800 years ago), which are characterized by long, graceful arrowheads and adzes; as well as the "cabinet of curiosities," featuring natural specimens that served as its first exhibits.

Plan to spend about two hours at the museum, which is located on the grounds of the statehouse complex on State Street in Augusta. It's open Tues through Fri 9 a.m. to 5 p.m., and Sat 10 a.m. to 4 p.m. Admission is $3 for adults, $2 for children (ages 6-18), and free for seniors (ages 62 and older) and children (under 6). For more information call (207) 287-2301 or visit mainestate museum.org.

Near the east end of the museum building you'll come upon a bronze statue of **Samantha Smith**, Maine's young "ambassador of goodwill." Samantha gained unexpected national and international fame after she wrote a letter to former Soviet leader Yuri Andropov questioning his commitment to peace. Andropov responded, inviting the Manchester, Maine, girl to Moscow and setting her off on an early career of diplomacy. That promising career was cut short when Samantha died in a local plane crash in 1985 at the age of 13.

While on the statehouse grounds, take the time to wander around to see government in action. From the museum, walk to the south entrance of the **Maine State House**, an imposing granite edifice originally designed by Charles Bulfinch, the architect of the US Capitol in Washington, D.C. You can learn about the architecture and history of the building during a self-guided tour. Historical markers guide visitors from one station to the next, pointing out various clues to the building's history, such as the 1907 expansion that greatly changed its profile. The south entrance was also the former site of the state museum, as evidenced by the display cases filled with moose, deer, fish, and beaver. The state house is open to the public year-round, Mon through Fri, 8 a.m. to 5 p.m. Guided tours are offered hourly from 9 a.m. to noon.

From the upper floor of the statehouse, be sure to step out onto the open veranda, where you may see legislators and lobbyists chatting in cane-seated rockers. From this vantage you get a fine view eastward across the Kennebec River. Directly below and across State Street is *Capitol Park*, where you'll find *Maine's Vietnam Memorial* as well as the tomb of Enoch Lincoln (a relative of Abraham), the Maine governor who moved the capital from Portland to Augusta in 1827, seven years after statehood. The park also was used as an encampment during the Civil War.

Across the Kennebec from downtown Augusta is *Fort Western*, a relic of the days when the river was the state's central trading route. The fort, built in 1754 by the Kennebec Proprietors (a group of major land owners), served as a garrison and supply station to protect traders venturing into the interior. The Arnold expedition passed by in 1775 en route to Quebec, but the structure was never used in combat.

Today the original 100-foot-long garrison house survives in nearly pristine condition, and the grounds have been augmented by a replica stockade fence and two blockhouses. Visitors take a self-guided walking tour, with informative history lessons offered by costumed interpreters. In the garrison house you'll see clues to the various identities that the building assumed both during and after its service as a fort—at one time or another it was a store, officers' quarters, and even a tenement in the 1920s. Look for intriguing bits of Americana, including an ingenious mousetrap that uses a falling block of wood to capture its prey.

Fort Western is on the east bank of the Kennebec at 16 Cony St. It's open in June and Sept on Fri, Sat, Sun, and Mon from 10 a.m. to 4 p.m.; and daily in July and Aug from 10 a.m. to 4 p.m. Admission is $10 for adults and $6 for children (ages 6-14). For more details, visit oldfortwestern.org.

Gardiner and Hallowell

Head 2 miles downstream from Augusta along the Kennebec's west bank (follow ME 27), and you'll pull into the quiet riverside town of *Hallowell*. Many of the younger state employees live and congregate in Hallowell, lending it a more spirited character than many Maine towns of its size (and in this area). Water Street, a compact thoroughfare of stout brick buildings, offers surprisingly upscale places to dine and drink, as well as a number of good antiques shops for browsing. Much of the 19th-century commercial architecture has

Maine Food

When traveling around Maine, make it a point to stop in at smaller restaurants and eateries, the kind where you'll find the locals. You'll sample local delicacies here, as well as find some of your new favorite Maine dishes—those aforementioned fiddleheads, for example, or specialties such as red flannel hash, American chop suey, and fresh smelts.

Red flannel hash is made from leftover boiled dinner ingredients: ham, turnip, potato, carrot, and cabbage. Beets are added to this, and everything is chopped and then heated. A dash of cider vinegar complements the flavor perfectly.

American chop suey bears no relation to its namesake. It is a hearty mixture of cooked macaroni, tomato sauce, onions, green peppers, and lean ground beef. Served with grated Parmesan cheese, it's Maine's answer to authentic Italian cuisine.

Finally, when a restaurant advertises **fresh smelts**, it means truly fresh smelts—as in just caught. Fried to a golden brown, Maine's rainbow smelts are an epicurean delight.

When in Rome, as they say: While in this great state, be sure to try some of the local fare. It's a fine opportunity to discover Maine off the beaten path.

been well preserved, and the gentrification has been subtle rather than obnoxious. Among the popular spots along Water Street are *Slate's* (slatesrestaurant .com; 207-622-9575), a watering hole and restaurant where you're liable to run into a state legislator or two; and the *Hydeout at the Wharf* (hydeoutat thewharf.com, 207-248-6317), which has an adjoining billiard hall with old-fashioned pool tables and low brass fixtures lighting the felts. Also on Water Street you'll find the *Hallowell Antique Mall* (207-430-8315; hallowellantique mall.com)—which embraces the irony of its position by calling itself the quaint town's "largest antique store." More than 30 dealers provide it with an eclectic variety of items.

Gardiner, a few miles downstream, is in the throes of reinvention and revival. Start out at a historical hangout: The *A-1 Diner* at 3 Bridge St. This 1946 Worcester chrome dining car is one of those classics sought by diner fans nationwide. Manufactured by the Worcester Lunch Car Company in its central Massachusetts namesake city, it features black-and-white tile floors, age-burnished wooden booths, art deco stools, and neat wood trim. As for the menu? It's not so classic. Alongside comfort food faves like pot roast and mashed potatoes, there are creative and delicious dishes such as Greek lemon soup, pad Thai, and Siamese chicken curry. Don't overlook the delicious tapioca pudding, served with a righteous heap of whipped cream. The A-1 (207-582-4804) is open Mon through Thurs 7 a.m. to 8 p.m., Fri and Sat 7 a.m. to

8:30 p.m., and Sun 8 a.m. to 1:30 p.m. They don't have a website, but you can find them on Facebook.

If you're an architecture buff—or just looking for an opportunity to walk off your meal—make a point to wander Gardiner's commercial and residential neighborhoods, which have benefited from recent renovation. There are numerous historic buildings scattered throughout town; one of the most notable is the former home of Pulitzer Prize-winning poet Edwin Arlington Robinson, located at 67 Lincoln Ave. The nonprofit Gardiner Maine Street offers a wealth of information and a variety of maps and podcasts. Visit gardinermainstreet.org.

Gardiner was also the staging point for one of the richer episodes involving the Kennebec River: the Arnold expedition in the fall of 1775. General Benedict Arnold, whose name is now synonymous with "traitor," led one of the more tragic endeavors in the American Revolution while attempting a surprise attack on Quebec. The expedition, which was made up of about 1,150 men, endured horrendous conditions through the Maine wilderness and failed miserably to take the city during an attack in December 1775. Arnold himself was wounded. An excellent fictional narrative dealing with the Arnold expedition may be found in Kenneth Roberts's novel *Arundel*, which is available in both new and used bookshops, as well as online.

Learn more about this ill-fated expedition at the **Colburn House**, managed by the **Arnold Expedition Historical Society**, downstream from Gardiner on the river's east bank in **Pittston**. This fine historic building, home to the Colburn family for more than 200 years, is furnished with period antiques from 1765. Visitors get a quick education in the history of decorative arts and architecture in seeing how the house evolved over the years. The guide will also tell you about Major Reuben Colburn, the original resident, who hosted General Arnold and Aaron Burr for two nights while the final arrangements for the expedition were laid out. In the barn you'll find two early bateaux (flat-bottomed boats), which may or may not have been used in the expedition, as well as a half-dozen replicas commissioned for a 1975 reenactment. ·

A designated state historic site, the museum is off ME 127 in Pittston, south of Randolph and Gardiner. The grounds are open 9 a.m. to sunset daily, and tours are offered on weekends in the summer. Call ahead for details (207) 624-6080, or visit arnoldsmarch.com.

Sagadahoc County

With less than 250 square land miles and a population base not quite reaching 40,000, **Sagadahoc** is Maine's smallest county—but it is as rich with history as many of its larger counterparts. Much of the state's early (and present) ship-building heritage can be traced to Sagadahoc, and that heritage is reflected in many magnificent homes in towns and villages from Merrymeeting Bay up the Kennebec and along the lower Androscoggin River. The terrain is gentle, with thick forests opening for farmers' fields and the occasional settlement.

Richmond Area

South of Gardiner you'll come to the once-prosperous town of **Richmond**, where many sea captains settled in the years prior to the Civil War. Handsome brick buildings line commercial streets, and elaborate Greek Revival and Italianate homes are tucked away on side streets. Richmond has by and large been overlooked by the years; it has a slightly unkempt appearance, but it lends itself to fruitful explorations and many opportunities for unique photographs. (Locals embrace the distinction of their town being "walkable" before it became a cool hipster thing.)

In your wanderings, you might find it strange to pass **Saint Alexander Nevsky Church** with its onion domes. Russians began settling here five decades ago, and in the 1940s the town caught the attention of Vladimir Kuhn von Poushental, a Russian émigré (and former count under the czarist rulers) who found Richmond's climate and terrain much like that of Moscow (See? There's a reason to complain about the cold). He bought up dozens of farms and buildings around Richmond, advertising parcels for sale in Russian immigrant newspapers. Transplanted Russians responded, moving in great numbers in the 1950s and 1960s. At the peak of the Russian influx, nearly 500 immigrants lived in this quiet riverside town, and Russian Richmond boasted its own restaurant, bootmaker, and three churches where Russian dramas were regularly staged. Since its peak around 1970, the community has significantly dwindled, but the distinctive language can still be heard here and there from yards and open windows.

Just a hundred yards or so from the Richmond town landing is the long and shallow **Swan Island**, a 4-mile-long state-owned island managed as the Steve Powell Wildlife Management Area. The island sits in the northernmost reach of **Merrymeeting Bay**, the largest tidal bay north of the Chesapeake. Six rivers feed into the bay, including the Kennebec and the Androscoggin, and some 1,755 acres of islands and mudflats are managed for wildlife conservation. Thousands of waterfowl and other birds stop over during their spring and fall migrations along the Atlantic flyway. Species include Canada goose, teal, pintail, and common goldeneye, among many others. Driving around the bay, keep your eyes to the sky for bald eagles—one of the greatest concentrations of nesting eagles in the state is found along these shores.

This inland bay measures some 4,500 acres, but much of the shoreline is privately owned, making a visit problematic. Swan Island offers the best way to have a glimpse of the bay's wildlife. The state's Department of Inland Fisheries and Wildlife offers a motorboat shuttle from Richmond to the island between May 1 and Labor Day, and limited camping is available. Reservations are essential. The day-use fee is $8 per adult and free for children (ages 3 and under). Admission includes a boat shuttle. Overnight camping is $14 per adult and free for children (ages 3 and under). For reservations for either day or overnight visits, call the reservation clerk at regional headquarters, (207) 547-5322. For general information call (207) 737-4307 or (207) 287-8000; on the web, visit maine.gov/ifw.

Several miles outside the village is the ***Richmond Corner Sauna***, one of the most unusual accommodations you're likely to find anywhere in Maine. Opened in 1976 by former aerospace engineer Richard Jarvi, this lodge, located on a quiet dirt road, embraces the "clothing-optional" lifestyle (which means you can go with clothes—or without; neither is preferred or required). It is housed in a fine 1831 home with six guest rooms, a baby grand piano in the dining room, and a well-stocked library.

Though the accommodations are homey and comfortable, what really attracts people is the rustic building next door, where you'll find saunas, a hot tub, and a swimming pool. (Bathing suits are also optional here.) Lodging prices include use of all the facilities, or if you're just passing through, you can stop by for a sauna or swim. The six saunas are wood fired and sufficiently steamy, with the hot tub and pool just outside the door, making for a short dash in winter.

Lodging begins at $100 per night. The price includes full use of the sauna, hot tub, and swimming pool. Jarvi also offers daytime nude sunbathing, swimming, and massages. Sauna hours are Tues through Sun from 6 to 10 p.m. in the summer, and Tues through Sun from 5 to 9 p.m. in the winter; closed Mon. Richmond Sauna is 1.1 miles west of I-95 on ME 197. Turn left on ME 138, then make the immediate left on Dingley Road. For more information call (207) 737-4752 or (800) 400-5751, or visit richmondsaunamaine.com.

Bath and Environs

Nearing the ocean you'll come to the historic town of ***Bath***. It's long been known as the "city of ships"—and it doesn't take long to figure out why. At the small downtown park along the Kennebec, a sign greeting visitors by boat heralds this history: WELCOME TO BATH, MAINE—CITY OF SHIPS—HOME TO THE BEST SHIPBUILDERS IN THE WORLD. If arriving by boat, you've already been made aware of the city's main industry—notably by having passed the imposing drydock of **Bath Iron Works**, where an Aegis-class destroyer or other navy ship may be undergoing repairs. Even arriving by car, though, you most likely figured out Bath's prominence: The towering red-and-white-striped crane of the shipyard—the fourth largest in the country—dominates the landscape, providing a navigational landmark for those traveling by road and river alike.

The shipyard was founded here in 1884, building a variety of private, commercial, and military vessels (most ordered by the US Navy) over its 130-plus years. Today it's a subsidiary of the General Dynamics conglomerate and isn't open to the public, but you can get a good introduction to Bath's venerable shipbuilding history at the **Maine Maritime Museum** just south of the iron works. This is one of Maine's most informative museums, founded in 1962 and located on the former grounds of the Percy and Small Shipyard, which built forty-two schooners between 1894 and 1920. In 1909, the largest wooden ship ever built in America, the 329-foot *Wyoming*, was launched from ways that can still be found in the marsh grass at the edge of the river.

Having recently merged with Portland Harbor Museum, the Maine Maritime Museum features an array of artifacts, including more than 140 boats ranging from a rare antique birch bark canoe to the deteriorating hull of the *Snow Squall*, the last American clipper ship in existence. There's also an immersive lighthouse experience giving visitors a sense of what it's like to stand sentinel in a lantern room, via a panorama of the Gulf of Maine and time-lapse video projections of the changing tides and seasons.

The museum has particularly strong interpretive exhibits, including an engaging lobstering display and a blacksmithing shop. Adults and kids alike who've harbored quiet fantasies of casting off lines and setting sail for points unknown will enjoy themselves at the Apprenticeshop, where boat builders employ traditional techniques in building craft sturdy enough to brave Maine's often tempestuous waters. The builders are happy to entertain any and all questions from visitors. All told, there's an incredible amount of detail and information here on maritime history throughout Maine and beyond. Visitors can get their own seaside experience with a ride on the 1906 Schooner *Mary E.*

Museum hours are from 9:30 a.m. to 5 p.m. daily (except Thanksgiving, Christmas, and New Year's Day). Hours are extended to 7:30 p.m. during the week in July and Aug. Admission is $17.50 for adults, $16 for seniors (65 and older), and $10.50 for children (ages 6-12). The museum is at 243 Washington Ave.; look for blue swallowtail pennants directing the way from various points around town. For more information visit mainemaritimemuseum.org or call (207) 443-1316.

Bath's historic brick downtown is also worth exploring. This area has much of the charm of Portland's Old Port Exchange, but with a less aggressive quaintness. For lunch there are a number of eateries along Front Street and Elm Street. A walk to the top of Centre Street toward the old Sagadahoc Courthouse will bring you to *Mae's Cafe and Bakery* (207-442-8577; maescafeandbakery .com), housed in a pair of 19th-century homes connected by a light and airy atrium. Mae's is well known for its pecan buns, which are about as rich and dense as you'll find anywhere. Expect to wait for seating on weekend mornings, when the brunch attracts folks from Portland and beyond.

Ringing the downtown is a wonderful assortment of handsome homes that reflect both the prosperity of the town in the late 19th century and the creativity of local architects and builders. Among the most impressive are those lining Washington Street just north of downtown. Check at the local visitor information centers or the town library for a copy of the informative and helpful brochure "Architectural Tours: Walking and Driving in the Bath Area." The guide provides a good overview of the exuberant styles you'll see while touring the town, as well as thumbnail descriptions of specific properties. Or visit sagadahocpreservation.org for a printable version.

Mouth of the Kennebec

Where the Kennebec River empties into the Atlantic, some 10 miles south of Bath, you'll find *Fort Popham*, a solid granite fortification that keeps watch over the broad river entrance. The fort was constructed during the Civil War, when the North realized how vulnerable Bath's shipbuilding industry was to Confederate attack. The war ended before the massive fort, ultimately spanning 500 feet in circumference, could be completed. And it never was; today it is a half-finished granite semicircle, quite imposing nonetheless, with 30-foot-tall walls and graceful stone staircases throughout. It's great for exploration, a family picnic, bird and animal watching, or just to take in the vast timelessness of

A Dismal Winter

About a half mile west of the fort is the site of the **Popham Colony,** or what could be called the sister city of Jamestown, Virginia. Both were established in 1607 during the first attempts by Europeans to settle the New World. Jamestown succeeded; Popham failed. About one hundred English settlers under the leadership of George Popham and Raleigh Gilbert landed here in August 1607 and constructed a fort and a storehouse. Called "Northern Virginia Colony" by the English, the settlement never took root. George Popham died during the winter, and Gilbert left for England the following spring. Disenchanted with their prospects, the remaining settlers drifted back to England the following summer, and the colony of Popham was relegated to a historical footnote.

the sea. The fort is open daily year-round from 9 a.m. until sunset; please note that the facilities are only open from April 15 to Oct 30. Parking is limited. For more information call (207) 389-1335.

Not far from the fort is 529-acre **Popham Beach State Park**. One of the state's most popular parks, Popham provides access to a broad sweep of beach with glorious views across smaller islands offshore and toward looming Seguin Island with its doleful lighthouse. Note that the beach parking lot fills up early on pleasant weekends. Fees of $6 for adult ME residents, $8 for adult non-residents, and $2 for Maine seniors are charged from Memorial Day through Labor Day for the day use area. Admission to the fort itself is free. For more information call (207) 389-1335.

araretreat

Sand beaches like those at Popham and Reid state parks are rare in Maine. How rare? Sandy strands account for only 2 percent of Maine's coastline—and cobblestone beaches only 3 percent. What's left? Mostly ledge or mudflats—two-thirds of the state's intertidal habitat falls into one of those two categories.

If you're planning to camp, **Hermit Island** is a spectacular private campground located not far from Fort Popham. In operation since 1952, it offers 271 sites (including several on the ocean) and a handful of cabins spread across the open, shrubby bluffs of the 1.5-mile-long island. Access is by car along a sandy spit, and only tents, pop-up, and small pick-up campers are allowed. Although Hermit Island has quite a few campsites, use is kept to a minimum: Only one car and two adults are allowed per site, and day visitors are not permitted. Those lucky enough to obtain a campsite (reservations are essential) have beaches, rocky bluffs, tidal pools, and trails aplenty to themselves.

The island can be reached by car off ME 209 south of Bath, and is open mid May through Columbus Day. Rates range from $43 to $70, depending on time of year and location. For more information call (207) 443-2101 or visit hermitisland.com.

On the east side of the Kennebec River (backtracking to Bath and crossing the Carleton Bridge to Woolwich) is **Georgetown Island**, connected to the mainland by bridge. This area is wooded and quiet, with a handful of low-key attractions, making it a worthwhile detour.

At the island's southern tip is **Reid State Park**, located on a former estate. Gorgeous in its expanse, the park has everything from picnic tables set in shady copses to rocky headlands and a mile-long sandy beach. It's a popular destination on balmy summer days, so head here early to stake your claim to a

A Different Kind of Shell

During World War II, towers sprouted up all along the Maine coast as the military mobilized for an offshore invasion. You can still see the stark, square towers along the coast, sprouting inelegantly skyward. Maine's bays were used as anchorages and some of its coastline for target practice. That history resurfaced in the winter of 1996–97, when about one hundred missiles and rocket motors emerged out of the sand at Reid State Park following a pounding from especially fierce winter storms. None of the armaments were active, but bathers stepped a bit more gingerly into the water in ensuing summer seasons.

table or plot of sand. The day-use fee is $6 for adult ME residents, $8 for adult non-residents, and $2 for seniors.

In driving to the park, you may have noticed the grand shingled mansion on your left near the turnoff to Five Islands. That's **Grey Havens Inn** (207-371-2616; greyhavens.com), a fine summer home that's now one of the region's better bed-and-breakfasts. Built in 1904, it is heavily imbued with the feel of a rambling summer cottage on the coast, with creaky steps, cobblestone fireplaces, and the tang of salt air. Many of the rooms have unrivaled ocean views; especially grand are the turret rooms, which come complete with binoculars to watch for whales and keep an eye on lobstermen. With names like "The Sunrise Suite," "The Tides" and "The Osprey Turret," rooms at Grey Havens start at $150 and climb to $395.

A few minutes' drive north of the inn, on Robinhood Road, is a great place to get coffee, breakfast, or brunch. Located in a spare and handsome early building that's been renovated to accent its clean lines, the **Robinhood Free Meetinghouse** (207-613-5682; robinhoodfreemeetinghouse.com) offers an eclectic menu that includes homemade waffles, scones and biscuits, as well as fried oysters or a smoked salmon and bagel plate if you want to get fancy—or good old Lucky Charms cereal if you don't. Most menu items are $12 or less.

Places to Stay in the Lower Kennebec Valley

AUGUSTA

Best Western Plus Augusta Civic Center Inn
110 Community Dr.
(207) 622-4751
ihg.com
Moderate
Near Augusta Civic Center and the University of Maine. Offers several vacation packages, including golf and movies.

Comfort Inn Civic Center
281 Civic Center Dr.
(207) 623-1000
choicehotels.com
Moderate
Offers free newspaper, pool, hot tub, exercise room, parking, and continental breakfast. Close to shops and of course, the Augusta Civic Center, which offers a wide variety of shows and symposiums.

Senator Inn & Spa
284 Western Ave.
(207) 622-5804
senatorinn.com
Moderate
Runs the spectrum from economical rooms to luxury options with fireplaces and jacuzzi tubs

BATH

The Inn at Bath
969 Washington St.
(800) 423-0964 or
(207) 443-4294
innatbath.com
Moderate
Comfy feel plus gourmet food

Residence Inn by Marriott Bath-Brunswick Area
139 Richardson St.
(207) 443-9741
marriott.com
Moderate

WATERVILLE

Budget Host Airport Inn
400 Kennedy Memorial Dr.
(207) 873-3366
budgethost.com
Inexpensive
Near development strip, a cheap place to stay

Fireside Inn and Suites
376 Main St.
(207) 873-3335
firesideinnwaterville.com
Inexpensive
Pet-friendly, offers indoor and outdoor pools, hot tub, and fitness room

Places to Eat in the Lower Kennebec Valley

AUGUSTA

Cloud 9 at the Senator Inn & Spa
284 Western Ave.
(207) 622-0320
senatorinn.com/si_cloud9
.html
Inexpensive
Creative cuisine, popular brick oven pizza lunch buffet

Damon's Pizza and Italians
244 Western Ave.
(207) 622-0551
damonspizzaanditalians
.com
Inexpensive
Damon's has a faithful following with just one thing in mind—Italian sandwiches (the "true" Maine Italian, thank you very much). For a quick take-out snack, try a Damon's Italian.

Riverfront Barbeque and Grille
300 Water St.
(207) 622-8899
riverfrontbbq.com
Inexpensive
Has a wide variety of menu items, but the standout features are their Memphis dry rub ribs and their pulled pork and beef brisket

SELECTED CHAMBERS OF COMMERCE

Southern Midcoast Maine Chamber
8 Venture St., Brunswick
(207) 725-8797
midcoastmaine.com

Mid-Maine Chamber of Commerce
50 Elm St., Waterville
(207) 873-3315
midmainechamber.com/cms

Kennebec Valley Chamber of Commerce
269 Western Ave., Augusta
(207) 623-4559
augustamaine.com

Whipper's Pizza
9 Bangor St.
(207) 622-1471
whipperspizza.com
Inexpensive
Family-owned and operated since 1960. One of the first places in Central Maine to serve Italian sandwiches. Still serving Italians and going strong.

BATH

Beale Street Barbeque
215 Water St.
(207) 442-9514
mainebbq.com
Inexpensive
Features natural, organic food plus hormone-free meats in a St. Louis style.

Kennebec Tavern
119 Commercial St.
(207) 442-9636
kennebectavern.com
Offering a laid-back selection along the Kennebec River

Mae's Cafe and Bakery
160 Centre St.
(207) 422-8577
maescafeandbakery.com
Inexpensive
See main entry (p. 105) for full description.

GARDINER

A-1 Diner
3 Bridge St.
(207) 582-4804
Inexpensive
See main entry (p. 100) for full description.

Lisa's Legit Burritos
242 Water St.
(207) 203-2013
lisaslegitburritos.com
Inexpensive
Serving up classic Mexican food with Mid-Maine charm

Pastaz Italian Cuisine
304 Water St.
(207) 582-8222
pastazrestaurant.com
Moderate
Fresh sauce made daily from scratch; fresh fettuccine cooked to order

GEORGETOWN

Robinhood Free Meetinghouse
210 Robinhood Rd.
(207) 613-5682
robinhoodfreemeetinghouse.com
Expensive
See main entry (p. 107) for full description.

WATERVILLE

18 Below
18 Silver St.
(207) 861-4454
18belowrawbar.com
Raw bar, prime aged beef and small plates are its specialties.

Grand Central Cafe
10 Railroad Sq.
(207) 872-9135
thegrandcentralcafe.com
Moderate
A favorite of locals, its brick-oven pizza is among the best around.

The Last Unicorn Restaurant
8 Silver St.
(207) 873-9363
thelastunicornrestaurant
.com
Moderate
Known for its farm-fresh
organic vegetables and
ever-popular cheese dip

Mirakuya Sushi and Steak House
150 JFK Plaza
(207) 616-0088
mirakuyawaterville.com
Moderate

Midcoast

Looking at it on a map, Midcoast Maine is a series of long, spindly fingers raking the ocean. While beautiful, traveling it can present a series of logistical challenges. Much of the coastal area between Casco Bay and Penobscot Bay is spread out on these narrow fingers, separated by wide rivers—such as the Kennebec, Sheepscot, and Damariscotta—few of which are spanned by bridges. The upshot is that after you've navigated your way for miles to the tip of a peninsula, you won't get lost headed back—just turn right around and head out the way you came in.

But therein lies the area's charm: Because these peninsulas are geographic cul-de-sacs, they maintain a sense of solitude and seclusion that is rare in other coastal areas both here and elsewhere. Sometimes surprisingly, travelers can find old resorts and homes at the very tip of these stretches of land after a long drive—traces of a time when most people traveled this coastline by water rather than land. Abutting rocky shores, you'll find oceanside farms, leafy hardwood forests, and spruce groves. Many of these desultory roads are best wandered at a slower pace than can be offered by a car. Bicyclists particularly rave about gently dipping and twisting roads that pass through

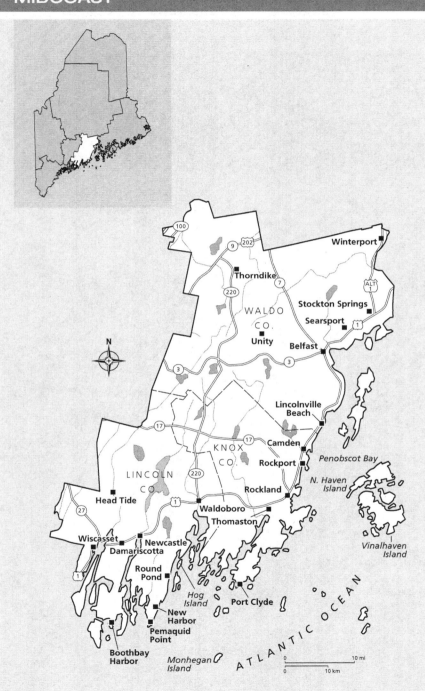

quiet forests and offer periodic glimpses of a distant ocean, with the inevitable fog heightening that pleasant sense of isolation.

Simply put, there is no place quite like Midcoast Maine.

Lincoln County

Lincoln County extends along the coast from Wiscasset to Waldoboro and inland to farm country around Somersville. There are two major peninsulas here: Boothbay Peninsula and Pemaquid Peninsula, both of which are blessed with at least two roads running down and back, allowing a loop tour. The fabled rugged Maine coast may be found in spots (notably at Pemaquid Point), but for the most part it's a gentle and wooded coastline, ideal for unhurried back-road exploration.

Wiscasset Region

If you're arriving in the region via US 1, one of the first towns you'll come to is *Wiscasset*, located on the western banks of the Sheepscot River. This now relatively small, quiet town was once a shipmaking hub—for a time the busiest one north of Boston (but that era abruptly ended with the embargo of 1807, when American ships were prohibited from trading in all foreign ports as the result of ongoing wars between Britain and France).

The rise and fall of this industry is evident in the story of *Castle Tucker*. Located just a few blocks off US 1, at the end of Wiscasset's High Street, visitors will no doubt be struck by this architecturally eccentric (and fittingly named) brick home overlooking the river and surrounded by more modest and contemporary structures. Particularly striking are two-story semi-circular protrusions that were added to either side of the original structure, as well as a piazza with floor-to-ceiling windows.

It was first built in 1807 by Judge Silas Lee, then widely modified around 1860 by Captain Richard H. Tucker, a sea captain who made his fortune in the cotton trade. Tucker added the grand three-floor piazza overlooking the river to the front of the Federal-era house, significantly altering the home's original character. Among other alterations inside, he converted a dining hall into a billiards room.

The mansion was owned by Tucker's descendants until 1997, when Jane Tucker donated it to Historic New England. She remained in the home until 2003, helping the nonprofit to catalog its thousands of objects spanning three generations. Parts of the house are now under restoration, but enthusiastic tour guides provide an intriguing look at the Tuckers, from the prosperous sea captain to his ancestors who had to resort to renting out its rooms as a boarding

FAVORITE ATTRACTIONS

The Lincoln County Museum and Jail	Monhegan Island
Town of Head Tide	William A. Farnsworth Art Museum, Rockland
Boothbay Railway Village	
Pemaquid Point, Pemaquid Peninsula	Penobscot Marine Museum, Searsport

house. There's a grand piano, an elaborately-carved billiard table and a beautiful Empire Crawford cast iron stove, as well as many portraits, medallion-backed Victorian furniture and numerous curios, ranging from a delicate egg collection to antique utensils. Architectural flourishes include an impressive freestanding elliptical staircase, a parquet floor, and plaster trim painstakingly painted to look like oak.

Castle Tucker stands at the corner of Lee and High Streets. Tours are offered every half hour Wed through Sun, 11 a.m. to 4 p.m from June 1 through Oct 15. Admission is $8 for adults, $7 for seniors, and $4 for students.

Nearby is a far different architectural specimen, the **Nickels-Sortwell House**. Also a Historic New England property, it was built in 1807 and is perhaps one of the region's finest examples of the high Federal-style. The three-story structure lords over Wiscasset's Main Street, and was built for then-successful ship captain William Nickels. As with many in Wiscasset, however, the Embargo of 1807 ruined Nickels; as a desperate act, he deeded the house to his business partner, who allowed his family to continue living there. Later, in the 1830s, it was operated as Turner's Tavern, then it served as a hotel, and at the turn of the 20th century it was bought as a summer house by the Sortwell family (whose riches were derived from the railroad and mining industries). Today, it is a fusion of contemporary and colonial styles, boasting heavy timber floors, a unique three-story lunette window, and antiques such as a gloriously carved four-poster bed and banjo clocks—but it has been updated with modern amenities, as well, and is available for vacation rentals. It is open from June 1 through Oct 15, Fri through Sun, 11 a.m. to 4 p.m. Tours are offered every half-hour. Admission is $8 for adults, $7 for seniors, and $4 for students. For more information on Castle Tucker or the Nickels-Sortwell House, visit historic newengland.org or call (207) 882-7169.

Just north of the village center on Federal Street (on the way to Head Tide), you'll pass the **Lincoln County Museum and Jail**, built in 1811 on a gentle hill overlooking the river. Tours of the jail reveal small dim cells seemingly carved out of a single block of granite—even the ceilings and floors are made of granite slabs. It may come as something of a surprise to learn that this jail, based on plans drawn up by John Howard, an early proponent of prison reform, was thought to represent state-of-the-art prison design. Prior to this time, most prisoners were held in large open spaces; the individual cells were thought to be a more humane approach. (An unexpected benefit was no doubt the fact it's extremely difficult to find an escape route through giant hunks of heavy, hard-to-penetrate granite.)

The impressive stonework of the three-story building, which was built with rock slabs ranging from 10 to 41 inches thick, is almost overshadowed by the fascinating graffiti left by early sailors, who, visitors can only assume, were arrested for, well, acting like sailors. The cells range from a grim isolation chamber with a narrow slit for a window, to somewhat airier rooms on the third floor used for women, debtors, and the insane. The jail was shuttered in 1913, considered a relic of the past and treated as such. It did serve another (quite different) purpose before becoming a museum: During Prohibition it was used to store confiscated contraband liquor.

The tour also includes a walk through the adjoining jailer's house, where the warden and his wife lived and prepared meals. The home features a restored kitchen and a bright exhibit area with examples of the jailer's craft, including early shackles, handcuffs, and photocopies of prison logs. The Lincoln County Museum and Jail is open June through Oct, Sat and Sun from noon to 4 p.m. Admission is $5 for adults, and those under 16 get in free. For more information call (207) 882-6817 or visit lincolncountyhistory.org.

While driving around town, you'll probably wonder about that long line of people waiting patiently along the slanted sidewalk outside a tiny boxcar building. That's **Red's Eats** (207-882-6128; redseatsmaine.com). Located just at the Wiscasset Bridge on Water Street, it's widely regarded as having the best lobster roll in Maine. There's always a line at the roadside stand, but it's worth the wait; Red's lobster rolls are full of succulent chunks of lobster (with mayonnaise served on the side) dished up in a hot-dog-style bun. (NOTE: The market price for lobster varies widely within season and by the year.) In addition to what it calls its "roll of fame," the 80-year-old eatery offers traditional hamburgers, crab cakes, fish and chips, as well as twists on beloved summertime snacks—one example includes a "puff dog" stuffed with cheese and bacon, then battered and deep fried. Red's offers takeout only, so first and foremost be patient; when your order is ready, wander down to the waterfront park as you savor it. Red's is open daily in the summer from 11:30 a.m. to 9 p.m.

East of the river and slightly south you'll come to the **Fort Edgecomb State Historic Site**, which sits on three acres at the south tip of **Davis Island**.

TOP ANNUAL EVENTS

JANUARY

US National Toboggan Championship
Camden, late Jan
(207) 236-3438
camdensnowbowl.com/
toboggan-championships

JUNE

Strawberry Festival
Wiscasset, late June
(207) 882-7184

Windjammer Days
Boothbay Harbor, late June
boothbayharborwindjammerdays.org

Damariscotta Oyster Celebration
Along the Damariscotta River, June

JULY

Great Schooner Race
Rockland, early July
greatschoonerrace.com

Maine Lobster Festival
Rockland, late July/early Aug
(800) 576-7512
mainelobsterfestival.com

AUGUST

Windjammer Weekend
Camden, Labor Day Weekend

OCTOBER

Great Fall Auction
Owls Head Transportation Museum
Owls Head, late Oct
(207) 594-4418
owlshead.org/events/detail/
great-fall-auction

The fort was built following the aforementioned Embargo Act of 1807, when Americans were concerned that it could lead to British attacks, thus building fortifications along the Maine coast as a reactionary measure. During the War of 1812, the fort was the scene of some skirmishes, which visitors can learn about in great detail while walking its attractive grounds. Particularly distinctive is its two-story octagonal blockhouse; dating to 1809, it is generally considered to be one of the best-preserved early forts in the country.

The historic site is open daily and year-round, from 9 a.m. to sunset. Please note that the gate and facilities are closed from September to May, but visitors are welcome to walk in and enjoy the grounds. Admission is $4 for adults, and $1 for seniors and children (ages 5-11). For more information call (207) 882-7777.

Inland Lincoln County

This area is decidedly off the beaten path (with few established "attractions," per se), but its peaceful, pastoral, and historic landscape serves as a delight in and of itself, and is well worth the diversion. Eight miles north of Wiscasset is the village of **Head Tide**, located in the tiny town of Alna (population less than 1,000). There's nothing in the way of major or minor attractions here, but the fourteen historic buildings wedged in a narrow valley along the Sheepscot make up a virtual museum of early-19th-century architecture. Head Tide was once a major commercial center where millers harnessed the energy from the falls at the head of the tide (thus the expository name). Floods in 1896 and 1924, however, destroyed the mills and doomed the local economy. As a result, Head Tide feels like it's been left behind by time and history. Take a drive around town, where you'll pass by the 1789 Meeting House; the six-room Center School built around 1796; Head Tide Dam; and Head Tide Church, whose simple white steeple is as classically New England as it gets. If the weather is warm (or even if not, depending on your hardiness), there's a fine swimming hole located beneath the old milldam next to a small parking area off the road. There are also meandering trails at **Trout Brook Preserve** and **Bass Falls Preserve**, both located off ME 218 and easily marked. Visit the town website for detailed information: alna.maine.gov. You can return to US 1 via ME 194 through Alna, continuing southward on ME 215 after ME 194 ends.

En route to the Augusta area is the **Pownalborough Courthouse**, situated on the Kennebec River in the town of **Dresden**. This handsome 1761 building in its peaceful bucolic setting is the only remaining pre-Revolutionary courthouse in the state and one of only about a dozen nationwide. Built on the parade grounds of 1752 Fort Shirley, it was constructed by the Kennebec Proprietors shortly after the county was incorporated. During its thirty-two years of service, the courthouse heard cases mostly involving land disputes in this remote part of the state.

After the county seat was moved and the building sold, the old courthouse served a variety of purposes but remained in the same family from 1793 to 1954, when the Lincoln County Historical Society acquired the building and 75 acres around it. Gradual restoration revealed a trove of small treasures: the original paint on the wainscoting in the tavern room; a carving of the sloop *Polly* by a British soldier who was held prisoner here during the Revolutionary War (which had been was plastered over and thus preserved for 150 years); and the carved initials of James Flagg, the architect's son and the courthouse's builder.

Visitors approach the courthouse down a short dirt road. A magnificent maple tree, thought to be as old as the courthouse itself, stands before this exceptionally well-proportioned building. The tour lasts between an hour and an hour and a half, depending on how many questions you muster, and includes an appealing exhibit on the once-flourishing Kennebec ice trade, when Kennebec River ice was shipped as far away as Calcutta. The courtroom proper is on the second floor and is far more spare and less grandiose than its latter-day equivalent. The most subtle indicator of the rich era in which this building was constructed is on the third floor, where you can see a 52-inch-wide pine plank, a sign of the extraordinary bounty of the early forest.

The courthouse is east of Richmond on ME 128, 1.3 miles north of ME 197. It's open from Memorial Day through Columbus Day, Sat 10 a.m. to 4 p.m., and Sun noon to 4 p.m. Those hours expand in July and Aug to Tues through Fri, 10 a.m. to 4 p.m. Tours cost $5 for adults, and children under 16 are free. For more information visit lincolncountyhistory.org or call (207) 882-6817.

Pack rats will enjoy snooping around ***Elmer's Barn*** in the tiny village of ***Coopers Mills***, about 21 miles north of Wiscasset on ME 17. Here you'll find three floors chock-full of what some might charitably call "stuff." (In the warmer months, those tend to overflow outside). But treasure is subjective, so you might just find your own as you poke around. The sign out front does a pretty good job of summarizing: FURNITURE, BOOKS, PLUNDER, TOOLS, SOMETHING FOR ALL. Elmer also has a rustic playground for kids to occupy themselves while the parents are rummaging, but as his brochure notes, "Not liable for any accidents or injuries (not a day-care center)." It is open year-round daily 9 a.m. to 5 p.m. For more information call (207) 549-7671, or look for them on Facebook.

Boothbay Peninsula

The ***Boothbay Peninsula*** between the Sheepscot and Damariscotta Rivers is one of the major stops on the contemporary tourist's pilgrimage along the Maine coast (the others include Camden and Acadia National Park). As such, the town of ***Boothbay Harbor*** is often inundated with travelers—and has been since the 1870s, when steamer service to Bath was established. Parking is tight, and the shops tend to reflect the interests of tourists more than of typical Mainers. If time is an issue, bypass it in favor of the Pemaquid Peninsula, farther east, which many find is more dramatic, intriguing, and historical.

If you have time, be sure to sample one of the boat tours out of Boothbay Harbor, with cruises ranging from a short jaunt of the harbor to daylong trips to ***Monhegan Island***. Whale watches and puffin cruises also are an option, as are deep-sea fishing trips. Clearly, tours are plentiful—there are more than a dozen excursion boats in the harbor. Wander the waterfront to peruse brochures and discuss options with tour-boat captains.

Among the best places for a simple lobster lunch or dinner is the ***Boothbay Lobster Wharf***. Cross the footbridge to the harbor's far side and head right on Atlantic Avenue until you see it. This cooperative of local lobstermen serves up lobsters fresh from the sea—you can watch them being unloaded in the afternoons. There's also an on-site fish market. Order your lobsters at one window, french fries, or other extras at another window, then settle in at one of the picnic tables overlooking the harbor. The working Maine lobster pound is open daily beginning one week before Memorial Day through Columbus Day weekend, from 11:30 a.m. to 9 p.m. The store, meanwhile, is daily and year-round, from 9 a.m. to 6 p.m. Visit boothbaylobsterwharf.com or call (207) 633-4900.

If you'd like to pilot your own boat in the harbor, try a sea kayak. ***Tidal Transit Kayak Company*** (207-633-7140; kayakboothbay.com) has a small fleet of rugged plastic craft at their dock near the Boothbay footbridge. Two- and three-hour tours are offered, providing a unique way to view the working lobster boats and pleasure craft that clot the picturesque harbor. The company offers three tours each day.

Across the harbor at McKown Point Road is the ***Department of Marine Resources Aquarium*** (207-633-9559; maine.gov/dmr/rm/aquarium), which reflects the state's ongoing research into marine life. The attractive pavilion-style building has a variety of lobsters (including rare blue lobsters and even a 20-pound lobster), an 850-gallon shark and skate tank, and exhibits about salmon aquaculture. Kids love having a chance to touch the invertebrates in the touch tank, along with petting the live shark. (Don't worry; it's harmless.) The aquarium is open Memorial Day through Sept, daily from 10 a.m. to 5 p.m., and those same hours on Wed through Sun in Sept. Admission is $7 for adults, $5 for seniors, and $3 for children (ages 3-12).

A short drive north of Boothbay Harbor on ***Barters Island*** is ***Coastal Maine Botanical Gardens***, which opened in 2007. Situated on 126 acres along quiet waters, its overseers don't want anything fussy and pretty—the nature contorted into a remote ideal setting that you might often find at garden destinations. They're more interested in enhancing the beauty of the native forest and its plants. The garden leads visitors into a quiet wonderland on pathways that often surprise and delight, and there are permanent sculptures on display, as

mainetrivia

Maine once had 5,000 billboards lining its highways. But in the 1970s all billboards were banned statewide, and that law remains on the books—despite frequent attempts to overturn or weaken it.

well as changing exhibits from artists exploring the theme between nature, culture, and place. The location is evolving in its own right, having recently opened a new visitor center, as well as a caterpillar lab, where the insects will be reared, researched, and photographed. All told, this quiet spot is perfect for recuperating from an overdose of the plethora of ice-cream and T-shirt shops cluttering the coast.

The gardens are open from April 15 through Oct 31, 9 a.m. to 5 p.m. daily (extended to 6 p.m. in July and Aug). Admission is $16 for adults, $14 for seniors (65 and older), and $8 for children (ages 3-17). The gardens run various special programs, with varying fees, throughout the season. To get there from Boothbay Center, follow ME 27 to the monument (at the stop sign), then bear right. Make your first right on Barters Island Road and drive 1 mile to the stone columns on your left. For more information, visit mainegardens.org or call (207) 633-8000.

For other woodland retreats in the area, stop at one of the Boothbay information centers and ask for a free guide to the lands owned by the **Boothbay Region Land Trust** (207-633-4818; bbrlt.org). The trust oversees eight parcels, all of which are open to the public and many of which feature inviting trails that make for peaceful summer rambles. Visit their website for maps and information on trail conditions.

Continuing on the woodland walk theme, swing by the **Dodge Point Preserve** on the northeast side of the peninsula just south of Newcastle. This attractive riverside parcel is open to the public for quiet recreation. A peaceful lane runs in a loop around the property, past vast stands of red pine, along a pond and marsh, beside stone walls, and beneath towering oaks. The entire loop may be hiked in about an hour; add more time if you stop for a swim at Sand Beach along the tidal river.

The preserve is located slightly over a mile south of the town of Newcastle. Look carefully for a small sign reading FL 30 (Fire Lane 30) on the east side of the road. The fire road is gated; park alongside River Road. A crude map is posted near the gate to enable visitors to get their bearings. Open daylight hours. No camping.

Also of note is the **Boothbay Railway Village**, with an extensive walkable re-created town featuring a town hall dating to 1847, as well as a chapel, hardware store, farm equipment shed, blacksmith shop, and one room schoolhouse. There are displays of antique internal and external combustion engines, carriages, antique automobiles, and period toys, as well. This is also the only place in New England where visitors can take a ride behind an authentic steam locomotive. The museum is located at 586 Wiscasset Road (ME 27). It is open from late May to mid Oct, daily from 10 a.m. to 5 p.m. Admission is $14 for adults, $12 for seniors (65 and older), and $7 for children (ages 3-18). Visit railwayvillage.org or call (207) 633-4727.

Pemaquid Peninsula

The **Pemaquid Peninsula** is a long wedge driven into the Gulf of Maine between Johns and Muscongus Bays. From the attractive river town of

Damariscotta to bold Pemaquid Point, the entire peninsula is well worth exploring at a leisurely pace. Stop to enjoy the historic buildings, investigate tide pools, or have a lobster while relaxing ocean-side. Take the time to explore both arms of this peninsula, **Pemaquid Point** itself and **Christmas Cove**.

Just north of South Bristol, a pleasantly unadorned fishing village, you'll pass the **Thompson Ice Harvesting Museum** on the east side of the road. An icehouse has been located here for decades; the present structure was built in 1990, modeled after one that previously stood at the site. The museum is on land donated by the Thompsons and operated by volunteers who feared that this unique part of Maine history would be lost forever.

This modest museum isn't merely a historic display; it's an operating icehouse. Each winter, generally in Feb, community members assemble on the ice pond and use old tools to harvest the ice. First the workers score the pond's surface into blocks of 20 by 30 inches. With both machine and handsaws, they then cut out the blocks along the scoring and clear a "canal" the length of the pond. The foot-thick ice blocks are then floated along using pick poles and ice tongs, loaded onto a massive conveyor, and transferred into the shed, whose walls are packed with 10 inches of sawdust insulation. The 7-foot-high pile of ice is then topped with an insulating layer of hay and sealed up to wait for summer sales.

As such, this Maine attraction is more active in winter than summer; if you do visit in the balmy months, there's little activity but plenty of information. A shed adjoining the storage room displays tools of the trade, and there's an outdoor display featuring photos of the ice-harvesting operation. Visitors can scramble up a ladder to look down on the blocks of ice (not melted!) glistening through the hay. The ice is sold throughout the summer to local fishermen, who use it to keep their catch fresh.

The Thompson Ice Harvesting Museum is on ME 129 north of South Bristol. It is open in July and Aug on Wed, Fri, and Sat from 1 to 4 p.m. Even when the museum is closed, the site is always open to the public. Admission is free.

The museum also hosts several seasonal functions. Each year on President's Day weekend, the public is invited to a day of old-time ice harvesting. Although a modern truck hauls the ice away, a team of horses is present to show how ice harvesting was undertaken in the old days. The event begins early in the morning, around daybreak, and usually ends around 3 p.m. The group serves hot soup, hamburgers, and hot dogs to visitors. In summer, meanwhile, the July 4th weekend brings an old-fashioned ice-cream social, featuring ice cream made with stored ice. For details, visit thompsonicehouse.com, or call (207) 644-8808.

By far, the best way to see the Maine coast is by yacht—preferably a very large and expensive one. Can't afford such an endeavor? You can get a taste

Return of the Puffin

The southernmost nesting ground for the common puffin is **Eastern Egg Rock**, which lies at the outer reaches of Muscongus Bay. Sometimes called the sea parrot, the puffin has a comic-book visual appeal, with stumpy legs, a round body, and a truncated, colorful beak. The birds were popularly hunted for their feathers in the 19th century and were nearly made extinct as a result. The Puffin Project was established in Maine to reintroduce the birds to offshore islands, which had been colonized by voracious gulls that survived by destroying puffin eggs. The project used various means, including tape recordings of hostile birds, to keep gulls away while the puffins were being resettled. The project has been gloriously successful, and puffins are now breeding on several offshore islands.

These birds rarely venture close to shore; you'll need to hop a boat to view them. From New Harbor you can sail aboard the *Hardy III*, a 60-foot boat with an enclosed cabin and open top deck that was built in Kennebunk. Puffin watches sail at 5:30 p.m. daily and last about ninety minutes. The price is $34 for adults and $15 for children (12 and younger). Visit hardyboat.com or check in at its waterside ticket booth.

More serious birders might consider signing up for Hardy's advanced **Windward Bird Expeditions**, which is the "enhanced" service focusing on migrating birds. Depending on your interest, you can arrange more extensive birding endeavors, or can partake in trips to Monhegan Island to see puffins, razorbills, and a variety of terns (not to mention the isle's historic lighthouse).

of the posh lifestyle at the ***Coveside Bar and Restaurant*** (207-644-8282). It's located at Christmas Cove, which was named by prolific explorer John Smith (he lent titles to locations far and wide across the northeast), who is said to have anchored here on Christmas Day in 1614. It's well off the beaten path for those traveling by car but a convenient and well-protected harbor for those cruising by boat. The food at the Coveside isn't all that distinguished, but the atmosphere more than makes up for it. The restaurant overlooks the scenic harbor, and yacht flags from around the world hang from the bar's wall like an unruly shag carpet. Large and impeccably maintained yachts are often moored near the docks, and regular visitors include celebrity yachtsmen.

The fastest and best way to cross from Christmas Cove to Pemaquid Point is by way of Old Harrington Road. Along the way, stop at the spare and handsome ***Harrington Meeting House*** (207-563-5270), one of three meetinghouses built in the area in 1772. (Only one other remains: the Old Walpole Meeting House off ME 129.) The Harrington Meeting House, located between two cemeteries with a view to the harbor beyond, was meticulously restored between 1960 and 1967. The interior is austere and elegant, built with massive hand-hewn timbers and an extraordinary eye for proportion and form. An intricately carved pulpit looks out over box pews. The second-floor galleries were left open to allow for a small museum, which displays arrowheads, portraits of local personalities, and a collection of photographs of early-20th-century ships. The meetinghouse is open seasonally.

Farther down the peninsula is **Colonial Pemaquid**, the site of one of Maine's earlier settlements, ca. 1625. Since 1965 excavations have been ongoing here, the earth gradually yielding up clues about this village and its settlers, who endured many years of privation as well as attacks from the French and Indians. Today Colonial Pemaquid is maintained by the state. Excavations pock the broad, grassy field overlooking the Pemaquid River and Johns Bay, and a small museum on the grounds displays artifacts uncovered during the digs. Abundant historical markers help make sense of the holes, where visitors may view stone foundations of former barracks.

The centerpiece of the park is **Fort William Henry**, a 1907 replica of a massive stone fort built on the point in 1692. One of many forts built on the site from 1630 onward, Fort Henry was one of the earliest stone forts constructed in the United States and was widely thought to be impregnable. Such assumptions were soon put to rest; the fort was rather easily destroyed by the French led by Baron de Castin, whose name was lent to the east Penobscot Bay town of Castine. The fort is open to the public and offers fine views across the waters. Next door is a fine old captain's house, built in 1790, which is closed to the public.

Colonial Pemaquid is open daily from Memorial Day through early Sept, 9 a.m. to 5 p.m. Admission is $2 for adults; seniors (65 and older) and children (12 and under) are free. This includes entry to both the museum and the fort. The restoration is located west of the town of New Harbor. Turn right off ME 130 just south of the intersection with ME 32. For more information visit friends ofcolonialpemaquid.org or call (207) 677-2423.

Rock of Ages

The Maine coast is famous for its rugged, rocky shoreline. Be sure to take the time to notice how it changes and evolves as you travel up and down the coast.

Around **Casco Bay** the ancient layers of rock strata were folded into an upright position, where the sea then eroded away softer rock, leaving a series of thin, vertical slatelike slabs that flake easily. As a result, the footing can be treacherous, and the consequences of falling on a shoreside scramble can be dire.

Pemaquid Point, in contrast, has broad, horizontal slabs of bedrock that have been washed smooth by the sea. Around Stonington you'll find pillowlike mounds of pink granite that look as if they would be soft to the touch. Wherever you go, look for the parallel gouges in the coastal rock, carved out by smaller rocks embedded in glaciers as they slowly moved southward during the last ice age.

Continuing south on ME 130 will bring you to dramatic, windswept **Pemaquid Point**. Near the tip is the scenic **Pemaquid Lighthouse**, built in 1827 and visible on a clear night 14 miles to sea. Visitors have the rare opportunity to mount the spiral staircase to its lantern room; many of the state's lighthouses can only be viewed from the outside or from afar. Although the point is a popular destination, visitors always sense an air of remoteness and foreboding, even when they share the experience with other people. Pemaquid Point is quintessential Maine coast, particularly when a storm sends waves exploding up the fissures in the rocky point.

Inside the former lightkeeper's house is the **Fisherman's Museum**, filled with all sorts of information and exhibits relating to the sea. There's an informative map showing the sixty-one lighthouses of Maine; displays of netting, traps, and buoys; and a monumental twenty-eight-pound lobster, which, somewhat disappointingly, was caught off Rhode Island. Be sure to take time to wander through the museum and the nearby gallery featuring works of local artists—although the real draw is the smell of the salty air and the surge of the surf. The museum is open seasonally.

Heading back toward US 1 up the east side of the peninsula on ME 32, you'll pass by the harbor that lends New Harbor its name. One of the better-known lobster pounds in the state may be found here at **Shaw's Fish and Lobster Wharf**, where you can enjoy a crustacean while watching the lobster boats come and go through the narrow inlet that provides access to the open sea. For more information call (207) 677-2200.

The **Rachel Carson Salt Pond Preserve** is a short drive north on ME 32. Plan to arrive at low tide, when the seas have receded to leave a quarter-acre tidal salt pond in a broad cobblestoned cove. The pond is perfect for exploring marine life, as author and naturalist Rachel Carson discovered during the countless hours she spent here collecting information for her best-selling book *The Edge of the Sea*. The preserve, which is owned and managed by the Nature Conservancy, was dedicated to Carson in 1970. Look for starfish and green sea urchins, and dig through the seaweed for blue mussels, green crabs, and periwinkles. At the registration box, you'll find a brochure describing some of the indigenous marine life. Some seventy wooded acres across the road are also owned by the Nature Conservancy and are open for walking during daylight.

If you'd like to be better informed about the range of wildlife you're bound to see around here—either on land or in tide pools—consider signing up for one of the programs at **Hog Island Audubon Camp**, located just off Keene Neck south of Medomak in the town of Bremen. Most of the weeklong sessions

Oyster Revival

The estuary of the Damariscotta River is one of Maine's most productive regions for oyster farming, which—along with shellfish aquaculture as a whole—is making a significant comeback all along the eastern seaboard. Oysters have been a food source for locals of the region for thousands of years—evidence of this has been found in "middens," essentially ancient waste heaps that include shells among their discarded and decaying items, lining the Damariscotta and many of Maine's islands. (One of these is the **Whaleback Shell Midden State Historic Site** in Damariscotta.) To celebrate the (once-again) burgeoning industry, several local organizations and educational institutions have come together to present the **Oyster Trail of Maine**. It features the state's handful of oyster farms and the dozens of restaurants that support them. Download a copy at seagrant.umaine.edu/maine-oyster-trail. Check out **Glidden Point Oyster Farms** in Edgecomb, which offers half-hour tours of its facilities daily at 1 p.m., as well as private water-based tours along the Damariscotta that bring visitors to its growing sites and allow them to sample bivalves fresh out of the water. Call (207) 315-7066 or visit gliddenpoint.com. Other local harvesters include **Mook Sea Farm** (maineoysterfarm.com), **Nonesuch Oysters** in Scarborough (nonesuchoysters.com) and **Bangs Island Mussels** in Casco Bay (bangsislandmussels.com). Meanwhile, **Damariscotta River Cruises** offers tours dedicated to the growing industry and its history (207-315-5544; damariscottarivercruises.com). And then there's the **Damariscotta Oyster Celebration** (damariscottaoyster.com) held annually in June. All told, Maine is filled with opportunities to get your shell on (or, more accurately, off)!

offered throughout the summer focus on hands-on bird science, field ornithology, habitat restoration, spring migration, and marine biology. Adult and teen "campers" live in rustic cabins at the 333-acre island wildlife sanctuary. Program fees start at around $1,000 per person and increase from there depending on program focus and depth. For more information or to register, visit hogisland.audubon.org.

Visitors are welcome to walk the trails on the island, which is part of the Todd Wildlife Sanctuary, but there's a catch: You've got to provide your own transportation across about 150 yards of water from Hockomock Point. The Audubon motorboat shuttle is for program participants only. There's another option: Audubon's mainland headquarters offers a mile-long nature trail with classic Maine views down island-filled Muscongus Bay. Stop by the office and ask for a nature trail guide, then spend an hour or so exploring *Hockomock Trail*, reading about forest and field ecology as you walk along. To reach the trail, look for Keene's Neck Road off ME 32 about 5 miles north of Round Pond. Drive to the end and follow signs for visitors' parking.

Waldoboro and Vicinity

Back along US 1 in **Waldoboro,** consider stopping for lunch at **Moody's Diner** (207-832-7785, moodysdiner.com). If Maine decided to establish an official Maine State Restaurant, Moody's would be a strong contender. It's a scene, although one where tourists are increasingly pushing out the locals, at least in midsummer. The diner has been a popular destination among lobstermen, locals, and truckers for decades and serves heaping portions of basic fare at reasonable prices. Don't gorge too excessively on the main course, though, since you'll want to leave room for some of Moody's famous cream pies. The diner is open Mon through Thurs, 5 a.m. to 9 p.m, Fri and Sat 5 a.m. to 9:30 p.m., and Sun 6 a.m. to 9 p.m.

Native food of another sort may be found a pleasant drive north of US 1 in North Waldoboro. **Morse's Sauerkraut and European Deli** can trace its roots back to 1910, when Virgil Morse began making sauerkraut in his basement for descendants of the German immigrants who had settled in Waldoboro's environs. Old Verge, as he was known, made a tart and tangy kraut that was widely popular and available in local stores. After Virgil's death in 1963, his son and his widow ran the business until finally selling it in 1988. As can be the case of many small enterprises (particularly in the restaurant game), it's had its ups and downs since then (once going out of business for about a year). But it's once again offering its tangy kraut made of cabbage cultivated in the broad fields across the road from the barn. Also visit its new German restaurant, which serves a variety of German specialties, from schnitzel to liverwurst to the monumental "Reubenator," a "mountain of meat" that costs $35.

Morse's Sauerkraut and European Deli is 7.6 miles north of US 1 on ME 220. With the exception of Wed, the store is open from 9 a.m. to 6 p.m. daily; the restaurant from 10:30 a.m. to 4 p.m. Both are open year-round. For more information call (207) 832-5569 or visit morsessauerkraut.com.

Knox County

Named after Revolutionary War officer Henry Knox, one of the area's chief proponents and earliest developers (see Montpelier in the next section, Thomaston and Environs), **Knox County** contains some of Maine's popular coastal destinations, including Camden and the islands off Rockland. Monhegan Island also is included here, even though Monhegan is actually in Lincoln County, since access is commonly from Port Clyde on the St. George peninsula. As with much of Maine, the inland townships contain mostly small farms and villages with few attractions but plenty in the way of peacefulness and charm.

Thomaston and Environs

The otherwise hospitable and historic town of **Thomaston** is dominated by an imposing structure: the spire of the Dragon cement factory that sticks up jaggedly into the sky. Established in 1928, Dragon remains in operation, employing hundreds of locals and producing materials for highways, bridges and buildings. A building on the other side of town, meanwhile, is dedicated to commerce of a very different sort (it's also one of the more unusual gift shops in Maine). This is the **State Prison Showroom** (207-354-9237) located on Thomaston's main street. Inside you'll find a variety of items made (or at least assembled) by prison inmates. These range from ashtrays crafted from Maine license plates to lobster-trap tables, cedar boxes, and simple pine furniture. Not everything is made by inmates, though; to be sure, look for a tag or stamp on the bottom of the item marked as such. Items for sale are mostly crafted of wood, but there are also some leatherwork and fabric goods represented. The cash register is staffed by uniformed prison officials, and the store is open daily from 9 a.m. to 5 p.m. except on Thanksgiving, Christmas, and New Year's Day.

Fans of the art world often make a detour from Thomaston to the **Olson House**, which is located in the nearby village of **Cushing**. This stern, hulking house was the subject of countless studies and paintings by revered American painter Andrew Wyeth. One of the most famous of those is *Christina's World*, which depicts Christina Olson in the fields below the house. The dark-haired girl is half-sitting, half-laying, facing away from the viewer toward the house; there is an air of both casualness and alertness about her. The house deteriorated until it was purchased by John Sculley, the former Apple Computer CEO, who donated it to the Farnsworth Art Museum in Rockland, which now administers it.

The 14-room farmhouse is about 10 miles south of Thomaston at the end of Hawthorn Point Road. It's open Memorial Day weekend through Columbus Day weekend, Wed through Sun from noon to 4 p.m. Tours depart on the hour. Admission is $20 for adults, $18 for seniors, $15 for students (17 and older), and free for children (16 and under). This price includes admission to both the Farnsworth Homestead and Olson House. For more information call (207) 596-6457 or visit farnsworthmuseum.org.

Just east of the Thomaston center, at the intersection of US 1 and ME 131, you'll see a massive Federal home set on a hillside. This is **Montpelier**, home of Henry Knox, Revolutionary War major general, the first secretary of war, and one of Maine's principal landowners during the early days of the republic. (Knox came into his vast landholdings largely through a fortunate marriage.) Seeking to build a country estate not unlike Washington's Mount Vernon or Jefferson's Monticello, Knox set about constructing Montpelier in 1793. But the

Montpelier, Thomaston

Tours run about forty-five minutes and include both floors of this sprawling mansion. Among the architectural elements that distinguish the building are the graceful oval front room, the semi-flying double staircase (also referred to as a "butterfly staircase"), and clerestory (elaborate church-like) windows high above the hallway. Note the detailing, including wallpaper reproduced from scraps of the original and the intricately carved moldings throughout the house.

Montpelier is open from late May through early Sept., Tues through Fri from 10 a.m. to 4 p.m., and Sat from10 a.m. to 1 p.m. The last tour departs a half-hour prior to closing. Admission is $10 for adults, $8 for seniors, $4 for children (ages 5-13), and $20 for families. For more information, visit knoxmuseum.org or call (207) 354-8062.

grand plan ended as a dismal failure. The Maine winters were ill suited to a house of this scale, and Knox proved to be a less-than-shrewd businessman, quickly dissipating his fortune. Montpelier was constructed but Knox never established roots.

The present building is actually a replica, built during the Great Depression, and is not on the original site. The home Knox built overlooked the St. George River and was demolished in 1871 to make way for the railroad. Other than a pair of supporting walls added on the second floor, the present Montpelier is a faithful reproduction of the original, and it is no less spectacular or grand. Located on 13 acres, the brick mansion boasts four chimneys, a roof walk, and is furnished with many items from the original homestead.

St. George Peninsula

Turning south on ME 131, you'll pass a few small fishing towns and soon reach the working waterfront at **Port Clyde**, the traditional departure point for **Monhegan Island**. (Island excursions are also available from Boothbay Harbor and New Harbor.) Even if you don't have time to visit the island, Port Clyde is worth the drive. It's a town of weather-beaten clapboards and worn shingles, clinging to a point seemingly at the edge of the earth. Stop for lunch or to browse the **Port Clyde General Store**, which has a deck out back overlooking the harbor. The general store seems right out of a tale spun by South Berwick author Sarah Orne Jewett, with creaky floorboards and a cracker-barrel atmosphere (although today's selection of beer and wine is undoubtedly better than Jewett might have found in the 19th century). A deli counter in the back offers sandwiches and pizza. Scattered around the deck are lumber, propane tanks, and other items destined for the scattering of outlying islands. Visit linda beansperfectmaine.com.

If you're just down for the day, be sure to make a detour to **Marshall Point Light**. The handsome white tower was first built in 1823, then rebuilt in 1858. (If it looks dimly familiar, it may be because this was where the bearded Forrest Gump turned around and headed back west during his long run across the country.) The lightkeeper's house, with its small museum focusing on local culture, is worth a visit. But the real draw is the view out toward lumpy Monhegan Island on the far southern horizon, along with closer Mosquito Island to the east with its open pasturage for sheep. Bring a picnic and revel in the sights, sounds and smells of the open ocean.

Access to **Monhegan Island** is via the *Laura B.*, a sturdy workboat, or the *Elizabeth Ann*, a more modern boat with a heated cabin and extensive seating. The 12-mile trip takes an hour and ten minutes. The boat (whichever you pick) passes several inshore islands before making the open-sea crossing to the misty pale blue knob of Monhegan. The boats sail there three times daily from late May through early Oct, and once daily the rest of the year. Reservations (207-372-8848) are encouraged. The round-trip fare for either boat is $38 for adults, $25 for children (ages 2-12), and free for children under 2. There is a $5 fee to bring pets. You can also find special puffin, nature, sunset, and lighthouse cruises. Schedules are available at monheganboat.com.

As becomes instantly clear to anyone who visits, it's more than coincidence that artists have been attracted to the distant shores of Monhegan—and have flourished there over the decades. Rockwell Kent, Robert Henri, and George Bellows all spent time on the island, and noted painter Jamie Wyeth (the most recent of the legendary Wyeth family to pick up a paintbrush) has summered here and on islands nearby. The isle overall is imbued with a stark natural drama and is often graced with a thin, almost Arctic light. The architectural style is also unique, putting its own island twist on the traditional Maine vernacular. In recent years it has become somewhat inundated with day-trippers who spend an hour or two wandering before returning to the mainland. The number of overnight accommodations has held steady, however, and seem about the right carrying capacity for the island. To get a real sense of this special place,

Maine Mountain Lions

The eastern cougar, or mountain lion, is officially considered "extirpated" (that is, extinct) by the Maine Department of Inland Fisheries and Wildlife (MDIF&W). However, that designation hasn't deterred Maine residents from filing reports of hundreds of cougar sightings in recent decades. The MDIF&W admits the probable existence of cougars in Maine, but maintains that the animals are escaped pets. It's a controversy that's not likely to end anytime soon.

plan to spend at least one night. You'll be doing yourself an injustice otherwise (after all, you came all this way, right?).

Monhegan has several inns and bed-and-breakfasts, but reservations are essential during the peak months of July and Aug; call or visit their websites for details (those you can find here: monheganwelcome.com/sleep). The *Island Inn* (207-596-0371; islandinnmonhegan.com) is the largest of the bunch, featuring a variety of rooms, two oceanfront suites, and a "cottage" for rent. Rates range from $160 to $445. The *Monhegan House* (207-594-7983; monhegan house.com) is rambling and picturesque and has the best front porch for idling and watching the quiet comings and goings of island byways. Continuously operated as a guest house since 1870, it now features 28 rooms on four floors, with rates starting at around $165. A particular favorite is the funky, casual *Trailing Yew* (207-596-0440, trailingyew.com), which has rooms spread about a rambling compound of 11 buildings, most offering views of the ocean. Family-style meals are served in the main building, and rates start at $110.

You'll find small stores, restaurants, a brewing company, a one-room school house, fish houses, and workshops spread across the island, as well as a small memorial library and a local history museum situated at its most dramatic point—the rounded hill capped with a lighthouse overlooking the village. Inside the *Monhegan Museum* (monheganmuseum.org) there's a compact collection of intriguing artifacts related to life at a remote outpost, as well as a small art museum featuring changing exhibits of island art. The museum also offers tours of the Rockwell Kent-James Fitzgerald House and Studio.

Be sure to bring hiking boots or sturdy shoes, since walking is the thing here. About two-thirds of the island is undeveloped and features 12 miles of trails ranging its expanse from dense, quiet forests to open meadows atop dramatic headlands. If you're spending the night, you'll have time to walk the *Cliff Trail* around the island's perimeter, as well as explore some of the inland trails, including the intensely peaceful *Cathedral Woods Trail*. For swimming, the only safe option is the aptly named *Swim Beach*; but even there, you have to be careful. The water is cold and the tide runs hard. For more ideas and options, visit monheganwelcome.com.

Rockland Area

Back on the mainland, continue eastward up the coast from Port Clyde. You'll soon make this discovery: You're actually heading more northward than eastward. That's due to *Penobscot Bay*, a massive indentation in the Maine coast extending about 50 miles from Port Clyde to Bucksport. Three major islands with year-round communities are located in the bay, along with dozens of smaller uninhabited islands. Following US 1 along the western edge of the bay affords occasional views, but, as always, you'll get a better sense of the area if you leave the security of the main highway and venture along smaller byways.

From the attractive and still-bustling seaport town of **Rockland**, make a detour to the **Owls Head Transportation Museum**, another one of those attractions that at first sounds dreary and dull but turns out to be quite fascinating.

Housed in a series of multicolored hangars adjacent to the Knox County Regional Airport, its cavernous exhibit space is filled with vehicles meant for the road and air, many of which show an attention to extravagant aesthetics that has long since been abandoned by designers. The collection runs the gamut of transportation, from bicycles, to carriages, automobiles, motorcycles, aircraft, even space craft—serving as a sort of real-life timeline of the history of humans getting from one point to another. There are gliders, biplanes, stagecoaches, buggies, and highwheelers. Special finds include a 1910 Harley Davidson motorcycle ("Does the work of three horses," its advertisement claimed), and a 1929 Rolls Royce Phantom I Tourer. There's also a replica of a 1911 Burgess-Wright Model F, the Wright Brothers' first production plane. For the more mechanically inclined, there's a room called the Engineerium, which displays the museum's impressive collection of internal combustion engines.

Most Maine museums are best visited on weekdays, when the crowds thin out. That's not the best advice for Owls Head; special events are usually scheduled for Sat and Sun in the summer, during which the fine museum pieces are brought out of the hangar and taken for a ride or flight. The museum's collections are often joined by other privately owned museum-quality pieces that are driven or flown in from around the region.

The museum is 2.8 miles south of Rockland on ME 73. It's open daily and year-round, from 10 a.m. to 5 p.m.; but closed on Thanksgiving, Christmas, New Year's Day, and other specified holidays. Admission is $14 for adults, $10 for seniors. Those under 18 are admitted free. For more information call (207) 594-4418 or visit owlshead.org.

While in Rockland, you don't want to pass up a visit to the **William A. Farnsworth Art Museum**. One of the state's finest museums, the Farnsworth was established in 1935 when the reclusive Lucy Farnsworth died at the age of 96, bequeathing her estate of more than $1 million to endow a museum in her father's memory. The museum contains a superb selection of American impressionists, including Childe Hassam, Maurice Prendergast, and Josephine Miles Lewis (also distinguished as the first woman to graduate from Yale University). Many of the Monhegan artists also are featured here, among them Rockwell Kent, George Bellows, and Robert Henri. In addition, the museum has an extensive collection of works by Rockland native and internationally acclaimed sculptor Louise Nevelson.

In June 1998 the museum opened the Center for the Wyeth Family, where works are on display from all three generations of Wyeth: N. C., Andrew, and Jamie. Included in the center is Andrew and Betsy Wyeth's personal collection of Maine-related art. Another major expansion into an adjacent storefront occurred in 2000, increasing gallery space even further. The museum also operates the *Farnsworth Homestead* on Elm Street. This 1850 Greek Revival home is where benefactor Lucy Farnsworth lived and died. It's open throughout the summer and has been preserved as a typical Victorian show home. Entrance is included in the price of museum admission.

Located in downtown Rockland at 352 Main St., the museum is open daily from 10 a.m. to 5 p.m. June through Aug, those same hours Tues through Sun in Nov, Dec, Apr, and May; and Wed through Sun from 10 a.m. to 4 p.m. Jan through Mar. There are also extended nighttime hours on Wed and the first Fri of every month. Admission is $15 for adults, $13 for seniors, $10 for students (17 and older), and free for children 16 and under. For more information call (207) 596-6457, or visit farnsworthmuseum.org.

Interested in more experiential and modern works? Check out the *Center for Maine Contemporary Art* (cmcanow.org) on 21 Winter St. There you'll find a variety of exhibits that push artistic boundaries. Its building is a visual feat itself; it was designed by the renowned Toshiko Mori and features a saw tooth roofline. The Center for Maine Contemporary Art and the Farnsworth are both located in Rockland's arts district, with dozens of art galleries and the Strand Theatre clustered around them; take time to walk around and check things out.

Also in the downtown area, the recently refurbished *Maine Lighthouse Museum and Maine Discovery Center* is home to the largest collection of lighthouse lenses, lighthouse artifacts, and Coast Guard memorabilia in the United States. (Don't be deceived by its small appearance; it is decidedly filled with all you need to know about lighthouses in Maine.) And housed inside the Gateway Visitor Center is the Lighthouse Depot, which bills itself as "the world's largest retailer of everything for the lighthouse lover."

The museum, store, and visitor center are located at 1 Park Dr. in Rockland and are open Mon through Fri from 9 a.m. to 5 p.m., and Sat and Sun from 10 a.m. to 4 p.m. Admission is $5 for adults, $4 for seniors, while escorted children under 12 are admitted free. For more information call (207) 594-3301 or visit mainelighthousemuseum.com.

Nearby you'll find a welcome center of an altogether different sort: *The Project Puffin Visitor Center*. Run by the National Audubon Society and opened in July 2006, it celebrates the successful return of the puffin to the area through lectures, films, maps, and a variety of exhibits on the unique avian. Visitors can also learn about Audubon's "Adopt a Puffin" program; in return, they receive a certificate of adoption, a biography of their adopted bird, and the book, *How We Brought Puffins Back to Egg Rock*. The center is located at 311 Main St.; it is open daily from June 1 to Oct 31, from 10 a.m. to 5 p.m. (Wed night that is extended to 7 p.m.). It also has limited hours in May and Nov. Visit projectpuffin.audubon.org or call (207) 596-5566.

In Rockland you'll also find the terminal of the state ferry line that services the large Penobscot Bay islands of **North Haven** and **Vinalhaven**. Both have year-round communities, but Vinalhaven tends to harbor more fishermen and be a bit earthier than old-money North Haven. Vinalhaven is also a bit more accommodating to tourists, offering overnight lodging in several B&Bs and motels. Both islands have paved roads winding through forest and field, affording outstanding views of the ocean and offshore islands. If you're disinclined to bike, mopeds may be rented on Vinalhaven. The ferry schedule varies throughout the year; for current information call (207) 596-5400.

In addition to the ferries, one of the larger windjammer fleets in the world is based on Rockland's no-nonsense industrial waterfront, offering trips that range from an afternoon to a week. The wooden ships with their towering masts are an impressive sight tied up at dock, but the best way to appreciate them is under sail. Overnight accommodations aboard vary from the cramped to the moderately luxurious.

Rates for windjamming run from $545 to $975 for a three- to six-day cruise. Prices vary slightly among different ships. Your best bet for scheduling a windjammer vacation is to contact the **Maine Windjammer Association** for information well in advance of your arrival (800-807-9463; sailmainecoast.com). If you're already in Rockland and would like to see if anything's available, stop by the Rockland Chamber of Commerce office at the public landing, where you

Do It Up like a Scotsman

Descendants of Scottish settlers are numerous in Maine, and so Apr 6 the state celebrates **Tartan Day**. On that day it is not unusual to drive past a golf course and see kilted players or to hear the piercing strains of the Highland bagpipe in the distance. And Maine has its own tartan, too. In fact, it is the oldest US state tartan. The colors of the Maine State Tartan were specially selected as representative of the Pine Tree State: azure blue for the sky, royal blue for the water, and dark green for the state's forests and trees; the thin red line is for the Scottish bloodline of Maine's people.

can find windjammer brochures. There are also Windjammer cruises available out of Camden and Rockport.

One of the great bargains of coastal Maine is the ferry to the island of Vinalhaven. The ferry departs from the Maine State Ferry Terminal off US 1 north of downtown Rockland and round-trip passage costs $11 for adults, $5.50 for children (11 and under), and $30 for cars (trucks cost a little more depending on their size). Bringing a bike? It's $20 for adults and $10 for children. And the sights you'll see! You'll pass the unique *Breakwater Light* at the end of the 4,346-foot-long Rockland Breakwater, then catch a glimpse of *Owls Head Light* to the south before starting across the vast expanse of western Penobscot Bay. Before the ferry docks at Carver's Harbor in Vinalhaven, you'll wend through an archipelago of thickly forested islands, and on a clear day this trip is one of Maine's finest sights. Plan to stay on the island for a few hours. It's fun to simply walk around and soak in the atmosphere. Call ahead at (207) 596-5450 for schedule and fare information.

Within walking distance of the ferry is the *Tidewater Motel* (15 W. Main St.; 207-863-4618; tidewatermotel.com), which is well suited as a base for exploring the island. The motel has a particularly unique feature: Constructed on the granite footings of a disused bridge, the tides flow directly underneath its rooms. Overlooking the waterfront and featuring balconies, its rooms offer a cozy atmosphere; you can sit back, relax, and watch the goings-on in the harbor. Bikes are for rent, as well, although most fit into the category that some would call "beaters." Rooms for two range from $195 to $330 during the peak summer season.

Camden and Rockport

The scenic harbor town of *Rockport* has a more genteel feel than its neighbor Rockland to the south. As such, it is a great place to wind down, walk around, and take in the classic coastal atmosphere around you. The harbor, the former home of André the Seal of book and movie fame, is smaller and more scenic; attractive homes and estates cluster along the flanking hills. (Head down to Marine Park along the waterfront, where you'll find a statue of André, along with three intriguing early lime kilns.)

On US 1 at the western edge of Rockport, watch for *Sweet Sensations Pastry Shop* and *3 Dogs Café*, whose bakery features an extravagant selection of pastries and exotic baked goods. Among the most sought-after snacks are its humble macaroons, which are baked to perfection. Stop by and stock up with a bunch for the road. The shop is at 309 Commercial St. (US 1) and is open from 9 a.m. to 5 p.m., with slightly curtailed hours in the winter. Call (207) 230-0955 or visit 3dogscafe.com.

When John Smith sailed up this coast in 1605, he noted "the high mountains of the Penobscot, against whose feet the sea doth beat." In later years the town of **Camden** flourished at this very location, attracting fishermen and the wealthy rusticators, both of whom saw advantages in the well-protected harbor. For a long time Camden was something of a secret, a gem hidden between mountains and sea.

That's no longer the case, however. Camden has been discovered by just about every traveler to Maine (tour bus operators included). Still, a number of elegant inns dot the hillsides around the harbor, and Camden boasts some excellent restaurants and shops. A walk around town should include the attractive town park, designed near the turn of the 20th century by the firm of Frederick Law Olmsted, the designer of New York City's famed Central Park. Camden's park offers an excellent view of the harbor, which throughout the summer is packed tightly with tall-masted sailing ships and all other manner of watercraft.

One spot in particular comes well recommended for libations and snacking. **The Waterfront** is a handsome restaurant whose deck hangs out over

Camden's Castle

What's that immodest stone "castle" you see along US 1 just north of Camden's village center? That's **Norumbega**, a picturesque pile built in 1886 by Joseph B. Stearns. Born in the Maine mountain town of Weld, Stearns was not a natural businessman—he had managed to accumulate significant debts before turning 20. Nevertheless, he went into the telegraph business, mastered it, and invented duplex telegraphy, which allowed two messages to be sent along a telegraph wire simultaneously. Royalties on the invention rolled in from around the globe, and Stearns was able to retire nicely by the time he was 54. He headed to Camden to build his mansion, using rough stone and timber to construct a rambling, Queen Anne-style building overlooking a beautiful panorama of Penobscot Bay. The home has been remarkably well preserved (it was owned for a time by newspaperman Hodding Carter III). If you're feeling frisky of wallet, you can follow in the footsteps of millionaires by booking one of thirteen rooms at Norumbega, which is now an inn. With regal names like "Versailles," "Windsor," and "Kensington," rooms range from around $200 to more than $600. If you can afford it, it's well worth the price; its rooms are each uniquely elegant, with stone wall architecture, four-poster beds, jacuzzi tubs, large bay windows—and one is even incorporated into the castle's original library. Call (207) 236-4646 or visit norumbegainn.com for reservations or more information.

For a great view of the inn (and a less expensive lodging option), head next door to **Castleview by the Sea**, which is housed in a more modest Cape Cod-style home dating to 1850. Call (207) 236-2344 for reservations; on the web visit castleviewinn .com. Rooms are $189 to $245 in the peak months, with off-season rates slightly less.

the harbor. If the weather's nice, you won't find a better spot to spend a late afternoon watching the comings and goings of yachts, kayaks, and other pleasure boats. Too many places dotted along the coast take shortcuts on their food while the view distracts their customers; this is not one of them. It's located off Bayview Street and is open daily from 11:30 a.m. to 9 p.m. for lunch and dinner. Call (207) 236-3747 or visit waterfrontcamden.com.

An oasis of serenity amid Camden's commotion may be found just off US 1 south of town. ***Merryspring Nature Center*** is a 66-acre floral preserve dedicated to the planting and preservation of Maine flowers and shrubs. Although barely a third of a mile from the highway, it's well off the tourist track; if anyone's here when you visit, it's almost sure to be a local gardener or volunteer. An information kiosk near the parking area has maps for the taking. Trails meander through a variety of terrain, with pleasing views of the surrounding Camden Hills. Don't miss the extensive and exuberant herb garden near the entrance, featuring medicinal, culinary, and medieval herbs. The park is open daily year-round from dawn to dusk, and no admission is charged (although donations are accepted and encouraged). From US 1 on the Camden–Rockport town line, head west on Conway Road. The center offers regular classes, lectures, and events. Contact (207) 236-2239 or visit merryspring.org.

Two of the most prominent of the ***Camden Hills*** are located within 5,700-acre ***Camden Hills State Park: Mount Battie*** and ***Mount Megunticook***. Battie's 800-foot summit is accessible by car up a short toll road, as well as by a foot trail. On the summit is a plaque commemorating one of Camden's most illustrious residents, the poet Edna St. Vincent Millay. The ledges on the southeast face of Mount Megunticook are accessible via a forty-minute hike up a well-marked but rocky 1-mile trail. From either Battie or Megunticook, outstanding views of Penobscot Bay lie before you, including the island of Vinalhaven and the open ocean beyond. Try to arrive at one of the peaks early in the morning, before the crowds ascend, when you can enjoy the sun glinting through the mist on the ocean's surface. The park is open year-round from 9 a.m. to sunset daily. General admission is $6 for adults, $2 for seniors, and $1 for children (ages 5-11). Those under 5 and over 65 get in free. Call (207) 236-3109 (in-season) or (207) 236-0849 (off-season).

landsailing

In 1830 a 30-ton vessel was built on the north side of Megunticook Mountain, in Camden. The vessel was hauled from there to Megunticook Lake and was then pulled another 6 miles over the ice to Penobscot Bay, where it entered the fishing and lime-hauling trades.

Six miles north of Camden in **Lincolnville**, look for **Windsor Chairmakers**, located just past Lincolnville Beach. At this handsome shop you can see classic Windsor chairs being made by hand and shop for wonderfully made chairs, beds, dining room tables, and more. If you don't have room in the car, the shop can ship your purchases. It's open daily July through Oct, from 10 a.m. to 5 p.m., and from Nov to June, Mon through Sat, 10 a.m. to 4 p.m. Call (207) 789-5188 or visit windsorchair.com.

Waldo County

Founded in 1827 shortly after Maine's statehood, **Waldo County** includes the northeast part of Penobscot Bay. Renowned as a major poultry region early in the 20th century, the county (like many slung along the coast) now relies more on small businesses and tourism. It's also a magnet for artists, who have been migrating in large numbers to its pleasant communities—in particular, the county seat at Belfast.

Belfast and Vicinity

The town of **Belfast** was first settled by the Scotch–Irish in 1770; it then went through a series of economic booms and busts related to shipbuilding and the poultry industry. In recent years it has found a fair degree of prosperity as a haven for artists, who live along the coast and in the nearby hills. Their work may be found in several galleries in downtown Belfast—which consists of two commercial streets, one paralleling the harbor a hundred yards above it and one descending to the water's edge. Many fine Federal and Greek Revival homes line the residential streets nearby, especially the **Primrose Hill District** along High Street (coming from the south, follow the first downtown Belfast sign).

Old-timers from Belfast just returning home after many years away would hardly recognize their hometown. Most of the stores and shops have long given way to artsy-craftsy-type establishments. But a select few of the original stores remain. Prominent among these is **Colburn Shoe Store**. This is the oldest shoe store in America; it first opened its doors in 1832 and has remained in business ever since. Visit this small shop for a trip down a footwear-style memory lane. Its walls abound with period advertisements, most of which have remained in situ since first placed there so many years ago. Of course Colburn carries all the newest styles of shoes, too. For more information call (207) 338-1934 or visit colburnshoe.com.

Young's Lobster Pound, aka Young's Lobster Shore Pound Wharf, located about a mile east of town on US 1, is a must-do when visiting Belfast. What makes Young's so special is this: The lobsters, crabs, and clams are

Seaside Artifacts

When a glacier ripped off a large section of gray rhyolite, or "Kineo flint," from Mount Kineo, in the middle of what is now Moosehead Lake, it became a benefit to early man. Rhyolite flakes under pressure, and Maine's Indian tribes soon learned to use it for tool and weapon making. The glacier terminated at the seashore in what is now the Midcoast region; therefore, when native peoples later filtered into the area, they were spared the 100-mile trek to Kineo to collect the rhyolite. Today, you can still regularly find faceted bits of the waxy gray flint along the area's stony beaches.

always freshly harvested and are kept alive in circulating seawater. The fourth-generation business and restaurant cooks on the spot and also packs its seafood to go. The cooker—a huge, steaming vat—tantalizes the nostrils from afar. The juice of lobsters and clams that have been previously steamed intermingle with freshly cooked seafood. This produces a one-of-a-kind flavor that you must experience to appreciate.

yardsale(ing)

On the first warm Saturday in spring, Mainers are likely to ask each other the question "Want to go yard saleing?" This Maine term refers to the practice of spending at least part of a day going from one to another of the various lawn, garage, and yard sales that are held in nearly every Maine town, village, and hamlet from spring until late fall.

Young's is not visible from the main road. Look for a sign just past the former Jed's Restaurant, and follow the narrow road down to the water. The building is a double-decker, situated directly over the harbor. Here you can sit and enjoy the freshest lobster while enjoying what some say is the best view possible in the city. Young's is open daily and year-round, holding hours in the summer from 7:30 a.m. to 8 p.m. It's also open from 7:30 a.m. to noon on Thanksgiving Day and Christmas Day. (Coastal Mainers often prefer lobster to turkey as the main course of holiday dinners.) Call (207) 338-1160 or visit youngslobsterpound.webs.com.

Northern Penobscot Bay

Passing through **Searsport** on US 1, you'll see an attractive complex of white clapboard and brick buildings on the north side of the highway. Make a point to stop here. Inside these buildings are some of the most intriguing nautical items anywhere in the state. The **Penobscot Marine Museum** has been somewhat eclipsed in recent years by the rapid growth of the Maine Maritime Museum in Bath, but this extensive collection still has the power to enchant. Like Bath, Searsport was an important shipping town, launching more than

3,000 vessels between 1770 and 1920, and serving as a home to 286 ship captains in the 19th century. The ships and captains are long gone, but ample evidence of their existence may be found at the museum, which unfolds in room after room, revealing its treasures slowly and pleasurably.

Well-presented exhibits throughout inform visitors about trade routes, ship design, and the sailor's life. The Douglas and Margaret Carver Gallery contains one of the finest collections of marine paintings in the state; there's also an extensive display of chinaware and lacquered tables brought back from trading missions to the Far East. A portrait gallery highlights the classic weathered faces of the ship captains who sailed from Searsport. Two unusual exhibits include the whaling room, with its centerpiece four-panel Dutch painting of whaling in the Arctic (formerly in Hearst's San Simeon), and rare scenes by accomplished amateur photographer Ruth Montgomery, who accompanied her father on a sailing trip to Argentina aboard the Portland bark *Carrie Winslow* in 1902. Montgomery deftly captured the joys and hardships of life at sea through her lens.

The Penobscot Marine Museum is open daily Memorial Day weekend through the third weekend in Oct., Mon through Sat from 10 a.m. to 5 p.m., and Sun from noon to 5 p.m. Admission is $15 for adults, $12 for seniors, $10 for children (ages 8-15), and free for children 7 and under. For more information call (207) 548-2529 or visit penobscotmarinemuseum.org.

Halfway between Belfast and Searsport on US 1 is the 40-acre **Searsport Shores Ocean Campground**. While having the usual amenities—recreation hall, laundry, showers, and restrooms—this place is far from the typical campground. The owners have taken pains to keep the campsites as private and as close to nature as possible. Some sites are directly on Penobscot Bay; others have fine views of the water; and still others are in a natural woodland setting. For campers who don't like being crammed into side-by-side sites, this is the place to go. Additionally, the staff is happy to cater to individual needs. Group lobster bakes can be arranged. These are also regularly held on a communal basis and include fresh local seafood and produce. It's a great opportunity to stroll along the beach and watch lobstermen hauling their traps, spot seals and porpoises, and view a variety of seabirds.

The campground features 125 sites across its 40 acres. All varieties of campers are welcome, from tents to RVs and pull-along trailers. Also featured are community gardens, travel trailers, and cabins for rent, and a dog park. Daily tent rates range from $14 to $94, while cabins and trailers go from $82 to $168. For more information, call (207) 548-6059 or visit maineoceancamping.com.

Just Barb's, a small restaurant located on US 1 in **Stockton Springs**, advertises itself as "the best-kept secret in Maine." And for fish-and-chip fans, this boast may be accurate. While not fancy or refined in any sense of the word, Barb's serves what may just be the best fish-and-chips in Maine. There's more, too. It's on an all-you-can-eat basis. Other offerings are equally good, and quantities are liberal. Don't expect elegance here, but if you're hungry and want a hearty dose of good Maine food, this is the place to go. Barb's is open Tues through Sat 7 a.m. to 8 p.m., and Sun 7 a.m. to 2 p.m. Call (207) 567-3886.

Fort Knox, on the Penobscot River across from the mill town of *Bucksport*, is not to be confused with the place where the US government used to hoard all its gold bullion. But it is well worth exploring, particularly if you're traveling with children. This massive fort seems a valiant exercise in overkill, even considering the strategic importance of the river. Started in the 1840s, the fort was manned during the Civil War and the Spanish–American War but was never attacked. Perhaps with good reason. Visitors today can marvel at the extensive earthworks and sheer granite walls sited dramatically on a bluff overlooking the Penobscot's narrows at Verona Island. The fort is a sprawling labyrinth, full of dim hallways, irregular courtyards, wondrous angles, and echoes that endlessly fascinate both children and adults. Much of the masonry work is exceptional, particularly the graceful spiral staircases of hewn granite. In an inspired marriage of art and architecture, Macbeth was staged here for two summers in the 1950s. One can only hope for a revival.

Fort Knox (207-469-6553) is on ME 174 just west of US 1 at the Penobscot River. Managed as a state historic park, it is open daily from 9 a.m. to 6 p.m. Admission is $5.50 for adults, $2.50 for seniors (65 and older), $2 for children (ages 5-11). Those under age 5 and over 65 get in free. A flashlight is helpful for exploring some of the long, dark, eerie chambers.

You can't miss the twin suspension bridges right next to the fort; this is the recently constructed *Penobscot Narrows Bridge and Observatory*. Entrance to the observatory is on fort grounds via a tunnel, and visitors can take a one-minute elevator ride to the top. The Observatory is one of only four bridge observatories in the world—and at 420 feet above the Penobscot River, it stands as the world's tallest. Don't skip the opportunity; it offers spectacular views of the Midcoast and Downeast. The observatory is open from May 1 through Oct 31 from 9 a.m. to 5 p.m., and in July and Aug from 9 a.m. to 6 p.m. The cost to visit both the fort and the observatory is $8 for adults, $5 for seniors (65 and older), $4 for children (ages 5-11), and free for those under 5 and over 65. Visit the website of the Friends of Fort Knox at fortknox.maine guide.com for a wealth of information.

Located at 279 South Main St. in *Winterport*, the *Winterport Winery* is a welcome newcomer to the area. Featured here is a tasting room and art gallery. The wines produced at this family-run business are fermented from a variety of fruits (apples, pears, apricots, blueberries, cranberries) and are sold in stores and restaurants throughout Maine. This is a place to check out a new variety of wine before plunking down your money, and it also presents the perfect opportunity to choose a special wine for that hard-to-please friend or relative. The tasting room is open in Mar and Apr on Fri and Sat from 11 a.m. to 5 p.m. From May through Oct, it's open Tues through Sat from 11 a.m. to 5 p.m. It is closed in Jan and Feb and on holidays. Call (207) 223-4500 or visit winterportwinery.com.

Just across the river in the town of Bucksport is another fascinating find: **Northeast Historic Film**. Housed in the old Alamo Theatre, which opened in 1916, the group is dedicated to preserving New England's film and video heritage. It collects old films by New Englanders and about New England, shows them at screenings at the Alamo and at festivals, and runs a three-story vault that holds 10-million-plus feet of film. In the old lobby of the theater you can peruse exhibits on the history of movies and moviegoing in New England. Particularly in this day when film and video are going the way of the dodo in lieu of digital options, it's well worth a visit. It's open Mon through Thurs, 9 a.m. to 4 p.m., and on Mon and Fri by appointment. Admission to the shop and exhibit is free; there's a charge for screenings. Enter from the Elm Street entrance. For more information call (207) 469-0924 or visit oldfilm.org.

Places to Stay in the Midcoast Region

BELFAST

Belfast Bay Hotel
72 Main St.
(207) 338-5600
belfastbayinn.com
Expensive
Beautiful boutique hotel setting in a Greek Revival row house. Features eight unique suites in the heart of downtown.

Belfast Harbor Inn
91 Searsport Ave.
(207) 338-2740
belfastharborinn.com
Moderate
Offers a variety of well-equipped suites for your Belfast getaway

Fireside Inn & Suites
159 Searsport Ave.
(207) 338-2090
firesideinns.com/maine hotels
Moderate
Great views of Penobscot Bay. Ask for a room in back with a bay view. (And pet-friendly, too!)

BOOTHBAY HARBOR

Cap'n Fish's Waterfront Inn
63 Atlantic Ave.
(207) 633-6605
capnfishmotel.com
Inexpensive
Situated on the busy, working harbor. Features whale-watch tours.

Five Gables Inn
107 Murray Hill Rd.
(207) 633-4551
fivegablesinn.com
Moderate
Victorian charm plus five-star breakfast

Ocean Point Inn and Resort
191 Shore Rd.
(800) 552-5554 or
(207) 633-4200
oceanpointinn.com
Moderate
Visitors can fish for flounder, pollock, and mackerel from their pier.

Spruce Point Inn Resort & Spa
88 Grandview Ave.
(800) 553-0289 or
(207) 633-4152
sprucepointinn.com
Moderate
This regularly voted "best of" resort and spa has all the amenities.

Topside Inn
60 McKown St.
(888) 633-5404 or
(207) 633-5404
topsideinn.com
Moderate
No one leaves here hungry after the full breakfast.

CAMDEN

Blue Harbor House
67 Elm St.
(207) 236-3196
blueharborhouse.com
Moderate
Quaint rooms with easy access to harbor, shopping, and outdoor activities

Camden Riverhouse Hotel and Inns
11 Tannery Ln
(207) 236-0500
camdenmaine.com
Moderate
On a quiet street just moments from downtown. Complete with two-acre backyard.

Towne Motel
68 Elm St.
(207) 236-3377
camdenmotel.com
Moderate
Building is ca. 1810. Features exceptional breakfast and a gentle atmosphere.

FRIENDSHIP

Outsiders' Inn B&B
4 Main St., ME 97
(207) 832-5197
Moderate
Relaxed, casual atmosphere—people like to come back here.

MONHEGAN ISLAND

Monhegan House
1 Main St.
(207) 594-7983
monheganhouse.com
Moderate
See main entry (p. 130) for full details.

NEWCASTLE

Mill Pond Inn
50 Main St., Nobleboro
(207) 563-8014
millpondinn.com
Moderate
Lakeside living near town, with fishing, wildlife viewing and casual walks in a rural setting

---

SELECTED CHAMBERS OF COMMERCE

Boothbay Harbor Region Chamber of Commerce
P.O. Box 356, Boothbay Harbor 04538
(207) 633-2353
boothbayharbor.com

Damariscotta Region Chamber of Commerce
67A Main St., Newcastle 04553
(207) 563-8340

Penobscot Bay Regional Chamber of Commerce
P.O. Box 508, Rockland 04841
(800) 562-2529
camdenrockland.com

ROCKLAND

Lime Rock Inn
96 Limerock St.
(800) 546-3762 or
(207) 594-2257
limerockinn.com
Moderate
Chill out on its wonderful
wrap-around porch.
Featuring the best in lazy
elegance.

The Lindsey Hotel
5 Lindsey St.
(207) 596-7950
lindseyhotelmaine.com
Moderate
Boutique and classically
old-timey, but with all
modern conveniences

Samoset Resort
220 Warrenton St.
(800) 341-1650 or
(207) 594-2511
samoset.com
Expensive
Set on a seaside golf
course overlooking the
Rockland Breakwater and
Lighthouse

Trade Winds Motor Inn
2 Park Dr.
(800) 834-3130 or
(207) 596-6661
tradewindsmaine.com
Moderate
Features fresh lobster
served seven different ways

Places to Eat in the Midcoast Region

BELFAST

Darby's
155 High St.
(207) 338-2339
Moderate
Once a working-man's bar,
now turned a fashionable
restaurant. Intricately
carved trim around bar
with a giant, old-time mirror
behind.

Seng Thai
139 Searsport Ave.
(207) 338-0010
sengthaime.weebly.com
Inexpensive
Authentic Thai food, with
daily specials. Unbeatable
curries.

Young's Lobster Pound
2 Fairview St., East Belfast
(207) 338-1160
youngslobsterpound.webs
.com
Expensive
Lobster, clams, and
mussels, caught locally and
cooked in sea water; some
of the best around

BOOTHBAY HARBOR

Boothbay Lobster Wharf
97 Atlantic Ave.
(207) 633-4900
boothbaylobsterwharf.com
Inexpensive
See main listing (p. 118)
for full details.

Lobsterman's Wharf
224 Ocean Point Rd.
(207) 633-3443
lobstermanswharf.com
Inexpensive
Try their clam chowder
while sitting on a picnic
table on the deck. Fine,
traditional, and not-so-
traditional (as in tuna
sashimi) fare.

Rocktide Inn and Restaurant
35 Atlantic Ave.
(207) 633-4455
boothbayharboroceanside
resort.com
Moderate-Expensive
Offers casual dining as well
as formal (jacket required
for men, ladies dressed
accordingly). Overlooking
harbor.

Tugboat Inn & Restaurant
80 Commercial St.
(800) 248-2628 or
(207) 633-4434
tugboatinn.com
Moderate
Enjoy lodging and food
inside a real tugboat.

CAMDEN

Belmont Inn
6 Belmont Ave.
(207) 236-8053
thebelmontinn.com
Moderate
Quiet, charming. Great
breakfast, well-maintained
flower garden.

Peter Ott's

16 Bayview St.
(207) 236-4032
peterotts.com
Moderate
Some special must-try
items include sautéed
crabcakes, butternut
squash ravioli, and brown
ale–steamed mussels.

The Waterfront
Restaurant

48 Bayview St.
(207) 236-3747
waterfrontcamden.com
Moderate
More than 30 years strong.
Patio or interior dining on
the water; casual setting.

LINCOLNVILLE

Whale's Tooth Pub

2531 Atlantic Hwy.
(207) 789-2500
whalestoothpub.com
Moderate
On the beach, great views
of Islesboro (an island on
Penobscot Bay)

ROCKLAND

Cafe Miranda

15 Oak St.
(207) 594-2034
cafemiranda.com
Moderate
In addition to absolutely
fresh local seafood, Café
Miranda offers Thai, Mex,
Asian, and vegetarian treats.

Rock City Cafe

316 Main St.
(207) 594-4123
Inexpensive
Coffee is roasted and
ground on the premises. A
delightful aroma pervades.

TENANTS HARBOR

East Wind Inn

21 Mechanic St.
(207) 372-6366
eastwindinn.com
Moderate
Make sure to try the
steamed mussels, which
are highly acclaimed.

Down East

Where "Down East" Maine begins is a matter of debate and conjecture. The term dates back to early sailing days, when vessels heading east had the prevailing coastal winds and currents at their stern, making an easy go of it from Portland to Eastport. Heading back the other way? Well, that was a different matter altogether.

Eighteen-wheelers have long since supplanted cargo ships, but the term lingers. Today it refers almost as much to a notion as a destination. The classic *Down East* landscape ranges from rocky promontories ceaselessly battered by surf to quiet harborside towns filled with lobster boats in various states of disrepair. The image of Down East Maine may vary, but it's unified by a sense of remoteness and isolation, as well as by the idea that it's populated by a laconic, hard-bitten breed that forges ahead despite considerable adversity. Although pockets of Down East Maine may be found west of Penobscot Bay, for the most part it doesn't appear in earnest until east of the bay. And for real aficionados of rugged Maine, Down East doesn't quite start until you get past Mount Desert and the tides start to exceed 20 feet.

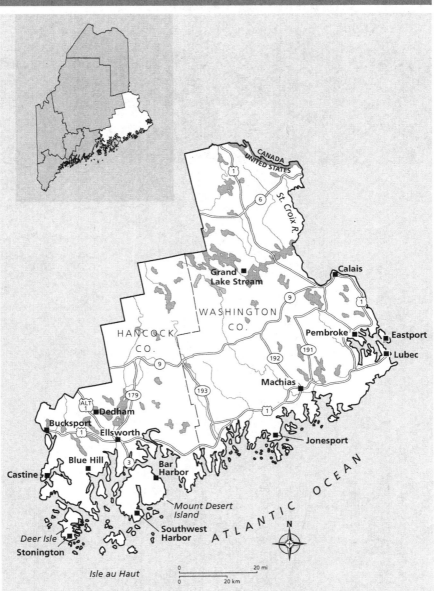

No matter where that imaginary Down East line is drawn, classic coastal Maine starts east of Bucksport. The farther east you head, the fewer tourist amenities you'll find—and the grittier and more ineffably authentic the towns become. And then there's the fog, which seems to cling tenaciously to the coast through much of the year. If a fog bank muffles you, don't be discouraged; it's beautiful in its own right. Take the time to note how the fog enhances the richness of the foliage, particularly the forests in the Deer Isle area, the lichen-mottled rocks of Mount Desert, and the heaths near Cutler.

Hancock County

Hancock County contains Maine's crown jewels: ***Mount Desert*** and ***Acadia National Park***. But don't be blinded by this dazzling display. Be sure to explore the rest of the county, particularly Deer Isle, which doesn't attract nearly the numbers as its more famous island cousin to the east. The county also extends far inland to the northeast, where you'll find remote lakes, good fishing, and unpretentious small towns.

Castine Area

If you've ever wondered what America looked like before Dutch elm disease, head to the quiet coastal town of ***Castine***, about 16 miles south of US 1. This regal village, where the occasional house that's not of white clapboard is the one that stands out, is overarched throughout by more than one hundred towering, majestic elms. Look closely and you'll see small numbered tags on the trees, indications of the town's tireless efforts to keep the canopy healthy and alive. When signs of Dutch elm disease appear, arborists rush in like a SWAT team. Castine's success rate is admirable, and it's hard not to get a little nostalgic about all the long-gone elms that once graced cities and small towns across the country. Fittingly, a local Castine saying is "Under the elms and by the sea."

But they're just part of the allure here. Castine also has a rich—and sometimes bizarre—military history. In the 17th and 18th centuries, the town passed back and forth between the French and British at a dizzying rate. Among the luminaries who made appearances in Castine was Miles Standish, who in 1635 was dispatched to aid the British colonists in their resistance against French usurpers. The small band accompanying Standish was unsuccessful, and the French maintained control except for a brief interregnum when the newly aggressive Dutch prevailed. Around the year 1700 the British once again reclaimed the town and held it, more or less, until the Revolution.

It was during the Revolutionary War that one of the more ignominious American defeats took place: Forty-four American ships failed to capture a conversely thinly defended British fort. A British fleet then forced the Americans to retreat upriver, where the colonists scuttled all ships to avoid capture, returning to Boston on foot. Captain Dudley Santonstall was later cashiered and forever banned from future command as a result of the embarrassing loss. Meanwhile, Lieutenant Colonel Paul Revere (who holds a place in history for his actions in Lexington and Concord) was in command of the artillery train. However, he didn't suffer Santonstall's fate; Revere later sought and won a court-martial, where he was acquitted of all charges. You can learn about these historic episodes at more than 100 markers spotted throughout town, as well as at the earthworks marking the sites of *Fort George and Fort Madison*. On your way into Castine, look for the remains of the British canal between Hatch's and Wadsworth Coves, which was constructed during the War of 1812 (when the British *again* occupied Castine).

The best way to enjoy Castine is to take a walking tour of the quiet, shady streets. Ask for one of the well-written, highly informative walking-tour brochures produced by the Castine Merchants' Association, available for free at many shops and restaurants.

In addition to the walking tour, several sites lend themselves to brief visits, including *Dyce's Head Light* at the westernmost point of town; follow Battle Avenue to the western end. Although this 1828 lighthouse is closed to the public (it was replaced by an offshore navigational beacon in the 1930s), there are a couple of trails that lead below it to rocky bluffs overlooking Penobscot Bay. Look for the small sign near the lighthouse indicating the way to the public trail; it's perfect for an afternoon picnic or an evening sunset walk.

On Perkins Street, stop by the *Wilson Museum* and the adjacent Perkins House. This small brick museum overlooking the water was built in 1921 to house the anthropological collections of local resident John Howard Wilson. Represented are crafts and tools from native cultures worldwide—including

FAVORITE ATTRACTIONS

Acadia carriage roads, Bar Harbor

Asticou Terraces and Thuya Gardens and Lodge, Northeast Harbor

Haystack Mountain School of Crafts, Deer Isle

Nellieville, Deer Isle

The Museum of Telephony, Ellsworth

Roosevelt Campobello International Park and Natural Area, Campobello Island, Canada

West Quoddy Lighthouse and grounds, Lubec

Peru, Ethiopia, Angola, Oceania, and Venezuela. Spears and other weapons from Java and the Philippines are also on display, as are a number of rifles dating from 1580 to the 1880s. American-history lovers will enjoy the replica of the 1805 kitchen downstairs, as well as the operating blacksmith forge next door. And be sure not to miss the outbuilding dedicated to a macabre purpose: Assembled here are a number of winter and summer hearses.

At the ***John Perkins House*** next door you can tour the oldest home in Castine. Miraculously (or perhaps not so miraculously), the house emerged intact despite British bombardment during the wars. This is likely because the trim colonial house was appropriated for British officers' quarters during both the Revolution and the War of 1812. Guided tours of the house in the summer sometimes include demonstrations of open-hearth cooking, with guests invited to taste the results.

The museum is open daily from May 27 through the end of Sept. from 10 a.m. to 5 p.m. on weekdays, and 2 to 5 p.m. on Sat and Sun. Museum admission is free, but donations are accepted. The Blacksmith Shop, Hearse House, and Perkins House are open on Wed and Sun in July and Aug from 2 to 5 p.m. House tours are offered on the hour and cost $5. For more information call (207) 326-9247 or visit wilsonmuseum.org.

Castine is an almost perfectly preserved village, quaint, charming, and with a classically New England feel. There are steepled churches and characteristically shingled boathouses, and Colonial architecture is on full display; many houses bear American flags and are hemmed in by picket fences. Be sure to also stop by the ***Castine Post Office*** on Main Street—put into use between 1831 and 1833, it is the oldest continuously operating post office in the US. Housed in a two-story pale yellow building with burgundy accents and twin chimneys, its interior still features original gaslight fixtures.

To learn more about the town's history, check out the ***Castine Historical Society***, which offers walking tours in July and Aug, as well as special lectures and talks throughout the year. Visit castinehistoricalsociety.org for more details.

There is one towering anachronism in this otherwise picture-perfect locale: the ***State of Maine***, a hulking, gray, former oceanographic research ship berthed at the docks of the ***Maine Maritime Academy*** (it is just one of five academies nationwide that train merchant marines). The ship, which rises incongruously over the village, was built in 1990 by the US Navy before it was turned over to the academy as a training vessel in 1997. Cadets spend sixty days at sea during the course of their training, either as "deckies" or as engineers. The ship can house nearly 300 cadets and staff. Midshipmen give free guided tours of the ship that last about a half hour. Call ahead for details

The War of 1812 in Maine

England smarted and held a long grudge over the treaty of 1783, which marked the St. Croix River as the boundary between Maine and British-held Canada. Landing at Castine on September 1, 1814, they sailed up the Penobscot River to Bangor, burning towns and pillaging along the way. On September 3, Maine militia and British regulars sparred in a battle in Hampden. The British won, and its occupying troops finally left Castine on April 15, 1815, following the Treaty of Ghent that ended the War of 1812. The boundary dispute was not fully settled, however, for another three decades, when the Webster–Ashburton Treaty was proclaimed on November 10, 1842.

at (207) 326-4311. While it's in use for training, you can follow its progress at mainemaritime.edu/tssom-training-cruise-blog/track-the-ship.

Deer Isle

The drive from Castine to Stonington takes you through rolling countryside with glimpses of Penobscot Bay and beyond. (A driving detour through the Cape Rosier peninsula, a pastoral cul-de-sac of early homes and rich landscapes, is an appealing if somewhat indirect route south.) Near **Sargentville** you'll cross a high, narrow suspension bridge across Eggemoggin Reach to **Deer Isle**. As is the case with many locales throughout New England, Eggemoggin was named by the natives, who canoed back and forth across the passage centuries ago. The bridge was built in 1938, but Deer Isle still retains a subdued and islandlike feel in its villages and rural byways. Like so many coastal Maine communities, the villages of Deer Isle look out to the sea. The bridge, in a sense, offers access through the back door.

There are many wonderful, offbeat and out-of-the way treasures to be found here. Among those is **Nervous Nellie's Jams and Jellies** (follow ME 15 out of Stonington for 6 miles, then take a left onto Sunshine Road and follow the handcrafted wooden signs literally "pointing" the way). About 300 jars of its jams, jellies, and chutneys are cooked and poured four mornings a week (Mon through Thurs), made from Maine-grown wild blueberries, strawberries, raspberries, cranberries, and apples. Its creations are no doubt delicious, but perhaps one of the most interesting things about this jelly joint is its rambling sculpture village, "Nellieville." Crafted by owner Peter Beerits, it is a re-creation of an old western town, featuring a general store, lounge, saloon, county jail, all "inhabited" by life-sized abstract figures crafted of salvaged wood, metal and machine parts. They roam the woods beyond, as well, where there's a Medieval castle and a chapel. Beerits gives a roughly 40-minute tour of his creation, which he describes as assembled "on the shadowy margins of life," at 1 p.m. on select Sun throughout the summer. Visit nervousnellies.com or call (800) 777-6845 for more information on tours and Nellie's goods.

Along that same idea, a tiny village pops up seasonally along Stonington's Main Street—it features several small houses of varied architectural styles, barns, stores, and a church. Everett Knowlton began making the buildings in 1947, averaging about one a year until the 1970s. He displayed them at his home until his death, when they were donated to the town, and dedicated volunteers set them up when the months turn warm, heralding spring and summer's arrival.

For something different when it comes to the culinary side of things, meanwhile, there's **El El Frijoles**, a Mexican taqueria on Rt. 15 in Sargentville. Deer Isle is probably the last place you'd expect to find authentic Mexican food—but husband-and-wife team Michele Levesque and Michael Rossney saw (and have found) great opportunity here. The restaurant, well-reviewed by out-of-towners as well as a favorite of locals, features everything from quesadillas to tacos to burritos, all made from scratch, every day. Working with a limited amount of ingredients, the restaurant owners observe a "wear the hat" tradition—that is, the last person in line gets to don a ceremonial sombrero (if you're unlucky enough to get behind them, you're likely going to have to come back another day). Visit elelfrijoles.com or call (207) 359-2486.

A whole different epicurean tradition can be had nearby at **Stonington Seafood**. The restaurant is celebrated particularly for its finnan haddie, a Scottish method of cold-smoking haddock using green wood and peat. Although an acquired taste, it is versatile and used in everything from eggs benedict, to chowder, to pate, to kippers. Check out Chef Richard Penfold's variety of creations. Visit stoningtonseafood.com or call (207) 348-2730.

A scenic drive from the village of Deer Isle will take you along **Stinson Neck** to the nationally known **Haystack Mountain School of Crafts**. Commonly known as "Haystack," it is certainly one of the most scenic campuses anywhere in the nation. This summer crafts school offers instruction to about eighty students per session. Its campus was designed in the early 1960s by architect Edward Larrabee Barnes, who was faced with a rugged site consisting of a steep, spruce-studded hillside plunging into the waters of Jericho Bay. Instead of building at the top or bottom of the slope, as many presumed he would, Barnes daringly designed a campus hugging the slope, with dramatic water views from virtually every building and walkway. And instead of disrupting the delicate spruce, moss, and granite hillside with intrusive construction, he designed twenty small shingled buildings that were placed on footings above the ground and connected by "floating" wooden staircases and boardwalks. A

TOP ANNUAL EVENTS

JULY

Eastport Fourth of July
July 1-4
eastport4th.com
The largest fourth of July festival in the state

Folk Art Festival
Grand Lake Stream, late July
(207) 796-8199
grandlakestreamfolkartfestival.com

Bar Harbor Music Festival
Mount Desert Island, throughout the month
(207) 288-5744
barharbormusicfestival.org

AUGUST

Claremont Croquet Classic
Claremont Hotel, Southwest Harbor, early Aug
(207) 244-5036
theclaremonthotel.com

Sipayik Indian Days
Passamaquoddy Reservation
second Sun in Aug
(207) 853-2600
wabanaki.com

Machias Wild Blueberry Festival
Machias, mid-Aug
(207) 255-6665
machiasblueberry.com

Blue Hill Fair
Blue Hill, late Aug
(207) 374-3701
bluehillfair.com

SEPTEMBER

Windjammer Association Sail-In
Brooklin, early Sept
(800) 807-WIND
sailmainecoast.com

broad central stairway serves as a main hallway, descending to the Flag Deck with its spectacular vistas of gently domed offshore islands capped with the sharp tips of spruce trees.

When workshops are in session, visitors are welcome to walk to the Flag Deck, and visit the college store, Goods in the Woods, which sells art supplies and craft books. During the instructional sessions, the smells of the ocean and the spruce will more often than not mingle with the sounds of reggae and wood saws. A nature trail near the shop also is open to the public, but the studios are closed to visitors except during weekly tours, which are held at 1 p.m. on Wed from the first week of June to the last week of Aug. Cost is $5 per person. Incidentally, don't look for Haystack Mountain hereabouts. The school was named after a mountain near the campus's former location.

To reach the Haystack Mountain School of Crafts on Stinson Neck, drive south of the village of Deer Isle on ME 15, then turn left on Greenlaw District Road and follow the signs for 7 miles. The campus driveway is well marked. For more information call (207) 348-2306 or visit haystack-mtn.org.

Continuing southward on ME 15, you'll soon arrive at the village of **Stonington**. This southernmost point of Deer Isle can seem remote and desolate, particularly when the fog rolls in and the low, lugubrious moan of the foghorn reverberates along the coast. When the weather is clear, porcupine-back islands clutter the horizon, and in the distance the gentle peaks of Isle au Haut rise steely blue above the scene. Except for a couple of inns and some galleries and shops, Stonington is a true fishermen's village and still retains a salty, gritty feel. Keeping with this atmosphere, it offers basic food and accommodations in its restaurants, motels, and bed-and-breakfasts. Not to be missed is the **Stonington Opera House** (operahousearts.org; 207-367-2788), sitting halfway up a hill at the junctions of Main and School Streets. It's an otherwise relatively unassuming building of forest green—but you can't overlook the giant painted letters, stark black against white, simply stating its purpose: "Opera House." (Gotta love the period at the end for emphasis). Built in 1912 and owned, operated, and rescued from abandonment and disrepair by the nonprofit Opera House Arts, it is host to numerous events, including a regular music and film series, jazz festival, summer theater and other events covering the cultural spectrum—from down-home jug bands, to opera, to Shakespeare. You'll see locals and visitors alike intermingled in the crowds.

It's remote in Stonington, but fishing hasn't been the only industry. There were also its quarries, where much of the fine coastal granite was extensively mined for use in buildings in New York and beyond at the end of the 19th century. You can learn a great deal about the town's granite heritage at the **Deer Island Granite Museum** (deerislegranitemuseum.wordpress.com). The site's centerpiece is a large-scale working model of the Crotch Island quarry, the last in operation, showing how it would have appeared around 1900. The museum is open seasonally.

Weaving a Literary Web

Elwyn Brooks (E.B.) White is one of world's most beloved children's authors, having penned the classics *Charlotte's Web* and *Stuart Little* (not to mention his renowned revision of William Strunk Jr.'s *The Elements of Style,* an essential handbook for writers.) Born in New York, White spent much of his adult life in Maine, notably at his (now) namesake homestead in Brooklin. Located on a 40-acre-plus saltwater farm on Allen Cove overlooking Blue Hill Bay, it was said to be the setting for his renowned tale of the benevolent-hearted spider Charlotte and her pig friend Wilbur (and was where he wrote the children's favorite). He is buried in the Brooklin cemetery beside his wife, Katherine. His longtime home was subsequently owned by the Gallant family for more than 30 years; they put the legendary home on the market in late 2017.

If you really want to get a feel for the area, plan to abandon your car for a while. Two good alternatives are available. First, you can travel by sea kayak among the dozens of islands dotting the coast—an undertaking that, depending on your time and stamina, could take anywhere from a few hours to up to a week. Secondly, you can venture by mail boat to Isle au Haut to explore Acadia National Park's wildest and most remote section.

Looking out on the water from anywhere along the coast you're likely to see graceful, slender sea kayaks making their way across open waters to the islands. The sport has been compared to mountain biking on water, and that's an apt analogy. Among Maine sea kayakers the Stonington area is perhaps the most popular. Of the many small islands in the area, a good number are publicly owned and allow camping. The Nature Conservancy also owns several of them (available for day use only), one to pasture a large flock of sheep. Along **Merchant's Row**—the local name for the archipelago off Stonington—the islands are rimmed with weathered pink granite that becomes infused with an almost phosphorescent glow at sunset. Exploring one of these miniature wildernesses is an experience like no other in Maine.

With unpredictable wind and fog, the coast's weather conditions are highly volatile. It's best to have some oceangoing experience before renting a kayak and setting out on your own. Failing that, another option is to sign up for a trip with an established guide service. For that, you have several options in the area. New to Stonington is **Old Quarry Ocean Adventures**, a kayak rental and guide service located on ME 15 just outside the village (turn left at Ron's Auto). Entrepreneur Bill Baker has several kayaks at his waterside compound that features two launch sites. He's available for guided tours or lessons (he also offers hiking, sailing, and boat tours) and will rent kayaks to those who can demonstrate some past kayaking experience and paddling proficiency. If you're headed into the area for a few days, ask about campsites, bed-and-breakfast accommodations, and primitive "camping cabins," which share a bathhouse with tenters. For more information call (207) 367-8977 or visit Bill's website at oldquarry.com.

Other outfitters travel from around the state to lead tours among these wondrous islands. Try **Maine Island Kayak Company** on Peaks Island (207-766-2373, maineislandkayak.com) or **Maine Sport Outfitters** in Rockport (207-236-8797, mainesport.com). No experience is necessary, but you'll enjoy yourself more if you're reasonably fit and comfortable on the water. Gliding across the bay, you'll likely discover that there's something very peaceful about the pace and scale of kayaking (particularly across open water).

If your outdoor tastes run more to hiking, plan to board one of the mail boats to **Isle au Haut**, so named in 1604 by French navigator Samuel de

View with a Room

What could be more quintessentially Maine than spending the night in a lighthouse? Not much. And there's one inn that offers that experience. The **Keeper's House** on Isle au Haut occupies a striking 1907 lighthouse station on the island's northwest coast, with panoramic views out toward the Penobscot Bay islands and the Camden Hills. It's a great base from which to explore the island on foot or to just lounge in Adirondack chairs and watch the shifting light and fog play against the landscape.

The trim black-and-white lighthouse, sitting atop a granite pier, still operates and provides a beacon for fishermen returning to the island. It's not open to the public. But the gambrel-roofed, shingled station house next door serves as lodging, with views of the water from nearly every window. It's a rustic experience—there's no telephone or electricity, and light is provided in the evening by gas and kerosene lamps—but one of the best ways to get a sense of the remoteness of a keeper's life. Meals are provided to guests from the original kitchen. Advance reservations are essential, as there are just a handful of rooms for rent. There is a two-night minimum, and the price for a couple ranges from $850 to $1,000, depending on the room. Lodging here is available from June 1 to Columbus Day weekend. Call the innkeepers at (207) 335-2990 or visit keepershouse.com.

Champlain. (It means simply "high island.") About half of this big, brawny island is privately owned; the other half, about 2,800 acres, was donated to **_Acadia National Park_**.

Daily mail-boat runs take hikers to **_Duck Harbor_**, where five Adirondack-style lean-tos are maintained for primitive camping. Sites are $25 per night for up to six people; reservations are essential, and camping is limited to three nights in the summer and five nights during the spring and fall. Camping is not allowed from mid Oct. through mid May. A special use permit is required, and can be found online at the National Park Service website or by calling Acadia National Park at (207)288-3338. After disembarking, follow Western Head Road—a grassy, wooded lane—to Western Head Trail. This connects to Cliff and Goat Trails, which wind their way between spectacular rocky shoreline and damp, dense forests of fir, spruce, moss, and lichens. From the Goat Trail you can climb to the bald summit of **_Duck Harbor Mountain_**, which provides surprisingly open views of the island and eastern Penobscot Bay, including the eastern shore of Vinalhaven Island. From here you can return to the harbor in plenty of time for the return boat. Be sure to pack a picnic lunch to enjoy along one of the many cobblestoned beaches, since no food is available in the park due to (well-founded) concerns about animals and litter. A water pump for drinking water is located at Duck Harbor; fill up your canteens before you set off. Visitors usually have about six hours to explore the island. A ranger meets incoming boats to provide maps and hiking information.

Round-trip fare is $40 for adults and $20 for children under 12. For a current schedule call (207) 367-5193 or visit isleauhautferryservice.com to purchase advance tickets. Plan to arrive at the dock thirty minutes before departure.

The restaurant selection in Stonington is limited, but recommended is an unvarnished seafood spot called **Stonecutters Kitchen** (formerly Fisherman's Friend), located on School Street a short drive up the hill from the harbor. The fish is freshly caught and prepared simply and deliciously. Prices are moderate; call (207) 367-2530 or visit stonecutterskitchenme.com. You'll also find the **Harbor View Store** here if you have a need to stock up on provisions.

Harbor Café offers what are quite possibly the freshest, sweetest steamed clams found in Maine. Locals come for these and other seafood delights and often wash them down with a "pail of beer," a metal bucket filled with a variety of delightful brews on a bed of ice. It is open year-round; hours are 6 a.m. to 8 p.m. Mon through Thurs, 6 a.m. to 9 p.m. Fri and Sat, and 6 a.m. to 2 p.m. on Sun. For more information call (207) 367-5099.

Before you depart Deer Isle, take time to visit the Nature Conservancy's **Crockett Cove Woods Preserve**, located a few minutes northwest of Stonington. This roughly hundred-acre preserve contains a "fog forest": a rich, quiet, mossy forest of mature spruce, fir, and pine that thrives in the damp, foggy environment prevalent along Deer Isle's south coast. Walking along the short self-guided nature path, you'll hear birdsongs filter through the forest and enjoy the contrast of the rough bark of the red spruce against the brilliant green of the soft mosses. Brochures describing some of the natural highlights may be found in the registration box near the entrance. The preserve is open during daylight hours, and no admission is charged. From Stonington, head northwest on the road toward the town of Sunset. Shortly after passing through the village of Burnt Cove, turn left on Whitman Road. Follow it along the cove until the pavement ends and a dirt road departs to the right. Drive 150 yards to a small parking area with a registration box.

Blue Hill and Environs

Continuing up Down East (which sounds like a misnomer), you'll soon pass through the coastal town of **Blue Hill**, named after the gently rounded 934-foot hill that dominates the relatively low terrain hereabouts. This aristocratic town, located at the head of Blue Hill Harbor, boasts dozens of historically significant buildings dating from the 19th century and earlier. For the last two decades or so, Blue Hill also has served as a magnet for a variety of potters, weavers, and other craftspeople, many of whom sell their wares in shops in the village and outlying areas. Blue Hill is also home to many fine inns and restaurants, and for many decades it has been a popular summer destination for those looking for a more low-key social season than you might find on Mount Desert Island.

If there's any one historical character who defines Blue Hill, it's **Parson Jonathan Fisher**, a Harvard-educated cleric who became the village's first settled minister in 1796. Parson Fisher, who lived in Blue Hill for more than half a century, is considered a New England original of the highest order: He was a respected painter, writer, minister, and tinkerer whose energies were indefatigable. His *Morning View of Blue Hill Village* is an enduring primitive American landscape (the painting can be viewed at the **Farnsworth Museum** in Rockland), and the journal he kept faithfully for 59 years remains a source of interest to scholars and historians.

The **Parson Fisher House**, built in 1814, is open to the public as a memorial to Fisher's many talents. The two-story, four-room house, which Fisher built himself (yes, he could do that, too), contains his elegant homemade furniture, copies of books he bound himself, prints and originals of Fisher paintings, maps of property he surveyed, and examples of the style of short-hand he invented. Of particular interest is a clock with wooden works Fisher made while at Harvard; its painted face represents the five languages he spoke (and used in delivering sermons)—Hebrew, Latin, French, Greek, and Aramaic. About the only thing this "versatile Yankee" wasn't interested in, according to historians, was politics.

The Parson Fisher House is about a half mile south of Blue Hill village on ME 15 and ME 176. It is open from July through Sept on Thurs, Fri, and Sat from 1 to 4 p.m., or by appointment. Suggested contribution is $5; children under 12 are free. For more information call (207) 374-2459 or visit jonathan fisherhouse.org.

Also in Blue Hill is the foursquare **Holt House**, home of the **Blue Hill Historical Society** (bluehillhistory.org). Located at the head of the harbor, the home was built in 1815 by one of the first families to settle in Blue Hill. The home was purchased by the Blue Hill Historical Society in 1970 and restored to its original appearance. Some of the original stenciling was found beneath the wallpaper and is reproduced throughout the home. The collection of local historic artifacts includes furniture, clocks, and kitchenware and continues to grow through donations and purchases. Holt House has the same hours as Fisher House, and it charges a small admission fee.

One of Maine's most noted potters is based in Blue Hill and runs a show-room that you can peruse (and where you can purchase some of the fine hand-thrown works if you so choose). The bowls, plates, and cups made of native clay at **Rackliffe Pottery** are marked by concentric rings, and some of the glazes are of a shimmering, rich cobalt blue that seems to mimic the sea. The workshop and showroom on Ellsworth Road (ME 172) is open year-round; call (888) 631-3321 for more information or visit rackliffepottery.com.

If the weather's cooperative, you might consider a hike up eponymous Blue Hill for a superb view across Blue Hill Bay to the mountains of Mount Desert Island. Drive north on ME 172 and turn left (heading westward) on a road just across from the Blue Hill Fairgrounds. Drive 0.8 mile to the sign marking the start of the trail on the right side of the road. The mile-long hike to the bald, craggy summit (topped with an unmanned fire tower) takes about forty-five minutes.

Ellsworth Area

In the minds of many, the town of **Ellsworth** is merely a gateway to Mount Desert Island and Acadia National Park. It's become the sprawl capital of Down East Maine, with a handful of outlets, Walmarts, and strip malls lining US 1 east of the town center. Look beyond this, though, and you'll find a couple of sites well worth visiting.

The **Woodlawn Museum**, aka **Black House**, located just west of town center, is a fine example of a modified Georgian brick residence. Colonel John Black was a land agent for William Bingham, owner of two million acres of Maine; Black constructed this house between 1824 and 1827. Tradition says that the bricks were shipped from Philadelphia and the laborers from Boston. Noteworthy are the triple-hung front windows (note the absence of a front door on the porch—residents entered and departed through the fully opened windows) and the handsome spiral staircase inside. Although the mansion was a full-time residence and office for the colonel, the house was used sparingly by his descendants. In 1930, the home, fully furnished right down to the original family linens, was donated to the county by Black's grandson.

The museum, set amid 180 wooded acres, is a treasure trove of life in the 19th century. The house contains a canopied bed with the original tassels, a rare Aaron Willard clock, and an exceptional collection of blue and white pottery (among many other items). There are a number of other Victorian flourishes, such as the stuffed peacock (which once roamed the grounds here) and a German silver bathing tub. The site offers a number of educational events, exhibits, talks, antiques shows, and high tea (of course!). It is undergoing an extensive campaign to transform its property by making various building enhancements and improvements to walkways, utilities, and parking areas. The Mansion is open in May and Oct on Tues through Sun from 1 to 4 p.m.; and in June through Sept, Tues through Sat from 10 a.m. to 5 p.m., and Sun from 1 to 4 p.m. Admission is $10 for adults and $3 for children. This includes an audio tour, which can run about forty-five minutes. The museum is located on ME 172, 0.25 mile south of US 1. Call (207) 667-8671 or woodlawnmuseum.com.

Parallels have long been made between the expansion of the internet around the globe and the extension of telephone/cell phone service in the latter half of the 20th century; you can explore the telephone's vast contribution to the world at the ***New England Museum of Telephony***, aka "The Telephone Museum." Founded in 1984, the museum explores the development of telephone services between 1876 and 1983, and particularly its impact on rural New England, where it helped to end (in some cases) centuries-long isolation on ocean points and in backwoods hamlets. (Similarly, the internet is still in the process of reaching some of these areas; reliable, high-speed service can be spotty in Maine the further north and west you go.)

Some of what is on display is quite utilitarian and industrial—such as a panel system from Brooklyn, New York, and "a complete #3 Crossbar system from Bradford, Maine"—but it's augmented by interactive exhibits: Visitors can wax nostalgic as they use hands-on switchboard systems, dial, rotary, and hand-crank magneto phones. Above all of the technical detail rises the scope and scale of the historic enterprise of communication. Every August a telephone fair here celebrates the history and technology of items that we now so often take for granted.

Rising from the Ashes

For years, the **Stanwood Homestead** and **Birdsacre Sanctuary**, along ME 3 about a mile south of Ellsworth, have provided shelter and recreation opportunities for avians and humans alike. However, in March 2014, the historic 1850 home here—which housed numerous historical items, heirlooms, photographs and artifacts belonging to the talented self-trained ornithologist **Cordelia Johnson Stanwood** (1865–1958)—was devastated by fire. Members of the Stanwood Wildlife Foundation, the site's owner and operator, have dedicated themselves to restoring, rebuilding and recovering what they can—all while continuing to care for the injured hawks, owls and geese that are housed on the site's 130-acre grounds. Standwood greatly contributed to the understanding of the natural history and migration patterns of many North American birds, often using the woods behind her simple Cape-style home as an outdoor laboratory. The property is laced with well-marked nature trails that wind past small ponds, across boardwalks and through shady glades and gardens, all maintaining a quiet and settled air—and after the fire, one that also embodies grace and hope.

To learn more about restoration efforts or to volunteer, call (207) 667-7851 or donate to the Birdsacre Phoenix Fund, c/o Bangor Savings Bank, 59 Foster St., Ellsworth, ME, 04605. Visit the foundation's website at birdsacre.com, for more information on its work and educational programs and Cordelia's legacy.

The New England Museum of Telephony is about 10 miles north of downtown Ellsworth off US 1A, at Lottie Bell Farm, 166 Winkumpaugh Rd., North Ellsworth. It's open in July, Aug, and Sept on Sat from 1 to 4 p.m. However, the museum's administrators stress that, should you come upon it "by chance," you're likely to find volunteers at work who will be more than happy to give you a tour. Other times may be arranged by calling (207) 667-9491 for an appointment or by visiting thetelephonemuseum.org. Admission is $10 for adults and $5 for children.

Mount Desert Island

Acadia National Park on *Mount Desert Island* is among the 10 most popular national park in the United States, joining the likes of the Great Smoky Mountains, the Grand Canyon, and Yosemite. Around four million park visits are recorded annually, and between July 4 and Labor Day weekend, the island can fill up, leaving no place to pitch a tent or rent a room. Reservations are strongly encouraged during the peak season. General park information can be found at nps.gov/acad or by calling (207) 288-3338.

Getting off the beaten path at Mount Desert is more a matter of strategy than of destination. Many visitors display a singular lack of imagination by

A Fire to Remember

The autumn of 1947 was unusually dry on Mount Desert Island. There had been no rain since May, and the woods were tinder crisp. It was a disaster just waiting to happen. And that disaster finally flared up toward the end of Oct.

How the fire started, nobody knows. But a small, insignificant wildfire up near Hulls Cove that had attracted some lackadaisical attention early in the week suddenly roared when fierce northwest winds whipped the flames into a frenzy. The fire moved down the east side of the island, destroying many of the extravagant cottages, hotels, and homes around Bar Harbor, then continued toward Eagle Lake and beyond. The island scene was one of chaos: Islanders were evacuated, guardsmen were called in to prevent vandalism and theft, and smaller fires flared all around as raccoons fleeing the flames carried their smoldering fur to new territory. The fire wasn't fully extinguished for two weeks.

The final toll: Five Bar Harbor hotels, 67 summer cottages, 170 homes, and 10,000 acres of Acadia National Park were destroyed. Today there's almost no trace of the fire—buildings have been rebuilt, forests have had many decades to recover. But when you approach Bar Harbor on Eden Street, notice the stone walls and fancy gates here and there. If they seem a bit excessive for the motels and modern buildings nearby, there's a good reason for it. This used to be the habitat of the grand estates.

stopping at Bar Harbor for an hour or two, then heading to the park loop road to drive from one parking lot to another, rarely walking more than a few dozen yards from the road. Admittedly, the coastal loop road is spectacular, with twists and turns and views across Frenchman Bay. But a motor tour provides only a glimpse of the spirit of this place—like viewing the countryside from an interstate highway. Detouring off the loop road and exploring by foot, boat, or bicycle offers a more intimate look at the extraordinary island.

Acadia National Park offers no backcountry camping and only three drive-in campgrounds, which fill up by early morning in midsummer. In addition to the numerous private campgrounds, there is another, little-known option for campers: **Lamoine State Park**, located on the mainland 11 miles from the Acadia visitor center. The 55-acre park is situated on Eastern Bay and has a number of pleasant campsites, including several overlooking the water. There's a boat launch, a pier for fishing, grassy fields, and picnic tables facing across the bay toward Cadillac Mountain and other Acadia peaks. It's a peaceful and quiet place and makes a good spot to further unwind after a day in the park. For more information call (207) 667-4778 (in-season); (207) 941-4014 (off-season).

Immediately after crossing the Mount Desert Island causeway on ME 3, you'll come to the **Thompson Island Information Center**. This is a good stop for basic information about island lodging, restaurants, and attractions. It's run by the island's chamber of commerce, but you also can ask questions about Acadia. It's open daily from 8:30 to 5:30 p.m. If you're more interested in park activities, continue on ME 3 toward Bar Harbor to the National Park Service's **Hulls Cove Visitor Center**. It's open daily from 8:30 a.m. to 4:30 p.m. and features exhibits on wildlife, a relief map, a short film introduction to the park, and a bookstore with trail handbooks and field guides. Ask for the free listings of carriage roads and hiking trails. For more information about the park, contact the park headquarters at (207) 288-3338.

It's not hard to imagine **Bar Harbor**, the island's undisputed commercial center, during its heyday, when corporate titans and others maintained magnificent summer "cottages" (really: palaces) along the coastal hills. Think of Bar Harbor in the early 1900s as Newport, Rhode Island—with moose horns. The Vanderbilts and the Rockefellers were among the families that established summer estates here; in fact, the national park's existence is due in large part to the generosity of these and other wealthy families, who purchased the more spectacular parts of the island and donated them to the US government. (John D. Rockefeller Jr. alone donated 11,000 acres.) Though many fine homes may be viewed at a distance from here and there, the majority were destroyed during an extraordinary conflagration in the autumn of 1947, a period of prolonged

Inside Outlets

Maine has two bona fide upscale outlet meccas attracting shoppers from throughout the Northeast—Kittery along US 1 and the entire village of Freeport.

So where do native Mainers head when looking for the best bargain? Neither of the above—they're too crowded and glitzy. Their destination is more likely to be **Marden's** and **Reny's**, two discount chains with a handful of stores statewide that offer salvage and seconds, often at tremendous bargains.

Marden's ("I shoulda bought it, when I saw it, at Mardens!") is the less conventional of the two. Marden's aficionados know they can never venture into one of its stores in search of something specific. Also, don't be thrown off by the jumbled and unkempt appearance; that's their signature. The best tactic is just to go and browse. You'll be amazed at how much stuff you suddenly realize you need. The eclectic stock is often gleaned from disaster areas—places that have been hit by floods, fires, or hurricanes—and you're certain to find imperfections, like smoke smudges or water stains. But there's usually a good if motley assortment of stuff, ranging from hiking boots and casual clothing to furniture and kitchen gadgets. The company gained a bit of nationwide notoriety with the election of former Republican Governor Paul LePage (2010 to 2018), who became well-known for his unminced partisan comments. He was general manager of Marden's from 1996 until he was elected in 2010.

Marden's stores are located throughout the state. The mother ship is in Waterville (458 Kennedy Memorial Dr.; 207-873-6112), and it's sprawling and huge. Other shops are in Biddeford, Brewer, Calais, Ellsworth, Gray, Houlton; at the Northwood Park Shopping Center in Lewiston (207-786-0313); Lincoln, Madawaska, Presque Isle, Rumford, Sanford, and Scarborough. Visit mardens.com for more information on individual stores and hours.

Reny's ("A Maine Adventure!") offers a more traditional range of merchandise. Its stores are cleaner and much more organized, with an emphasis on remainders rather than salvage goods. You can often find name-brand clothing, along with a growing assortment of foodstuffs, toiletries, bedding, office supplies, toys, tools, gardening and outdoor gear, and small appliances. The chain of department stores was founded in 1949 by its late namesake Robert H. Reny. It continues to be operated by his family, and has experienced significant growth in recent decades.

One of the largest shops in the chain is in Ellsworth (207-667-5166), just across from the L.L.Bean outlet. Others are in Bath, Belfast, Bridgton, Camden, Damariscotta (which has two—a main store and another at the "Underground"), Dexter, Farmington, Gardiner (this one's also big, stretching over three storefronts and two floors), Madison, Pittsfield, Portland (right on Congress Street), Saco, Topsham, Wells, and Windham The chain maintains its office and massive distribution center on ME 1 in Newcastle. Visit its website for details and individual store hours at renys.com.

drought that bred wildfires throughout much of the state. Downtown Bar Harbor was spared, as were some of its year-round homes.

Much of Bar Harbor today caters to the tourist trade, and visitors can select from a wide array of T-shirt shops, restaurants, and bars. One site that retains some of the flavor of the town's past is the **Criterion Theatre**, a magnificent 1932 building that has preserved its art deco extravagance. The interior of this 916-seat theater is awash with geometric patterns rendered in soft, earthy colors that seem enhanced in the dim glow of the central lamp. The theater, listed on the National Register of Historic Places, shows classic and first-run films and presents live musical performances throughout the warm-weather season. Light meals are served in the balcony. It is located downtown at 35 Cottage St; (207) 288-0829; criteriontheatre.org.

The Bar Harbor branch of the **Abbe Museum**, an institution dedicated to eastern Native American culture (with a strong emphasis on Maine), opened in 2001. Located just off the town's Village Green, this branch serves as an extension of the cramped Abbe Museum located within Acadia National Park at Sieur de Monts Spring. The institution has some 50,000 artifacts in its collection and, until recently, had been able to display only a small fraction of those. Ask about special programs, like classes in basket making.

Abbe Museum at 26 Mount Desert St. is open daily from May 1 to Oct 31, 10 a.m. to 5 p.m. Winter hours (Nov to Apr) are Thurs through Sat from 10 a.m. to 4 p.m. Admission is $8 for adults, $7 for seniors, and $4 for children (ages 11-17). The Abbe Museum at Sieur de Monts Spring is open late May through Oct, 10 a.m. to 5 p.m. It is closed in the winter. Admission is $3 for adults and $1 for children (ages 11-17). For more information visit abbemuseum.org or call (207) 288-3519.

Sometime around 1905 a rancorous local debate erupted over whether to allow automobiles onto the island. Progress, such as it was, eventually prevailed and horseless carriages were given the run of the island, forever disrupting its tranquility. One of the outraged opponents to cars was John D. Rockefeller Jr. Preferring to get even, rather than get mad, he set about designing and building a 57-mile network of quiet, leafy carriage roads on the east side of the island, concentrated mostly around **Jordan Pond**. Rarely has vengeance produced so exquisite a result. The peaceful lanes blend remarkably well with the landscape and include a dozen graceful bridges crafted of local granite. The roads deteriorated following Rockefeller's death in 1960, but a major restoration effort was launched in 1990, and eroded derelict lanes were returned to their former glory.

Carriages today are (not surprisingly) few, but mountain and hybrid bikes are plentiful and, it turns out, serve as perfect vehicles for exploring "Mr.

Rockefeller's roads." Pack a picnic lunch to enjoy along a stream, or take a side trip on foot for a summit view across the bay. You might also make a detour for outdoor tea and popovers at the *Jordan Pond House*, a longtime park landmark in Seal Harbor. The restaurant was opened in the 1870s, burned down, and was replaced with a more modern structure in 1979. It is open from mid May through Oct 15 daily, serving outdoor tea and lunch on a grassy promenade looking up the lake; the restaurant is also open for lunch and dinner. Hours are 11 a.m. to 9 p.m., and an all-day menu item features popovers, chowders, classic sandwiches, and entrées such as shepherd's pie, strip steak and (of course) lobster. You needn't be formally dressed for tea (cyclists in spandex are usually well represented), but you should expect a bit of a wait on warmer days. Call (207) 276-3316 or visit acadiajordanpondhouse.com.

If you didn't bring a mountain bike, rentals are available in Bar Harbor at *Acadia Bike* (48 Cottage St.; 207-288-9605, acadiabike.com) and *Bar Harbor Bicycle Shop* (141 Cottage St.; 207-288-3886, barharborbike.com). In *Southwest Harbor* try *Southwest Cycle* (370 Main St.; 207-244-5856, southwest cycle.com). Daily and hourly rates are available. Bike shops can provide maps of the carriage roads, and their staff is more than happy to make suggestions for day trips.

Educational, fun, and uniquely different is a trip with former Harbor Master Eddie Monat. Monat operates *Diver Ed's Dive-In Theater* on his boat *Starfish Enterprise*. While Monat sweeps the bottom of Frenchman Bay with his underwater video camera, bottom-dwelling sea creatures come to life topside on an LCD projector in the mini-theater. Lobsters, hermit crabs, scallops, sea urchins, starfish, sea cucumbers, and a host of other salty critters appear live and in color. As a finale, Monat surfaces, bringing with him a collection of live creatures for participants to view and even handle. At trip's end the critters are safely returned to the icy waters of the bay.

Diver Ed runs his sea-bottom adventures from late May through October. The *Starfish Enterprise* departs from the College of the Atlantic pier daily at 9:30 a.m., 1 p.m., and 4:30 p.m. Reservations are required for all trips. Admission is $42 for adults, $37 for seniors, $32 for children (ages 5 to 11), and $16 for "wee ones" (children under 5). Call (207) 288-3483 or visit divered.com.

Starfish Enterprise, by the way, is a relatively new boat (especially when you consider the backdrop of the maritime history here). Ed's old boat recently burned, and townspeople, as so frequently happens in Maine, came together to help buy him a new one. The name came about as a result of a "name-the-boat" contest among local children. "Starfish Enterprise" won hands-down.

If you're seeking a bit of a horticultural respite, head southward on ME 3 toward *Northeast Harbor*, where you can visit a pair of extraordinary hidden gardens that are as seldom visited as they are spectacular. The best (but not only) access to the *Asticou Terraces and Thuya Gardens and Lodge* is from a discreet parking lot off ME 3. Look for a small sign reading Asticou Terraces on the left as you wind around Northeast Harbor coming from Seal Harbor. If you pass the grand Asticou Inn, you've gone too far. If you're coming from the north, the lot is 0.5 mile south of the intersection of ME 198 and ME 3.

A paved trail leads down to the water and is worth a short stroll. But be sure to cross the highway and begin the climb up the granite steps and through a series of stone terraces overlooking the harbor. The landscaping is remarkable: It seems rugged and wild and ineffably Maine, but it is actually one of the finer bits of outdoor architecture in New England. The hillside was created by Boston landscape architect Joseph Henry Curtis (1841–1928), who summered here for many years and donated the land and his lodge as a "gift for the quiet recreation of the people of this town and their summer guests." At the top of the hill, Curtis's rustic Thuya Lodge (named after the scientific name for white cedar, *Thuja occidentalis*) is open to the public and contains an assortment of antiques and a fine horticultural library.

Behind the lodge, walk through the massive carved wooden gates into the formal Thuya Gardens, with its reflecting pool, gazebo, spectacular flower displays, and lawns trimmed as precisely as putting greens. If the weather's nice, you're certain to find people reading here, talking quietly, or examining the wide variety of common and exotic flowers. The garden was designed by Charles K. Savage, who borrowed elements from famed English designer Gertrude Jekyll and Maine landscape designer Beatrix Farrand.

The terraces and gardens are open daily from sunrise to sunset in May through Oct. The lodge is open daily from mid June to late Sept from 10 a.m. to 4:30 p.m. A $5 donation is requested of visitors to the gardens. The lodge and gardens also are accessible by car without ascending the terraces. Head toward Seal Cove from the terraces' parking lot for 0.2 mile, and turn left on the first road. This will bring you to the lodge. For more information call (207) 276-3727 or visit gardenpreserve.org.

Just north of the Asticou Inn is the *Asticou Azalea Garden*. These grounds, like the Thuya Gardens, also were designed by Charles Savage but have a vastly different structure and feel. Raked gravel walkways wind through the flower beds, with elements borrowed from both East and West. Benches are tucked into leafy niches here and there, providing for a quiet moment or two. A sand garden, designed after those found in Kyoto, Japan, in the late 15th century, invites a pause. The gardens are small—only two and a half acres—but in their design they recall a spacious home, with one private room opening into another. Although lush and inviting throughout the summer, the gardens are at

Sea Smoke and Floating Islands

Maine's coastal residents have a unique lexicon of terms to describe weather and climatic conditions. Delight in the keen wits that first coined these phrases. For instance, "sea smoke" occurs in extremely cold weather. It is a result of the water being warmer than the air. The resulting vapor looks like smoke—thus the name. Sometimes sea smoke is so thick that it obscures distant objects. Sit in the warmth of a seaside restaurant, enjoy some local fish, and frigid sea smoke as it drifts and wafts outside.

Another fun weather term is to "see under the islands." This is a frequently occurring mirage and usually precedes a storm: If you look out at sea toward a distant island, it appears as if it is floating slightly above the horizon; thus you "see under the island." And while sea smoke occurs only in winter, you can see under the islands any time of year.

their most spectacular during the last three weeks in June, when many of the fifty varieties of azalea are in bloom.

The garden is located about 100 yards north of the intersection of ME 3 and ME 198; look for a parking lot on the east side of the road. It is open during daylight hours from May through Oct., and a donation of $1 is appreciated. Call (207) 276-3727 or visit gardenpreserve.org.

Like Acadia, both locations offer an exquisite landscape—if of an altogether different sort than their nationally famous neighbor.

From picturesque and snug Northeast Harbor, boats depart regularly for the **Cranberry Islands**, a pleasant archipelago of flat, open islands dotted with summer homes and cranberry bogs. Several options are available to prospective visitors. You can travel with a National Park Service naturalist to outermost Baker Island and spend a couple of hours exploring the delicate, dramatic terrain; or take the scheduled ferry to either Great or Little Cranberry Islands and explore on your own. Neither island boasts much in the way of tourist attractions, and most residents would like to keep it that way. Great Cranberry has a gift shop, grocery store, and a small lunch spot that operates Thurs through Mon. Isleford, on Little Cranberry, has about the same with the addition of the Isleford Historical Museum, a small collection focusing on island history and maintained by the National Park Service. It's open during the summer and staffed by a park ranger.

Beal and Bunker (207-244-3575) offers a half-dozen boats daily in the summer to the Cranberry Islands. Round-trip cost is $32 for adults and $14 for children (ages 3-11). **Cranberry Cove Boating Co.** (207-244-5882) departs from Southwest Harbor six times daily; the company also runs a night boat.

Round-trip fares are $29.50 for adults and $22 for children under 12. For more info on ferries and "water taxis," visit cranberryisles.com/ferries.html.

In 1930 a Southwest Harbor plumber named Wendell Gilley set off to study a display of taxidermy at the Boston Museum of Natural History. What caught his attention, however, was a display of delicately carved wooden birds. Gilley returned to Maine to take up a new hobby. At the time of his death fifty years later, he had established himself as one of the nation's foremost carvers of birds. Carvings by Gilley and other master carvers may be seen at the **Wendell Gilley Museum of Bird Carving** just north of the town of Southwest Harbor on ME 102.

This modern and airy museum contains about 250 carvings ranging from miniature birds such as chickadees and mourning doves to massive life-size eagles and turkeys. After looking at some of Gilley's fine handiwork, you can watch a half-hour video about him and his wood carving, then see the most recent wood-carver-in-residence at work in the glass-walled studio. Wood-carving classes ranging from an afternoon to 10 weeks are offered throughout the year, and a small gift shop sells magnificently carved birds in a wide range of species and prices.

didyouknow?

Somes Sound is the only true fjord on the east coast of the United States. A fjord is a narrow, steep valley carved by glaciers that subsequently filled with rising ocean water.

The Wendell Gilley Museum is open June through Oct, Tues through Sun from 10 a.m. to 4 p.m.; in July and Aug, closing time is 5 p.m. In May, Nov, and the first two weeks of Dec, hours are 10 a.m. to 4 p.m. Fri through Sun. The museum is open by appointment from Jan through Apr. Admission is $5 for adults and $2 for children (ages 5-12). Children under 5 are admitted free. Call (207) 244-7555 or visit wendellgilleymuseum.org.

The **Claremont Hotel** in Southwest Harbor is one of the best surviving examples of a grand 19th-century island resort. What makes it so extraordinary is that it retains not just its architecture and gracefully simple decor, but much of its quiet, dignified character, as well. Built in 1884 on a low rise overlooking the mouth of **Somes Sound**, the distinguished four-story wooden hotel once attracted the eastern seaboard's gentry, who summered here for weeks at a time. It's been blessedly unchanged over the years and features nice touches, like rush-seated rockers on the porch and a pianist serenading guests during cocktail hour at its restaurant The Boathouse (it has two; the other is Xanthus with more gourmet offerings). A long-celebrated event has been the **Claremont Classic**, a croquet tournament that ends with a dance on the croquet court. It also has a lecture series and concert series.

The hotel offers a variety of elegant rooms as well as a handful of stately cottages. A room for two in season begins at $200; cottages start around $300. The hotel is open spring through the fall. Call (800) 244-5036 visit theclaremont hotel.com.

The west side of Mount Desert is less populated and more forested than the dramatic, congested east side. Acadia National Park maintains a handful of hiking trails here, and gentle winding roads touch the water at several points. Connoisseurs of country drives will enjoy exploring the roads around Bass Harbor and Seal Cove.

In the tiny town of **Bernard** across the inlet from Bass Harbor, look for an intriguing shop of interest to antique furniture collectors. **Antique Wicker of Bar Harbor** (formerly E.L. Higgins Antique Wicker) has a large selection of elaborate old wicker, the sort that one would expect filled the porches of the grand summer mansions hereabouts eighty years or so ago. It's not bargain priced, but it's a great selection, and much of it has been carefully restored. For information call (207) 244-3983 or visit antiquewicker.com.

The **Island Astronomy Institute**, an organization that offers online assistance and great information for beginning and seasoned stargazers, makes a point that, of all the locations east of the Mississippi, Maine—and Acadia National Park in particular—have the clearest of skies. That is, light pollution is barely a factor and those looking skyward at night have one of the best views in the country. The Milky Way shines brightly on a summer's night and even a modest set of binoculars reveals stunning images of distant galaxies and star clusters. The institute hosts an annual summertime **Night Sky Festival**. This includes talks, lectures, field trips, and a lot more, all under the crystal-clear skies of Acadia. For information, check out acadianightskyfestival.com, where you can find stunning images from past festivals.

On the northwest side of the island, stop at **Indian Point**, site of the Nature Conservancy's **Blagden Preserve**. This 110-acre property features

Rural Roads

Lots of town-maintained roads in Maine wind through terrain where (still to this day) electricity has not yet been introduced. These stretches of dark roads grow smaller with each passing year, but given their great number, it will be some time before Edison's discovery is totally ubiquitous throughout Maine. You can easily find stretches of road where there are no phone poles, no electricity, and no houses, and which are likely to stay that way for some time. Driving along them can be an atavistic experience—and, for the younger generation raised with devices, perhaps even a spooky one.

about 1,000 feet of shore frontage and a series of meandering, attractive walking trails through mixed hardwood and softwood forest. Bring binoculars and a book to the rocky shore, where the caretakers have scattered a dozen or so red Adirondack-style chairs facing westward across the water toward Blue Hill. Keep an eye out for harbor seals, which commonly haul themselves out to rest on the rocky ledges offshore on sunny days. In the forest near the shores you also might spot pileated woodpeckers or osprey.

The preserve is located off Indian Point Road. From the park visitor center at Hulls Cove, head south on ME 198 toward Somesville. Shortly after passing the Spruce Valley Campground, turn right on Indian Point Road. Proceed 1.7 miles to a fork; bear right for another 200 yards. Look for the preserve entrance on the right amid a row of handsome oaks. Stop at the red caretaker's cottage to sign in and pick up a preserve map.

One of the less-visited parts of Acadia National Park (remarkable when you consider it is accessible by car) is located a 45-mile drive eastward from Mount Desert. But **Schoodic Point**, an isolated, rugged promontory, is well worth the drive. From the town of Winter Harbor, follow the National Park Service sign for Schoodic Peninsula. A winding one-way road soon takes you along the east side of Frenchman Bay; on a clear day magnificent views of Cadillac Mountain open up through the spruce and pine. At the tip a broad expanse of salmon pink granite angles down to the water's edge, and the ocean tends to be at its most restless here. Bring a picnic; no food is available south of Winter Harbor. Another one-way road leads back along the other side of the spruce-clad peninsula toward the town of Corea. Take it slow and stop at the waysides to enjoy the unfolding show.

Washington County

East of Schoodic Point the coast's character starts to gradually change. You can find more shops and restaurants that cater to locals than to travelers. In the harbors, lobster boats far outnumber pleasure craft. Homes are maintained less to impress visitors than to provide sanctuary during the long months of winter. Coastal villages become somewhat more rough-hewn, reflecting a changing ratio of year-round residents to summer folk. Many consider this to be the true beginning of Down East Maine.

Heading eastward on US 1, you'll pass through the towns of Steuben, Millbridge, Cherryfield, and Harrington. Take time to enjoy the architecture, particularly in Millbridge and Cherryfield, where many of the mansions reflect the boom days of the lumber, shipbuilding, and fishing trades.

Jonesport and Vicinity

In *Columbia Falls* the *Ruggles House* is open to the public and offers a direct look into the region's past. This graceful but modest early-19th-century home was constructed for Thomas Ruggles, who moved to town in 1790 aiming to make his fortune in lumber. Ruggles succeeded in his quest and soon became a respected community leader; eventually he was appointed to a judgeship in Machias. In 1818 he commissioned a 22-year-old architect, Aaron S. Sherman, to design his home.

The interior has several elements of architectural distinction, including a magnificent flying staircase in the central hallway, "open Bible" keystones above the Palladian arches, and pine doors that were handpainted to resemble mahogany. Of particular note is the intricate wood carving throughout the parlor; local lore asserts that these were executed by a British craftsman who labored three years with a penknife (but that's never been validated). The home, which was restored from a state of severe dilapidation in 1950, now contains much of Ruggles's original furniture.

The Ruggles estate is open mid June to Columbus Day, Mon through Sat from 10 a.m. to 4 p.m., and Sun from noon to 4 p.m. Tours run about forty-five minutes, with the last tour starting no later than 4 p.m. Admission is $5 for adults and $2 for children under 12. The house is a quarter mile off US 1 in the village of Columbia Falls. For information call (207) 483-4637 or visit ruggleshouse.org.

Nothing to Get Bogged Down By

Maine has more bogs—and a diverse variety of them—than any other northeastern state. They're especially prevalent in Washington County, where the surface topography and cool, moist air off the ocean conspire to create these floating meadows.

Bogs form where there's little moving water to carry away rotting organic matter, which is often found in kettle holes that were left by retreating glaciers. (A kettle hole is a basin without an outlet, created where a massive slab of glacial ice that was buried in the ground later melted, leaving a broad, often circular depression.) Decades of dead leaves, twigs, and mosses accumulate and form a sort of thick mat that floats on top of the water. This eventually sustains a colony of specialized plants that have evolved to thrive in this hostile environment, which is by and large free of the nutrients typically found in soil.

Especially intriguing is the carnivorous pitcher plant *(Sarracenia purpurea)*. It survives by luring insects into its deep, tubular body, where they're trapped by downward-pointing hairs. Enzymes then digest the insects, providing life-giving nutrients to the plant. Early in the season they're easily spotted by looking for the red umbrella-like flower that rises on a slender stem above the red-veined pitcher below.

One of the Nature Conservancy's most spectacular Maine holdings is on **Great Wass Island**, located south of Jonesport and accessible by car via bridge and causeway. This 1,579-acre preserve, acquired in 1978, has more than 500 acres of jack pine—stunted, gnarly trees well suited to the harsh conditions on the island—as well as considerable areas of open heath and bog.

Two trails provide access to the eastern shore from a small parking lot. Twisting over rocky and root-covered ground that is relatively flat in terrain, the trails are linked via hike along the rocky shoreline, comprising a loop about 5 miles long. Take some time along the ocean's edge to watch the seals densely congregating on the ledges offshore and to enjoy the views of the Moose Peak lighthouse on the unfortunately named **Mistake Island** (also a Nature Conservancy holding). Just how did it get that name? It appears to be an English language corruption of the native word "Mooseabec," thought to mean "moose head." In any case, the teeny island intrigues with its unique (and ironically hard-to-forget) moniker. Allow about three hours for the entire loop, and be prepared for damp conditions; as can be common around here, fog often moves in with little warning.

The preserve parking lot is on the west side of Great Wass Island. From Jonesport cross the bridge to Beals Island and continue onward, bearing right at the fork after you cross the causeway to Great Wass. The pavement soon ends; continue until you pass a lobster pound at Black Duck Cove, then look for the lot on the left side of the road. Pick up maps and a birder's checklist at the registration box. Or visit The Nature Conservancy website at nature.org.

Machias Area

Here's a bit of Revolutionary War lore long buried in the footnotes: The first naval battle of the Revolution took place near the port town of **Machias**, when ambitious colonists succeeded in capturing the better-equipped British schooner *Margaretta*. The episode unfolded in June 1775, a month after the Battle of Lexington. The *Margaretta* arrived in Machias accompanying a freight ship to procure wood for building a barracks for British soldiers in Boston. This action (not surprisingly) didn't sit well with the citizenry of Machias, who hastily organized an expedition against the British ship. Aboard two smaller ships they successfully attacked the *Margaretta,* mortally wounding the captain and capturing the crew. The story didn't have an entirely happy ending for the colonists, however. The British vowed retribution, and in subsequent months returned to rout Machias soldiers and burn many buildings.

One place to learn a bit about the battle for the *Margaretta* is **Burnham Tavern**, a pale yellow gambrel-roofed building located on a small rise in the pleasant commercial town of Machias. Constructed in 1770 by Job Burnham, the tavern served as the base from which Jeremiah O'Brien and his townsmen formulated plans for the attack on the British schooner. Following the skirmish, it was in the tavern that *Margaretta*'s captain succumbed to his wounds and other British soldiers were nursed back to health.

The tavern was acquired and restored by the Daughters of the American Revolution in 1910 and today appears much as it did during the heady days of the War of Independence. The original tap table is on display, as are a tea set and a chest taken from the captured ship. Up the steep "good morning" stairs are several bedrooms, including one where local Masons first met in 1778. Today the rooms house a collection of tools and other historic objects. The house is just one of 21 in the US that has been designated as most significant to the American Revolution.

The tavern is open on Mon, Wed, and Fri in July and Aug from 10 a.m. to 3 p.m., and by appointment. It is in the center of town just north of the Machias River on ME 192. Tours last about forty-five minutes and cost $5 for adults and from $1 to $2 for children, depending upon age. For more information call (207) 255-6930 or visit burnhamtavern.com.

A wooden model of the *Margaretta* may be seen at the **Gates House** in the riverside village of **Machiasport**, several miles south of Machias on ME 92. Built around 1807, this home was in the Gates family for more than a century before it became the headquarters of the **Machiasport Historical Society** (207-255-8461; machiasporthistoricalsociety.org). Located on the tidal river, this classic clapboard home contains displays related to the marine history of the area and its early life and commerce. A kitchen displays early utensils; local period fashion may be seen upstairs. There's also a telescope offering views

Old-Fashioned Craftsmanship

So the saying goes, what is old is new again. In this age dominated by digital and proliferating with plastic, a vintage favorite has re-emerged, fueled by nostalgia: Log building sets; specifically, those made by **Roy Toy Manufacturing**. Originally founded by Roy Dennison in the 1930s in East Machias, the company went out of business following its namesake's death—and the plastic boom of the 1960s. (Cue the line from the 1967 classic *The Graduate*: "I want to say one word to you, just one word: Plastics.") The family took the old equipment apart and stored it away in attics, barns, and basements across town. Several decades later Dennison's grandson had an idea for a revival; after studying the old processes and equipment, he relaunched the business. Today, the company continues to makes log building sets that are crafted from hand-cut local pine and colored with nontoxic dyes. They range from the "original" 37-piece log cabin set first created by Dennison, to deluxe versions with more than 550 pieces. Visit roytoy.com or call (207) 255-0954.

down the river toward the open ocean. The house is open July through Sept, Tues through Fri from 12:30 to 4:30 p.m., or by appointment. Admission is free.

If you're continuing eastward toward Lubec, consider the somewhat longer but more scenic trip via ME 191 through the harbor town of **Cutler**. The road offers a fine view of coastal Maine at its most remote and least developed. Views of the ocean open here and there, and the road traverses broad heaths and blueberry barrens, which blaze a fiery red in fall.

Lubec Region

Maine's easternmost towns, located along Cobscook and Passamaquoddy Bays, are known for two major distinctions: the booming sardine industry that flourished here in the early 20th century, and the mighty tides that sweep twice daily in and out of the bays. The difference between high tide and low tide can be as much as 28 feet near Lubec and Eastport, and each tide generates fiercely powerful currents that can stymie unwary boat captains attempting to make headway at the wrong time and in the wrong place.

Lubec holds the distinction of being the easternmost town in the US. The **Lubec Historical Society Museum**, on ME 189 in town, gives visitors a glimpse into the area's past, and is fittingly located in the former **Columbian Fish Packing Plant**. Displays include merchandise (and prices) typical of a century ago. There's also a complete 1940s barbershop, an 1831 field cannon, a 1900s town watering trough, a lighthouse bell, antique farm and fishing tools in an array of working conditions, antique handmade quilts, and a wealth of log books, photos and military and other records. The adorably quaint museum is officially open from mid June until Columbus Day, Mon, Wed, and Fri from 10 a.m. to 3 p.m. Admission is free. For more information call (207) 733-2274 or visit lubechistoricalsociety.com.

Not far from town you'll find the easternmost point in the United States: **West Quoddy Head**. (East Quoddy Head, if you're wondering, is at the distant end of Campobello Island in Canada.) This narrow lobe of land extends off the mainland south of town and is anchored by a distinctive candy-striped red and white lighthouse, one that's appeared on postage stamps and countless wall calendars. On a clear day you can see from the lighthouse to the cliffs of Grand Manan, a brawny Canadian island 16 miles out in the Bay of Fundy. The lighthouse, first commissioned in 1807 and rebuilt in 1858, is operated by the Coast Guard and closed to the public. But visitors may explore the grounds, which are often blooming with daylilies and wild roses. A short shoreline trail runs southward along a jagged 50-foot precipice to **Quoddy Head State Park**, a 541-acre ocean-side park with picnicking and limited hiking. During midtide didyouknow?

Why is the West Quoddy Head Light striped red and white like a candy cane—the only lighthouse in Maine painted as such? It's simply following the lead of the Canadians just across the bay. Lighthouses in Canada are traditionally (and sensibly) painted with red stripes to make them stand out better in summer fogs and against snow-covered winter landscapes. Another interesting fact about West Quoddy: It is the first spot in the country to be hit by the morning rays of the sun.

you can witness the remarkable force of the currents as they eddy and curl around the offshore ledges and rocks.

The lighthouse grounds are open daily from 10 a.m. to 5 p.m. (only until 4 p.m. in May, June, Sept., and Oct). The state park is open daily May 15 through Oct 15 from 9 a.m. to sunset. Fee to visit the park is $4 for adults, and $1 for seniors and children (ages 5-11). When on the grounds, be sure to visit the recently rebuilt, wheelchair-accessible Visitor Center and Museum. This is located on the ground floor of the original 1857 Keeper's House. Features include regional and historical displays, artifacts, interactive exhibits (including a History of Fog Warning exhibit with push-button sounds—be ready to block your ears), and a small gallery of lighthouse and local art. Museum admission is free. Call (207) 733-2180 or visit westquoddy.com.

Campobello Island is accessible by bridge across the Narrows from the town of Lubec. Because the island is in the Canadian province of New Brunswick, you'll need to clear customs both coming and going. The United States has a stake in one section of the island: the *Roosevelt Campobello International Park and Natural Area*. This 2,800-acre park, located about 2 miles from the bridge, is managed by a special international commission with representatives from the US Department of the Interior and Canada's Department of External Affairs. It claims to be the only park of this kind in the world; at the very least it provides a bit of justification for including a wonderful Canadian destination in a book about Maine.

The park is named for US president Franklin Delano Roosevelt, who summered here almost every year between 1883, when he was 1 year old, and 1921, the summer he was stricken with polio. FDR's father, James Roosevelt, was first lured to the island's beauty and tranquility when Campobello was being touted as an exclusive resort for the wealthy. He purchased four acres and a partially built home, completing the residence over the next few years. In 1910 the family moved to a significantly larger eighteen-bedroom "cottage" nearby, which was originally built in 1897. The cottage is open to the public.

Get an overview of the island's history at the visitor center, where you can watch a short film about FDR's long relationship with the island. (He introduced

Salmon by the Pen

The towns along Passamaquoddy Bay once thrived on sardines, which were caught and canned here before being shipped worldwide. But with changing tastes, demand dried up. The seaport towns suffered. But another fish, now in high demand, is bringing new vigor to the area: the **Atlantic salmon**.

Where the roads touch along the bay, be sure to scan the waters. You may see what look like floating checkerboards off in the distance. But look closer. You'll see fish leaping, restrained from escape by netting draped over the water. The pens are especially prevalent in the coves around Eastport, where the nation's largest Atlantic salmon farming operation is located. You can learn more about the new industry, and take boat trips out to view the pens, during Eastport's longstanding annual **Salmon Festival**, which is held the second Sun of Sept.

golf to the island, which locals approved because they could graze their sheep on the greens, thus benefitting both parties.) The maroon-shingled Roosevelt cottage is a short walk behind the visitor center. A self-guided tour allows a leisurely wander through the spacious homestead, which is an appealing mix of the simple and the grandiose. It's hard to imagine an eighteen-bedroom house feeling like a cozy home, but somehow it does. Helpful guides are on hand to answer any questions. Spend a moment picturing the extended Roosevelt clan gathered in the massive kitchen on the east side of the house during one of the region's infamous foggy mornings.

Nearby is the equally elegant **Hubbard Cottage**, built in 1891 and often open to the public. (If it's closed, it usually means a conference or other event is being held there.) A visit to this classic shingle-style home at the edge of the bay seems a trip to a lost era. The magnificent view across the water to the town of Eastport through the oval window in the dining room alone makes a trip worthwhile. If you'd like to spend more time outdoors, be sure to obtain a map of the park grounds at the visitor center. The park maintains about 8 miles of walking trails that pass through a wide variety of terrain, including a dramatic 2-mile ocean-side hike from Raccoon Beach to Liberty Point. The park is open daily from mid May to mid Oct, from sun-up to sun-down. Admission to both the park and the cottage is free. For more information call (506) 752-2922 or visit fdr.net. Note that border security has tightened, and now a passport is required for a trip over the border to Canada.

Eastport and Vicinity

Turning away from the ocean and heading toward inland Washington County, you'll wind along beautiful and surprisingly remote Cobscook and

Passamaquoddy Bays. ***Cobscook Bay State Park*** (207-726-4412, maine.gov/cobscookbay) is one of the state's finest parks, with many of its secluded campsites located along the water on three peninsulas. A picnic area is near a broad, grassy meadow with fine views down to the water. The park is just off US 1 (look for the sign) between Whiting and Dennysville and is open daily year-round, from 9 a.m. to sunset. The day-use fee is $6 for adults, $2 for seniors, and $1 for children (ages 5-11).

Another commendable spot for a detour is ***Reversing Falls Park***, a scruffy municipal park 6 miles from the town of ***Pembroke***. This 140-acre park is located on Mahar Point, where Dennys Bay and Whiting Bay squeeze into Cobscook Bay between the point and Falls Island. Because of the extraordinary tides, water tends to back up here, creating a set of rapids heading one way at one tide and reversing at the next. There's a short walk through mixed forest to the rocky edge of the river; a couple of picnic tables invite a perusal of this natural phenomenon. You might even catch seals playing and leaping in the building current. The best time to visit, according to locals, is about two hours before high tide.

Small signs point you from Pembroke to the park. Sometimes. Other times they're torn down and not replaced for months at a time. Coming from the south, veer right at the Triangle store, then turn east at the IOOF (International Order of Odd Fellows) Hall. Travel 3.4 miles along Leighton Neck to a right turn. Follow this road, which becomes increasingly rugged, to the end and park. There is no charge for visiting the park, which is open during daylight.

Between Pembroke and the town of Eastport (continue north on US 1, then turn right on ME 190), you'll drive through one of several Native American reservations in Maine. The ***Pleasant Point Reservation*** (known to those who live there as "Sipayik") flanks ME 190 immediately before a series of causeways and islands that links to Eastport. Here the Passamaquoddy tribe maintains the compact ***Waponahki Museum*** on the east side of the road. It's dedicated to

Tide Bores

Off Eastport, Passamaquoddy Bay presents a thrilling spectacle with each tide change. Giant whirlpools, known locally as "tide bores," form with the fast-moving currents. These always occur in the same location, and, in fact, some are named. The Old Sow is one of the more spectacular tide bores. Some of these whirlpools are strong enough to spin a large boat around like a top. Kayak and canoe fanciers beware!

the preservation of the tribe's language and culture, and features photographs, beaded items, fishing artifacts, and baskets handmade of ash and sweetgrass that the tribe is well-known for.

Eastport, all told, is a small town with a lot of history. The downtown consists of doughty brick commercial buildings and clapboarded Cape-style homes. They sit on a gentle hill above the harbor, which is surprisingly active with freighters and pleasure craft. The town's main street offers several small shops that are great for browsing as you explore and take in the charm.

One unique option: **Raye's Mustard Mill**, located on the edge of town on Outer Washington Street, produces some of the world's finest mustards. That claim can even be backed up: The Down East Schooner (an American yellow mustard) won first place at a 1996 international mustard competition in San Francisco. The operation is now in its fourth generation of Rayes; the family founded the mill in 1903 to provide mustard for sardine packing. Raye's produces more than two dozen gourmet mustards, and the mill's products have generated legions of devoted fans both in Maine and across the country (and Canada to the north). You can try samples and pick some up for the road at its store, which is open daily in the summer from 8:30 a.m. to 4 p.m. (it opens at 10 a.m. on Sat and Sun). When the mill schedule allows, you can take a tour during the week and on some weekends. Call (800) 853-1903 or visit rayesmustard.com, where you can shop online.

On your way out of town, stop by **Shackford Head State Park** for a stroll to an open bluff with spectacular views of the bay. (Watch for a small sign across from the gas station at Country Road and Washington Street; drive 0.7 mile, then turn left on the dirt road and park in the clearing at the road's end.) The walk is about two-thirds of a mile and passes through spruce forest, near a profusion of berry bushes and across a boardwalk. The views from the cliffs are wonderful; from here you'll get a good sense of the extent of salmon farming in the area when you see the acres of floating pens bobbing in remote coves. For a longer, more rugged return path, follow the Schooner Trail, which runs atop rocky bluffs with sweeping views over Cobscook Bay.

eastporttrivia

In 1932 a 26-foot great white shark was caught near Eastport. It's still on the record books as the largest shark ever taken from the waters of Maine.

Heading north, continue to follow US 1. Between Robbinston and Calais there's a small island about a half mile offshore in the **St. Croix River** whose appearance is far overshadowed by its historical significance. **St. Croix Island** (so named after two large bays north of the island that appear to form the arms of a cross) was the site of the first attempted permanent European settlement in North America (north of Florida).

In 1604 a group of some eighty French colonists under the guidance of Sieur de Monts and his lieutenant, Samuel de Champlain, landed on the island with the intent of establishing a village and trading center. The colonists were so uncertain of what to expect that they brought their own timber for building homes. The island was reasonably secure from surprise attack but lacked a number of amenities, including a ready supply of drinking water. In addition, the island was swept by bitter north winds, prompting Champlain to note that there were "six months of winter in this country." (And you won't find many locals who argue with that statement.) The following summer the colonists abandoned St. Croix Island and resettled at Annapolis Royal in Nova Scotia.

St. Croix Island is managed as a national monument, but public transportation to the island is not available. A riverside observation area with historical markers is located along US 1 near the town of Red Beach.

Grand Lake Stream Area

From this eastern corner of Maine, US 1 heads north to Aroostook County (see The County), and the road's character changes dramatically. Once you turn and put the sea at your back, few early homes line the road and salt air is replaced by the smell of spruce and fir. Timber companies own and manage a great deal of this land, which is filled with vast lakes and wild lakeshores. The Grand Lake Stream region is highly popular among anglers, hunters, and canoeists. Two miles north of the Town of Princeton on US 1, look for an unnamed road on the left and a sign pointing to Grand Lake Stream. Turn left here and drive 10 miles to the village of *Grand Lake Stream*. The village, with its selection of lodges and boat access to numerous remote lakes, has been a favored base among many outdoorspeople for decades. (The bass and landlocked salmon fishing is especially good.) Among the lodges here are **Weatherbys Resort** (207-796-5558, weatherbys.com) and **Shoreline Camps** (207-796-5539, shore linecamps.com). Both traditionally cater to serious anglers, but the owners make others feel welcome as well.

Even if you don't fish or hunt, you might want to visit the **Pine Tree Store** while in Grand Lake Stream. This is virtually the only store in town and offers one-stop shopping in a wild setting. It was recently taken over by new owners after having been run by Kurt and Kathy Cressey for years. Besides that, the bench in front of the store is a local gathering place, and with patience, visitors can glean inside information on the area here. Prices on fishing tackle, clothing, and so on are reasonable, and in the fall the store is a game inspection station; the timber framework structure alongside it is there to weigh moose. The Pine

Tree Store is a great place to linger and soak up the atmosphere of this small rugged and rustic town. The store is open daily year-round from 6 a.m. to 8 p.m. Call (207) 796-5027.

The Maine Department of Inland Fisheries and Wildlife's **Grand Lake Stream Fish Hatchery** is located at the foot of West Grand Lake, behind the Pine Tree Store. Here Maine's premier sportfish, the landlocked salmon, *Salmo salar*, is propagated for stocking in Maine as well as other states and countries. West Grand Lake is one of the original homes of landlocked salmon, and fish culture has continued here since 1868. In fact, this hatchery is the world's largest source of landlocked salmon raised from wild stock. Note that taxonomically speaking, the landlocked salmon is nearly identical to the endangered Atlantic salmon.

The Grand Lake Stream Hatchery Visitor Center is open to the public. The most popular of the various attractions here is the 800-gallon viewing tank. It is filled with "brood stock," or large adult salmon used for propagation. Another tank features salmon fry, their tiny progeny.

The Visitor Center is open from 8 a.m. to 3 p.m. daily. Please call ahead at (207) 796-5580.

Drivers heading back south from Grand Lake Stream have a scenic alternative to US 1. It is **Maine Route 9**, locally known as "the Airline" (or Airline Road). About 13 miles south of Princeton on US 1, look for the ME 9 sign on the right. This straight shot across eastern Maine has roots back to 1857, when Calais citizens established a dirt path to improve mail service from the state's commercial hub at Bangor. In time the route was improved to accommodate stagecoaches, which made the trip daily except on Sun. The eighteen-hour trip was often brutal on passengers, but it was a full day quicker than traveling by steamship. When the steamship companies attempted to curb competition by depicting the route as populated by wolves and bandits, stagecoach ridership surged as adventurers shelled out the fare to claim they had survived the trip. Despite the incongruously modern-sounding name, the Airline is in fact the old name for the route. Old-timers say it is so named because the sensation when riding on it is similar to flying; the Airline is built on high ground.

Today neither wolves nor bandits present much of a problem for motorists, but ME 9 does provide a glimpse at an interesting cross section of Maine. The road passes through thick spruce forests and cutover timberland, across blueberry barrens and open heath. East of the town of Aurora, watch for the road to ascend a glacial esker (a tall ridge of gravel formed by currents running through massive tunnels beneath a melting glacier). The land seems to drop off on either side of the road as if on a human-made embankment; glacial bogs may be seen north of the road from a small rest area. There are few services along the road (an occasional motel, general store, or snack bar), but for the most part it's simply a well-maintained byway through some of Maine's most scenic country.

Places to Stay Down East

BAR HARBOR

Acadia Hotel
20 Mount Desert St.
(207) 288-5721
acadiahotel.com
Inexpensive, open year-round
Offers private parking, something that comes at a premium in busy, downtown Bar Harbor.

Bar Harbor Hotel–Bluenose Inn
90 Eden St.
(207) 288-3348
bluenoseinn.com
Moderate
A luxury resort with sweeping views of Frenchman's Bay

Bar Harbor Inn
1 Newport Dr.
(207) 288-3351
barharborinn.com
Moderate
On the waterfront and within walking distance of shops. Luxury spa onsite.

Bar Harbor Motel
100 Eden St.
(800) 388-3453
barharbormotel.com
Moderate
Guests can ride trail bikes or walk to Acadia National Park directly from the motel.

Bass Cottage Inn
14 The Field
(207) 288-1234
basscottage.com
Expensive
Yankee Magazine Best of New England Editor's Choice Winner

Ivy Manor Inn
194 Main St.
(207) 288-2138
ivymanor.com
Expensive
Storybook setting featuring authentic French cuisine

Villager Motel
207 Main St.
(888) 383-3211
barharborvillager.com
Inexpensive
Built in 1969. Clean, convenient and (an extra perk), it's on the path of the giant Bar Harbor 4th of July Parade.

Wonder View Inn
50 Eden St.
(207) 288-3358
wonderviewinn.com
Moderate
Concerning the view, the name says it all. Try to get a room with a balcony. Also pet-friendly.

BLUE HILL

Blue Hill Inn
40 Union St.
(207) 374-2844
bluehillinn.com
Moderate
Well-appointed rooms and baths, lots of little extras

CASTINE

Castine Inn
33 Main St.
(207) 326-4365
castineinn.com
Inexpensive
Check out the garden, which includes native plants of Maine as well as lots of other perennials.

SELECTED CHAMBERS OF COMMERCE

Bar Harbor Chamber of Commerce
2 Cottage St.
(207) 288-5103
visitbarharbor.com

Blue Hill Peninsula Chamber of Commerce
16 South St.
(207) 374-3232
bluehillpeninsula.org.

Bucksport Bay Area Chamber of Commerce
54 Main St.
(207) 469-6818
bucksportbaychamber.com

Belfast Area Chamber of Commerce
14 Main St.
(207) 338-5900
belfastmaine.org

Deer Isle–Stonington Chamber of Commerce
114 Little Deer Island Rd.
(207) 348-6124
deerisle.com.

Eastport Area Chamber of Commerce
141 Water St.
(207) 853-4644
eastportchamber.net

Machias Bay Area Chamber of Commerce
2 Kilton Ln.
(207) 255-4402
machiaschamber.org

Penobscot Bay Regional Chamber of Commerce
P.O. Box 508, Rockland
(800) 562-2529
camdenrockland.com

Pentagöet Inn and Restaurant
26 Main Street
(207) 326-8616
pentagoet.com
Moderate
Surrounded by historic sites. Be sure to take a walking history tour.

DEDHAM

Lucerne Inn
2517 Main Rd. (US 1A)
(207) 843-5132
lucerneinn.com
Inexpensive
Gracious inn with panoramic views of Lucerne Lake

DEER ISLE

Pilgrim's Inn
20 Main St.
(888) 778-7505 or
(207) 348-6615
pilgrimsinn.com
Expensive
An incredibly varied breakfast is included in room price.

EASTPORT

Kilby House Inn
122 Water St.
(800) 853-4557 or
(207) 853-0989
kilbyhouseinn.com
Inexpensive
Stay here to go on whale-watching tours and visit the historic downtown area.

GRAND LAKE STREAM

Chet's Camps on Big Lake
140 Chet Camp Rd.
(207) 796-5557
chetscamps.com
Moderate
Puts the traveler near some of Maine's best landlocked salmon, smallmouth bass, and white perch waters

Indian Rock Camps
15 Church St.
(800) 498-2821 or
(207) 796-2822
indianrockcamps.com
Inexpensive
Spend time along this historic stream. Be sure to visit the salmon hatchery.

Shoreline Camps
191 Pine Drive,
(207) 796-5539
shorelinecamps.com
Inexpensive
Comfortable camps, just
right for a salmon-fishing
vacation

Weatherby's Fishing and Hunting Lodge
(877) 796-5558
weatherbys.com
Moderate
A resort catering to fly-
fishermen (and other
outdoor-lovers, too)

HULLS COVE

The Colony Cottages
20 ME 3
(207) 288-3383
colonyathullscove.com
Inexpensive
Lawn leads down to
oceanfront tide pools. A
prime destination for nature
lovers.

MACHIAS

Micmac Farm Guesthouses and Gardner House Inn
47 Micmac Ln.,
Machiasport
(207) 255-3008
micmacfarm.com
Inexpensive
Steeped in history. Enjoy
river walks, woods, and
fields.

SOUTHWEST HARBOR

Claremont Inn
Clark Point Rd.
(207) 244-5036
theclaremonthotel.com
Moderate
Classic Maine summer
retreat. Built in 1884; listed
on the National Register of
Historic Places.

The Inn at Southwest
371 Main St.
(207) 244-3835
innatsouthwest.com
Moderate
A "stone's throw" from
Acadia. Overlooks
the harbor. Offers
breakfast and afternoon
refreshments.

Kingsleigh Inn Bed and Breakfast
373 Main St.
(207) 244-5302
kingsleighinn.com
Moderate
Elegant turreted Queen
Anne Victorian built in
1904 offering a unique,
eclectic designer decor and
gorgeous panoramic views
overlooking Southwest
Harbor

Lindenwood Inn
118 Clark Point Rd.
(207) 244-5335
lindenwoodinn.com
Moderate
Sea captain's home turned
cozy inn in the heart of
busy Southwest Harbor

Seawall Motel
566 Sewall Rd.
(207) 244-3020
seawallmotel.com
Inexpensive
Clean, quiet, and next to
the Sewall entrance to
Acadia National Park

STONINGTON

Inn on the Harbor
45 Main St.
(207) 367-2420
innontheharbor.com
Moderate
Relax on the deck built
directly over the harbor.

Places to Eat Down East

BAR HARBOR

Cafe This Way
14½ Mt. Desert St.
(207) 288-4483
cafethisway.com
Moderate
"Eclectic" casual dining. Try
their breakfast burrito with
eggs Benedict.

Havana
318 Main St.
(207) 288-2822
havanamaine.com
Expensive
In July 2010, US president
Barack Obama and first
lady Michelle Obama dined
here on lobster thermidor.
Havana is famed for its
mojitos and also for its
wine list, one of the best in
Maine.

Jordan's Restaurant
80 Cottage St.
(207) 288-3586
jordanswildblueberry.com
Inexpensive
Their homemade blueberry muffins excel. Excellent choice for a memorable breakfast.

Lompoc Cafe
32 Rodick St.
(207) 288-9392
lompoccafe.com
Inexpensive
Prides itself on being "unpretentious," but "a little different." Try their Coal Porter and Bar Harbor Blueberry Ale.

West Street Cafe
76 West St.
(207) 288-5242
weststreetcafe.com
Moderate
Family-friendly dining serving classic New England fare (yes, that means lobster).

DEDHAM

Lucerne Inn
2517 Main Rd. (US 1A)
(207) 843-5123
lucerneinn.com
Moderate
Fine food, friendly staff. Also great weekend specials for both lodging and dining.

EASTPORT

WaCo Diner
47 Water St.
(207) 853-4046
Inexpensive
Great water view. Established in 1924. Waco is Washington County, abbreviated.

NORTHEAST HARBOR

The Colonel's Restaurant and Bakery
143 Main St.
(207) 276-5147
colonelsrestaurant.com
Inexpensive
Family-run, family-friendly, casual dining

The Docksider
14 Sea St.
(207) 276-3965
Expensive
Specializes in seafood . . . no surprise, considering its location

OTTER CREEK

Burning Tree
69 Otter Creek Dr.
(207) 288-9331
Moderate
Worth the trip to Otter Creek just to eat here. Superb seafood as well as fresh, local produce, and herbs.

Jordan Pond House
Loop Road
(207) 276-3316
acadiajordanpondhouse .com
Moderate
See main entry (p. 164) for full description.

PERRY

The New Friendly Restaurant
1014 US 1
(207) 853-6610
Inexpensive
Family-style home cooking. Good food, good values. Try their lobster roll.

STONINGTON

Harbor Cafe
36 Main St.
(207) 367-5099
Inexpensive
Everything is good, but their fish and chips are especially so. Good portions.

Stonecutters Kitchen
5 Atlantic Ave.
(207) 367-2530
stonecutterskitchenme.com
Moderate
Lots of seafood specialties (not surprisingly), as well as specialty pizza and a la carte sandwiches.

North Woods

The North Woods consists of millions of acres of forestland, some of it as quiet and removed as when Thoreau traveled through and noted the "general stillness more impressive than any sound." This is the terrain of moose and loon; humans don't so much linger as pass on through.

The North Woods isn't for the garden-variety tourist. Because the region is so wild and undeveloped, car travelers may soon become frustrated at the lack of facilities and access. You can drive only so far on dusty logging roads through commercial timberland before you become a bit weary and start yearning for people and buildings of one sort or another.

The North Woods is best appreciated by those with outdoor inclinations: anglers, hunters, white-water rafters, and canoeists—especially canoeists (or kayakers). There are hundreds of miles of rivers and streams, as well as thousands of miles of lakeshore, that are best navigated by small private craft. Footpaths exist here and there—notably the Appalachian Trail—but for the most part the North Woods trail network is sketchy at best.

One more brief caveat before you visit the North Woods: This is not a wilderness area but an industrial forest, and there's

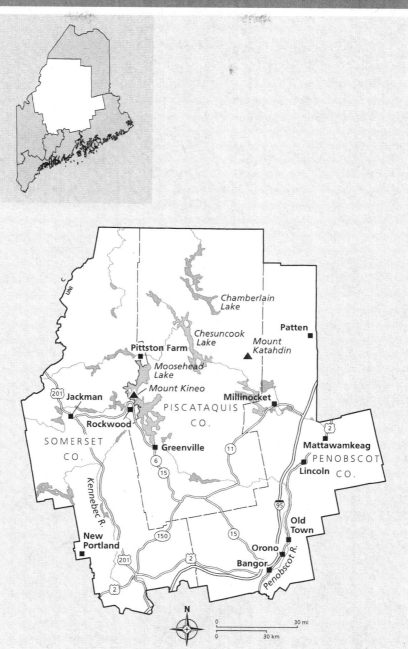

a big difference between the two. Pockets of undisturbed forest may be found throughout—isolated state landholdings and property owned by the Nature Conservancy—but much of the rest of the North Woods is privately owned by about two dozen timber companies. Virtually the entire forest has been cut at least once, and more likely twice or more. If you think of the North Woods as agricultural land, like a massive farm with crops on a forty-year rotation, you're on your way to understanding what this region is all about.

Penobscot County

Penobscot County includes Maine's second city, the lumber capital of Bangor. More likely, though, many know this city as the regular residence of horror master Stephen King, and influences for his iconic books can be found throughout. Ultimately, though, Bangor is a small urban oasis in a county that ranges from rural to wild. The county's borders extend far to the north, striking deep into the heart of the timberlands north of the mill town of Millinocket.

Bangor Area

Maine's North Woods begins at the city of *Bangor*, in both a geographic and historic sense. Between 1820 and 1860 Bangor prospered like no other town in Maine as timber merchants employed hundreds of men to cut pine and spruce along the Penobscot and its tributaries, then float the logs down the river during great spring lumber drives. Once at the mills downstream, the logs were cut and exported throughout the nation and abroad. In fact, Bangor was the largest lumber port in the world during the 1850s, and with that honor came tremendous prosperity. More than a few fortunes were made. But

Bangor Firsts

Among inventors, tinkerers, and the trivia obsessed, Bangor holds a special place. In the 19th century the city claimed several "firsts," beginning in 1850 when a young man developed the nation's first batch of chewing gum on his kitchen stove. He boiled spruce sap, added sugar, dusted the strips with cornstarch, and started peddling his new chewy concoction in the big cities. It didn't take long to catch on. Eventually he developed a business that employed 200 people producing gum for shipment nationwide. Bangor was also the first city to erect a Civil War memorial, building it at Mount Hope Cemetery a month before the Battle of Gettysburg. Bangor is the birthplace of the canvas-covered canoe, and the extension ladder. It also was the first city in Maine to have an electric trolley system, inaugurated in 1889.

America's Boogeyman

Well, the world's boogeyman, really. Forget about the glories of the timber baron days. Bangor today may be best known as the home of horror godfather **Stephen King**. As befits a writer of such novels in the modern Gothic tradition, King lives much of the year on a pleasant street of large handsome homes in an oversize Victorian house. It is reminiscent of the Addams Family house, only without prolific cobwebs and shutters all askew. By all accounts, King is a regular guy around town, involved in various civic and local affairs. If you're spending time in the area, you'll no doubt see the horror master out and about. He and his wife, Tabitha, who is also a novelist, have donated millions to various causes, including the construction of a world-class Little League field and the renovation of the public library. For those interested, there is a wealth of information online guiding to spots (including the town library, the standpipe, Mt. Hope cemetery) that inspired the author's writings and/or serve as prominent settings in his books.

Bangor began an inevitable decline in the 1880s as readily accessible trees were depleted and the timber industry moved west. Adding to this, a fire leveled much of the city in 1911. Nevertheless, Bangor retains much historical interest, and it's not hard to imagine it during its golden days more than a century ago. The city's proud woodland heritage may be best captured by the city's de facto symbol: the vaguely menacing 31-foot fiberglass *Paul Bunyan statue* on Main Street between Buck and Dutton Streets. Bangor claims that the legendary lumberman was born here in 1834. But not surprisingly, that's widely-disputed, with many other cities and towns, particularly in timber regions of the upper Midwest, claiming to be the bearded and burly lumberman's birth site and hometown.

A good place to get an overview of Bangor history is at the *Bangor Museum and History Center* at 159 Union St. The collections are housed in an uncommonly graceful brick home constructed in 1836 and now operated by the *Bangor Historical Society*. The Thomas A. Hill House was built for its namesake lawyer, architect and speculator by the renowned Richard Upjohn (best known for designing New York City's Trinity Church). It is furnished much like a typical upper-crust Victorian home, with medallion-backed chairs, soaring gilded mirrors, and intricate Oriental carpets. Be sure to note the exceptional craftsmanship of the carved frieze and the Corinthian columns in the airy double parlor. The museum and history center are open in the summer Mon through Fri, from 10 a.m. to 4 p.m., and Sat from noon to 4 p.m. A suggested donation for admission is $5 per person. The historical society also offers walking tours throughout town and provides materials for self-guided exploration, including at the historic *Mt. Hope Cemetery* (which King fans will know was a setting for *Pet Sematary*, both the book and film). For more information, visit bangorhistoricalsociety.org or call (207) 942-1900.

Fans of architecture will enjoy a stop at the **Bangor Public Library**. The original Beaux Arts structure, a handsome domed affair, was built in 1912 as the city was rebuilding itself after the devastating fire of 1911. By the 1990s the library was feeling its age; like many old buildings that can get a bit neglected with the years, it was crumbling and leaky. A massive campaign was launched by locals to restore and expand the building, and one of the nation's most prominent architects—Robert A. M. Stern—was hired to design a three-story addition. The new library is situated on 24 acres, and can be found at 145 Harlow St.; for more information call (207) 947-8336 or visit bpl.lib.me.us.

The **Maine Discovery Museum** makes exploration fun with the largest interactive children's museum in northern New England. It occupies the old Freese's Building at 74 Main St., and features three floors of hands-on exhibits. There is a dino dig, an introduction to nano science, a giant "body journey," and a "booktown" featuring scenes from favorite Maine children's books including *Goodnight Moon*. Kids can also sing karaoke, explore gravity, acceleration, and space, and bring out their inner artist in the museum's "artscape." The museum is open every day in the summer, Mon through Sat 10 a.m. to 5 p.m., and Sun noon to 5 p.m. During the rest of the year, it's closed on Mon as well as school holidays. Overnight stays for school and scout groups are welcome; call ahead for this. Admission is $7.50 per person, with those 12 months and under getting in for free. For more information call (207) 262-7200 or visit mainediscoverymuseum.org.

Outside downtown, near exit 45 off I-95, is the **Cole Land Transportation Museum**. This is more than your run-of-the-mill vehicle museum—it's

Thomas Hill Standpipe, Bangor

The **Thomas Hill Standpipe**, built in 1897, is one of the state's architectural eccentricities. Sited atop one of Bangor's beautiful and gentle hills, the standpipe is essentially a water tank with an observation deck built around it. If nothing else, this 110-foot-high white wooden hulk attests to the pervasive influence of the Shingle style in the late 19th century. With its clean lines, shingles, and colonnaded overlook circling the top, the standpipe also provides a heartening glimpse into a world where even something as utilitarian as a water tank benefited from an architect's eye. The 1.75-million-gallon tank is still used today to provide clean water to Bangor and is managed by the Bangor Water District. The standpipe observatory may be appreciated from the outside anytime, and it is open to the public from time to time for tours. Call the Bangor Museum and Center For History (207-942-1900) or the Bangor Water District (207-947-4516) for more details.

an eclectic collection of 19th- and 20th-century vehicles that extends back to the covered wagon days. You can view some 200 vehicles, from tractors to buckboards to sleds, housed in a modern and airy warehouse building. The museum is at 405 Perry Rd. and is open seven days a week from May through Nov, from 9 a.m. to 5 p.m. Admission is $7 for adults, $6 for AAA members, and $5 for seniors (62 and older). Children under 19 are free. For more information call (207) 990-3600 or visit colemuseum.org.

Orono and Old Town

About 8 miles north of Bangor in *Orono* is the principal campus of the *University of Maine*, which has about 11,000 students. The university began in 1868 as the Maine State College of Agriculture and Mechanic Arts but broadened its curriculum over the years to encompass liberal arts as well as forestry, business, and engineering. The campus was originally designed by noted landscape architect Frederick Law Olmsted, but the plan was modified and later additions have obscured Olmsted's original vision. With its attractive buildings and leafy trees, the campus still offers a pleasant place to stroll.

Here you'll find the *Hudson Museum* at the *Collins Center For The Arts*. This respected museum of anthropology and native culture occupies the performance center's second level, and its collections include gold and jade jewelry from the Aztec and Maya cultures of Central America, as well as an exceptional selection of masks and carvings from the native cultures of the Pacific Northwest (check out the towering and dramatic Haida house post). Other geographic areas represented include Oceania, the Arctic, and Africa, and there is a special emphasis on the native Penobscot Indians. Local crafts include cornhusk dolls, snowshoes, a birch-bark canoe, ceremonial beadwork, and split-ash basketry.

The museum is open Mon through Fri from 9 a.m. to 4 p.m., and Sat from 11 a.m. to 4 p.m., as well as during performance intermissions. It is closed on Sun and holidays. Admission is free. For more information call (207) 581-1904 or visit umaine.edu/hudsonmuseum.

Also on campus is the *Page Farm and Home Museum*. This small museum features a collection of everyday items that would likely have been found on a Maine farm a century ago. The museum is in the last original agricultural building (ca 1865) on the university campus; one of those simple white A-frame buildings that have come to signify Maine's rurality. There are exhibits on dairy and poultry farming, as well as a blacksmith shop and a one-room schoolhouse. The collections are a virtual compendium of life in Maine before 1940. The museum has never bought a thing—every bowl, beam, and bread-board was donated, and every item was likewise made and used in Maine. The

FAVORITE ATTRACTIONS

Bangor Museum and History Center

Baxter State Park

Gulf Hagas, Katahdin Iron Works Area

Mattawamkeag Wilderness Park

Old Town Canoe Company, Old Town

Moosehead Historical Society,
Greenville

SS *Katahdin*, Greenville

museum is open year-round, Tues through Sat from 9 a.m. to 4 p.m. Admission is free. For more information call (207) 581-4100 or visit umaine.edu/pagefarm.

Latter-day Penobscot and Passamaquoddy Indians still inhabit reservations around the state, remnants of the many early and inequitable land transactions between natives and European settlers. One of the more prominent reservations is located just north of Old Town. ***Indian Island*** was part of a 1786 treaty that deeded most of Maine to the European settlers; the Penobscots retained ownership of more than one hundred islands in the Penobscot River, Indian Island among them. The island, which is home to the Penobscot Nation, is connected via a bridge to the west bank. Visitors are welcome with the understanding that the island is an active community and not a tourist attraction.

New prosperity arrived at the island in 1972 following an $80 million settlement for outstanding land claims unearthed in early documents. The windfall has resulted in a handsome new school and the Sockalexis Memorial Ice Arena, named after the Sockalexis brothers, Andrew and Lewis, who went on to prominence in the Olympics and professional baseball in the early 20th century. To learn more about the Penobscot Nation (its various programs and educational initiatives, history, and culture), visit penobscotnation.org.

Indian Island also has the gravesite of ***Joseph (Joe) Polis***, the Penobscot Indian who served as Thoreau's guide and tutor during his travels through the forests of northern Maine. Polis taught Thoreau the Indian names for various flora and fauna, as well as the lore of the woods. As Thoreau noted, however, Joe wasn't entirely comfortable living off the land. "By George!" he purportedly told the celebrated transcendentalist, "I shan't go into the woods without provision—hard bread, pork, etc." Their relationship is one of the more intriguing of the 19th-century literary world.

To find Polis's grave, cross the main bridge to the island from Old Town and drive a short distance to where the road forks at a cemetery. Park and look for a granite stone topped with a small carved urn in the section of the cemetery closest to the bridge.

Old Town has become synonymous with canoes, thanks to the highly popular line of canoes manufactured by *Old Town Canoe Company*. Founded by George Gray in his hardware store in 1900, it is the largest and best-known canoe manufacturer—and these days it is well-known for its range of kayak styles, too. The company made its signature canvas-covered wooden canoes in buildings along the Penobscot that were originally constructed to manufacture shoes. As a point of fact, though, Old Town wasn't the first canoe maker hereabouts. That honor belongs to the White Canoe Company, founded in 1889, which was purchased by Old Town in 1984. Old Town phased out the White line in 1990. (And prior to that, of course, you can't forget the natives; they were crafting canoes from birch bark and other materials to cross the area's plethora of water bodies long before the "white man" set foot here.)

These days, Old Town, which is owned by Johnson Outdoors, still makes canoes with wood strips and brass nails; however, they cost closer to $2,500, a long ways from their original $40 price tag. The more commonly purchased Old Town canoes and kayaks are made of high-tech materials like Polylink 3, Kevlar, and complex laminates, and put together using processes and machines

TOP ANNUAL EVENTS

JANUARY

100-Mile Wilderness Sled Dog Race
Greenville, late Jan/early Feb
(207) 695-2421
100milewildernessrace.org

APRIL

Flower and Garden Show
Bangor, early Apr
(207) 990-1201

Kenduskeag Stream Canoe Race
Bangor, mid Apr
(207) 992-4490
kenduskeagstreamcanoerace.com

MAY

Moosemania
Greenville and Rockwood, late May or
early June
(207) 695-2702

JULY

Bangor State Fair
late July or early Aug
(207) 947-0307
bangorstatefair.com

AUGUST

The American Folk Festival
Bangor, late Aug
americanfolkfestival.com

SEPTEMBER

International Seaplane Fly-In
Greenville, Sept
(207) 695-6121
seaplanefly-in.org

Downstream, with Paddle

What to do if you're coming from afar and want to spend a few days in a canoe, but don't want to lug all that camping gear and a boat along on your whole vacation? Contact **Allagash Canoe Trips**. Experience? They've got plenty. They've been running guided canoe trips on Maine rivers since 1953. You can select from a variety of rivers, including the Allagash, Moose, Penobscot, and St. John. They provide all equipment, meals, and transportation. Lasting from five to seven days, trips start around $1,000. Call (207) 280-1551 or (207) 280-0191 or visit allagashcanoetrips.com.

that would certainly have confounded (but no doubt intrigued) Mr. Gray. For more information, visit oldtowncanoe.com.

Just across the Penobscot River from Old Town is Bradley where you'll find the *Maine Forest and Logging Museum*, whose center feature is the restored 18th-century logging community of *Leonard's Mills*. This is Maine's equivalent to Plimoth Plantation or Old Sturbridge Village: Essentially visitors "step back in time" to a 1790s-era logging and milling community where reenactors in period garb provide demonstrations of daily life, activities and commerce.

The little village centers around a water-operated sawmill, complete with wooden gears and a wooden waterwheel that makes a wonderfully syncopated thumping rhythm as it revolves. Maine's famous bean-hole beans and biscuits are made fresh, to the delight of old and young alike. A period blacksmith plies his trade, lumbermen drive steam-powered log haulers and split cedar shakes by hand with a vintage froe, while period merchants sell everything from musical instruments to pottery masterpieces. Visitors can also explore the *Grady Machine Shop* and take rides on an authentic bateau on scenic Blackman Stream, or in an historic wagon hauled by draught horses.

The Maine Forest and Logging Museum is open on Thurs from June through Sept; there are also special activities offered for families throughout the summer. Its grounds are open every day of the week for hiking, picnicking and enjoying Maine's natural beauty and history. Admission is $3 for adults (12 and older). For details call (207) 974-6278 or visit maineforestandlogging museum.org.

Northern Penobscot County

From the Bangor–Old Town area, the county narrows and extends far northward. Settlements become even more sparse, the lakes bigger and wilder. Many of the smaller roads turn to gravel with little warning. Summer communities thrive along some of the lakes, but for the most part the widely scattered residents are year-round, and many find their livelihood in the forest as lumber workers or guides.

One of the lesser-known destinations for campers in the North Woods is the **Mattawamkeag Wilderness Park** just outside the small town of Mattawamkeag, north of Enfield on US 2. The park isn't sparsely attended for lack of beauty; the place has a character that makes it seem like Baxter State Park's younger sibling. Relatively small at just over a thousand acres, this gem of a park sits alongside the wild Mattawamkeag River, a favored destination for serious white-water kayakers and anglers. White-water lovers are challenged by threatening rapids called the Heater and Upper Gordon Falls, both approaching Class V and portaged by all but the most experienced boaters. Those with less experience can enjoy some of the gentler white water above the falls. The park also features a network of hiking trails for exploring the riverside and flanking hills.

Mattawamkeag Park, which is owned by the town, has fifty drive-in campsites and eleven Adirondack-style shelters. Although it's called a wilderness park (some claim the forest has never been cut here), there are a fair number of amenities—including hot showers, Ping-Pong tables, and horseshoes.

The park is an 8-mile dirt-road drive east of Mattawamkeag, a tiny town of a few hundred people at the junctions of the Mattawamkeag and the Penobscot with the sparse human influence of a handful of small businesses. It is open from May through Columbus Day, with a day-use fee of $3 per person. Camping fees range from $22 to $35 (depending on whether you want a tent or a lean-to, and utilities such as electricity and water. For more information, visit mwpark.com.

It's hard to get a grasp of what life was like in the North Woods before the lumber roads changed the routine of loggers and lumber workers. The job is now much like any other: Workers commute to the woods from nearby towns, and then return home at night. Before the roads—and especially before the internal combustion engine—an entire subculture thrived in the forest as woodsmen spent weeks at their labors before returning to the civilized world.

One place to get a glimpse of that lost world is the **Lumbermen's Museum** just west of the town of **Patten.** Extensive collections fill its cluster of buildings, including one log cabin reconstructed from original 1860s loggers' cabins. This engaging museum, housing thousands of North Woods artifacts, was founded in 1962 when the lumbermen's trade was in full decline. Among the displays are early log haulers, a working sawmill, dioramas of the various types of logging camps that appeared in Maine, and hundreds of tools used by loggers, millwrights, coopers, and others who depended on the forest for their livelihood. Housed in an old Maine Forest Service building, the reception center features evocative logging murals painted by local artists.

The museum is open July through early Oct, Tues through Sat, 10 a.m. to 4 p.m. It is also open on Memorial Day weekend and on Fri through Sun in June from 10 a.m. to 4 p.m. Admission is $10 for adults, $8 for seniors (65 and older), and $5 for children (ages 4-12). The museum is located on ME 159/Shin Pond Road just west of ME 11 in Patten. Call (207) 528-2650 or visit lumbermensmuseum.org.

Continuing westward toward the mountains on ME 159, you'll cross the county line and come to the less-used northeast entrance to Baxter State Park, arguably one of Maine's foremost outdoor destinations.

Piscataquis County

Piscataquis (pronounced pis-CAT-a-kwiss) is the heart of Maine's timberland region and its least populated county. Even including the relatively populous towns of Dover–Foxcroft and Greenville, it can muster only about 17,000 residents, resulting in fewer than five people per square mile. Heavily forested, the county is marked by attractive hills and beautiful lakes.

Baxter State Park and Vicinity

If you visited the statehouse in Augusta, you may have noticed the bronze bust of one of Maine's former governor in the rotunda. That was Percival Baxter, who served between 1920 and 1925. The reason he's been granted this place of honor is immediately evident when you're traveling in north-central Maine. Scan the horizon on a clear day and you're likely to see the distinctive sloping ridgeline of Mount Katahdin set amid the lesser peaks of *Baxter State Park*, Percival Baxter's gift to Maine.

Baxter, both as state legislator and as governor, attempted to have the state acquire the land surrounding *Mount Katahdin*. The state legislature rebuffed those efforts. Stymied but not defeated, Baxter set about purchasing the land on his own, using a considerable fortune acquired in part from his father, James Phinney Baxter, one of the pioneers in the Maine canning industry. Between 1930 and 1962 Percival Baxter bought bits and pieces and donated them to the state until he had assembled a block of land totaling slightly more than 200,000 acres. Baxter's central stipulation in handing the property over to the state was that it remain "forever wild."

The state has done an excellent job carrying out Baxter's directive and self-described "magnificent obsession." The roads through the park are of dirt and often in rough condition. The 180 miles of foot trails running throughout it are sparingly maintained, making a hiking trip more of an adventure than a leisurely stroll. Not surprisingly, there have been some threats to the park's wildness over the years: Hundreds of hikers now scale Mount Katahdin's 5,267-foot peak on a cloudless summer's day, overburdening the trails and compromising the wilderness experience on the summit. But dozens of other park destinations still offer visitors a place to be alone with the impressive silence of the woods.

Unlike most North Woods locations, Baxter State Park is a hiker's park first and foremost and a canoeist's and kayaker's park second. Day hikers will find a number of excellent destinations that are less daunting—and less crowded—than the Katahdin summit. Try the 2.5-mile round-trip hike to Big and Little Niagara Falls from Daicey Pond or the 6-mile climb of Mount O-J-I west of Katahdin. The day-use fee is $15 per out-of-state vehicle per day (no charge for Maine residents). The most commonly used access point is the south gate, which may be reached from Millinocket along signed roads. If you plan to camp at the park, reservations are essential in the peak summer months. For some of its sites, Baxter employs a pleasantly anachronistic method of

The Mighty and Majestic—If Dim—Moose

Maine has by far the largest population of moose in New England, numbering more than 25,000. These are big animals—they can weigh upward of 1,000 pounds with their antlers alone topping 50 pounds or more (making for a heavy head in more than one sense of the word)—and are well designed for foraging for grasses and sedges, which they find so appealing. With long spindly legs and dense bodies, they're also perfectly designed for fatal collisions with cars. Typically, the front of the car knocks their legs out, and the body crashes through the windshield, often with grave results. The moose crossing signs you see throughout the state weren't placed there to entertain tourists: They're for real. There are dozens of moose-car collisions in the state (305 between 2015 and 2016, for instance, according to the Maine Department of Transportation; most of those occur at night in the summer and fall).

The moose is majestic, but few observers accord them much nimbleness of mind. Based on moose population, the state issues only a couple thousand moose hunting permits via lottery each year. Ninety percent of those permits go to residents, and 10 percent to non-residents. Generally, most of those permit holders bag their antlered prize. It doesn't take much to outwit a moose.

accepting reservations: You must reserve by writing, calling, or visiting the headquarters at 64 Balsam Drive in Millinocket, request specific dates, and include payment with your request. (This goes for sites at Chimney Pond, Russell Pond, Davis Pond, and Wassataquoik Lake Island, as well as for lean-tos, bunkhouses, and group sites.) All campgrounds are open mid May to mid Oct. To write, send a self-addressed-stamped-envelope to: Reservations, Baxter State Park, 64 Balsam Dr., Millinocket, ME 04462. Otherwise, call (207) 723-5140 or visit baxterstatepark.org.

West and north of Baxter State Park are timberlands under the oversight of **North Maine Woods, Inc.**, a consortium of nearly two dozen landowners who banded together to manage recreational access. These companies and families jointly own and manage 2.8 million acres of woodlands, which are open to the public for a fee. Don't expect pristine forest, even though your road map may not show any roads hereabouts. As mentioned, this is an industrial forest, managed for the production of fiber to supply paper mills. Recreational uses are secondary.

These woods hold few "destinations" for those who like their attractions neatly packaged. Access to the woods is on often dusty, unpaved logging roads, and you won't find much in the way of picnic areas or scenic turnouts. Along the way, drivers will see clear-cuts, regenerated forests, muskeg (a type of boggy ecosystem common to the northern woods), an occasional lakeshore, most likely a roadside moose or two, and periodic glimpses of distant mountain ranges. Most recreation involves fishing, hunting, and canoeing. Because

Along the Knife Edge

If you're physically fit and aren't afflicted with a fear of heights, one of the state's premier hiking pathways follows what's aptly called the **Knife Edge**, which links Mount Katahdin's two peaks. Those who've survived the trail like to boast that it is only a couple of feet wide in some sections, with drops of 1,000 feet or more on either side.

Technically that's true, but it's not quite as daunting as it sounds. The Knife Edge follows a boulder field that's been shaped to a narrow ridge by glaciers and the weather. At certain critical junctures you need to scramble atop massive boulders and inch your way across. And from atop these boulders you don't see much below except for the distant glinting of lakes and a dull mass of green that resolves itself into spruce spires only with the aid of binoculars. Acrophobia kicks in while scrambling over these boulders. Knees start to shake; breath becomes short.

In fact, if you peer over the edge, you might find yourself just 6 or 8 feet above other boulders that angle down sharply. It's not the sheer drop to eternity that it appears, but it's hard to convince yourself of that. Venture here at your own peril.

Running the Rapids

One of the more adrenaline-pumping ways to enjoy Maine's wilds is to sign up for a one-day rafting trip on the Penobscot or the Kennebec River. The West Branch of the Penobscot runs south of Baxter State Park and features one of Maine's most spectacular and demanding stretches of white water: a turbulent, rocky canyon called the Cribworks. After you maneuver through here, the remainder of the trip alternates between open river and quick, exciting plunges over short waterfalls and through narrow gorges. Exceptional views of Mount Katahdin open up along the way.

The upper stretches of the Kennebec River (near the Forks in Somerset County) offer larger waves similar to those found in the canyons of the West, and they're big enough to invoke genuine terror. The excitement runs its course fairly quickly, however, and you spend the rest of the day floating out of scenic Kennebec Gorge.

Around twenty firms are licensed to run guided rafting trips on the two rivers. Their base camps tend to be concentrated near Millinocket and the Forks, and prices generally range from $85 to $125 per person for a one-day trip, which includes a riverside lunch. Many outfitters also offer lodging options ranging from modern inns to campgrounds. The state's rafting companies are members of a group called **Raft Maine**, which will refer you to one of the member companies through its website, raftmaine.com.

of state cutting regulations and the cooperation of the timber companies, most lake and river shores have remained unharvested for many years and offer a dense backdrop of mixed and softwood forests. When traveling by canoe, expect to see loon, beaver, and plenty of moose. North Maine Woods maintains about 400 campsites, many of them accessible only by water. (They are available on a first-come, first-serve basis, and some require fire permits.)

Access fees are collected at various checkpoints around the perimeter (and note that they only accept cash or checks). Maine residents pay $10 per day per person plus an additional $12 per person for camping. Non-residents pay $15 per day plus $15 for camping. Those under 18 (no matter the state they're from) have free day use access and camping. Visit the organization's website at north mainewoods.org, for information on regulations, checkpoint locations, hours, and more. You can also call (207) 435-6213 or write North Maine Woods, P.O. Box 425, Ashland, ME 04732.

The region's early economic history isn't just a story of producing lumber, however. Well south of Baxter State Park is **Katahdin Iron Works**, a state historic site that provides some insight into how iron was made during the mid-19th century. Iron ore was first discovered by geographer Moses Greenleaf on Ore Mountain in 1843; within two years Katahdin Iron Works was built near the site. At its peak in the 1870s and 1880s, the works manufactured some 2,000 tons of raw iron a year, consuming upward of 10,000 cords of wood to fire the blast furnace. A small village thrived here, with many of the 200 residents involved in hauling logs and producing charcoal in beehive kilns.

There's little trace of a village today at this remote site deep in the woods, but historical markers provide information about the iron-making process. Take time to marvel at two restored structures: the towering stone blast furnace with graceful arches at its base, and the massive brick beehive kiln (one of fourteen originally situated here) with its domed roof. The ironworks checkpoint is open from mid May through mid Oct. To get there, drive 5 miles north of Brownville on ME 11, then turn left on a well-maintained dirt logging road, continuing on for 7 miles to a North Maine Woods gatehouse. The historic site is across from the gatehouse. Admission is free. For more information call (207) 965-8135.

Ask for directions at the gatehouse and pay the timberland access fee, then continue to **Gulf Hagas**, which has been billed as the "Grand Canyon of the East." That's a bit overly grand, but the 3-mile ravine is an impressive site. You'll find five waterfalls, a slew of rushing cascades, and sheer canyon walls topped with an austere northern forest. A trail follows the rim of the gorge, and other trails branch off and head down to the river, where you can take a cool dip on a summer's day. The land around the canyon is one of the few Maine parcels outside of Acadia owned by the National Park Service, which acquired it as part of its protection of the Appalachian Trail corridor.

The 100-Mile Wilderness

A recent series of land acquisitions has resulted in the **Appalachian Mountain Club (AMC)** becoming the owner of a stretch of woodland called the 100-Mile Wilderness. This begins, roughly, a bit northeast of Monson and extends all the way up to the Baxter State Park Boundary. The AMC operates a series of sporting camps in the wilderness. These include Little Lyford Lodge and Cabins, located on the West Branch of Pleasant River; Medawisla Wilderness Lodge and Cabins on Second Roach Pond; and the lodge, Gorman Chairback, set on the shore of Long Pond, with access to the Appalachian Trail.

Of these, Medawisla and Little Lyford are typical old-time Maine sporting camps. Fishing, skiing, snowmobiling, hunting, and hiking are all at their finest here. Plus, the main lodge at both these serves great, home-cooked meals at breakfast and supper. The lodge also provides cold meats, breads, fruit, and other goodies for visitors to take with them as a box lunch. The AMC also offers cross-country ski trails with shuttle service from one camp to the other—so guests can enjoy a day's skiing without worrying about carrying supplies; those will already have arrived at the next stop, via snowmobile. For more information visit outdoors.org/mainelodges.

Near Gulf Hagas (ask at the gatehouse) is a 35-acre Nature Conservancy sanctuary called *The Hermitage*. While not a virgin forest, it does include pines up to 120 feet high with diameters reaching 3 feet. The Appalachian Trail passes through the stand, and a few other short trails offer access to these quiet, stately pines. Let your imagination go a bit, and you'll see how the whole northern forest once looked before it became a plantation.

Eastern Moosehead Lake Area

The former frontier town of *Greenville* is located at the southern tip of *Moosehead Lake*, Maine's largest body of water. Lying at an elevation of just over 1,000 feet, Moosehead is some 32 miles long and ranges from 1 to 5 miles wide. With numerous bays and coves, the shoreline twists and turns for about 350 miles, providing home to osprey, eagle, deer, and moose. There are a few vantage points here and there for those traveling by car, but for the most part you'll be required to travel by means other than automobile to get a good sense of the lake's beauty and drama.

One enjoyable option is to take a cruise on the *SS* **Katahdin**, a restored steamship (converted to diesel) that's been plying the waters of Moosehead since 1914. The *Kate*, as she's called locally, was built at Bath Iron Works and shipped in parts to Moosehead Lake, where she was assembled and launched by the Coburn Steamboat Company. After a twenty-four-year career as a passenger ship, the 115-foot *Katahdin* was retired when the rise of the automobile made her obsolete. She was then outfitted as a boom boat and used by lumber companies for hauling logs (towing them encircled by a massive wooden boom) down the lake to the mills. The *Katahdin* participated in the state's last log drive, which took place in 1975.

To learn more about *Kate*'s history, plan a visit to the exhibits at the ship's parent organization, the *Moosehead Marine Museum*. It is located next to the dock in what passes for downtown Greenville. There's a small but fine collection of historical artifacts relating to Moosehead's history, including fascinating photos of the last log drive. Leave enough time to browse through the piles of scrapbooks, where you'll find insightful articles and mementos relating to the history of the lake, including pictures of the early fleet and menus from the original Kineo Mountain House.

The museum offers daily trips aboard the *Kate* throughout the summer. A three-hour cruise takes passengers up the lake past Moose Island and Burnt Jacket Point to the narrow pass between Sugar Island and Deer Island. This provides a good introduction to the size and wildness of the lake. A longer trip (5-and-a-half hours), offered only a couple times a month, will take you halfway up the lake to Mount Kineo, where you can disembark and explore the grounds of a once-venerable hotel. And for those who have an insatiable thirst for long boat trips, the *Katahdin* cruises occasionally to the head of the lake at Seboomook, an eight-hour journey that provides a cormorant's-eye view of the lake's entire shoreline. There is also a special dinner-dance cruise and a "first mates club" for children.

The *Katahdin*'s schedule varies, so it is best to call first. The *Kate* currently runs from late June to early Oct. Prices range from $35 to $60 for adults, $30 to $40 for seniors, $18 to $23 for children (ages 11-16), and $5 to $10 for children (10 and younger). For more information call (207) 695-2716 or visit katahdincruises.com.

The **Moosehead Historical Society** is located on ME 6 and ME 15 in **Greenville Junction** (just west of Greenville proper). The late-19th-century house is an interesting artifact for those curious about the history of decorative arts and architecture. (The carriage house also has displays of Native American artifacts upstairs and a lumbermen's exhibit in the basement that includes a collection of early outboard motors.) But more fascinating is the odd, melancholy story of the family, which you'll learn on a one-hour guided tour and which offers some insight into the social relations of the time.

In the early 20th century, Arthur and Rebecca Crafts, a prosperous couple with numerous local businesses, had two children, Oliver and Julia. Their son died tragically at age 16, after falling through the ice. The parents never really recovered from the death of the heir apparent; they kept his richly appointed room as it was when he died, and his mother delivered presents to the room each year on his birthday. She had a portrait of him commissioned and hung in an elaborately wrought gilded frame; a table beneath it was kept set with fresh flowers.

That left Julia, an attractive young woman whose bedroom was considerably less elaborate, to run the family enterprises. But society being what it was, she needed a husband. Not content to let her find her own, her parents contracted with a pleasant young fellow named Philip Sheridan, who worked at one of the family's hotels, to marry her. The contract stipulated that he needed to spend a minimum of three months each year with Julia at the home, for which he would be paid a salary.

Julia loved Philip quite a bit; but her affections evidently were not returned. Philip kept to the contract's terms to continue to receive his pay, but spent much of the rest of the year traveling and enjoying the finer things in life while Julia kept the family business going. ("He was quite the playboy," tour guides will tell you.) Even though Julia divorced him shortly before her death in 1967, the contract remained in force until Philip's death in 1992, and he continued to pocket his salary. He bequeathed the house to the historical society, which has adorned it with period furniture and objets d'art, some of it original to the Crafts.

The **Carriage House** on the property is open year-round, Tues through Fri, 9 a.m. to 4 p.m., and the **Eveleth-Crafts-Sheridan House** is open Wed through Fri 1 to 4 p.m., with tours given mid June through mid Oct. Admission is $5 for adults and $3 for children under 12. For more information call (207) 695-2909 or visit mooseheadhistory.org.

After visiting the house, head 0.4 mile north on Lily Bay Road and turn left at Preo Street, an easy-to-miss dirt lane. There's a small, unmarked lakeside park at the end of the street with a couple of picnic tables. If it's a pleasant day, this is a good place for a dip, too.

Not far away from here, lovers of the obscure and the abandoned can explore the wreckage site of a US Air Force plane. In January 1963, nine crew members took off from Westover Air Force Base in Massachusetts in a Boeing B-52C Stratofortress, a long-range, jet-powered strategic bomber. However, as it headed north, the aircraft hit extreme turbulence, resulting in its tail tearing off. Recognizing the inevitable, its pilot Lt. Col. Dante E. Bulli ordered its crew to abandon it—but only three of them had time to eject. Of those, only two lived; these were the captain and navigator Gerald Adler, who set a historical record he would have never expected. Adler was the only person to survive an ejection from an aircraft without his parachute opening. (It was a long recovery, according to the *Bangor Daily News*, and his leg had to be amputated due to gangrene and frost bite. He revisited the site of the crash on its 30th anniversary at a commemorative service sponsored by the Moosehead Rivers Snowmobile Club.) The men toughed it out in minus 29-degree temperatures and five feet of snow before being rescued.

Today, debris from the 160-foot-long plane—hunks of shredded metal, wheels, a half-intact tail cone, wires and other mechanical equipment—remains scattered across the forest floor at the base of Elephant Mountain. Some indiscernible bits of metal are still lodged in trees, becoming intermingled with their slow growth over the years. At what remains of the fuselage, there is a stone memorial to the crew. The site is well-marked and reached by a short walk, with signs along the way reminding visitors to be respectful and not to disturb or remove anything. To get there, follow Lily Bay Road north for roughly 6.5 miles until you see Prong Pond Road. Turn right and keep to the right for several miles as the road narrows and forks. You'll finally come to a trailhead and a small parking area.

For an eagle's-eye view of the Moosehead, **Currier's Flying Service** offers floatplane trips from its base in Greenville Junction on ME 15 next to the trestle. The planes fly high enough so you can appreciate the lake's size, but low enough to let you spot an occasional moose browsing in a marsh or along a river's edge. Currier's offers sightseeing and moose-watching trips in meticulously maintained vintage aircraft.

Even if you're not interested in a flight, it's worth stopping by the hangar at the edge of the lake to soak up the atmosphere and watch the planes take off and land. For more information, contact Currier's Flying Service (207-695-2778, curriersflyingservice.com) or *Jack's Air Service* (207-695-3020; jacksairservice .com). Of special interest is the annual *Sea Plane Fly-In* held the weekend after Labor Day. Competitions, exhibits, food, and more draw enthusiasts from across the country.

A half-day spent fishing is bound to please anyone interested in fast-paced action on brook trout, lake trout, and landlocked salmon. Or try a moose safari, deer and moose hunting, and upland bird hunting, complete with bird dogs. One good option is *Lawrence's Lakeside Cabins and Guide Service* at (207-534-7709; lawrencescabins.com).

A range of accommodations is available in the Moosehead area, from motels to B&Bs—but three inns, all rather expensive, deserve special mention. *The Greenville Inn* (207-695-2206; greenvilleinn.com) is located on a hillside overlooking the village and the southern tip of the lake. Housed in an 1895 mansion built by lumber baron William Shaw, this fine inn is a virtual catalog of turn-of-the-20th-century luxuries, ranging from marble showers to exceptional carved interiors of mahogany with cherry trim. The dining room serves excellent meals, with entrees starting around $20. The inn also has a comfortable front porch offering a view across the lake to the hills beyond. With a range of mansion rooms, suites and cottages, accommodations for two range from around $200 to $329 (with an extra $35 per guest, depending on the room). This includes a full breakfast buffet.

Continuing north on Lily Bay Road you'll come to two other impressive homes. The *Blair Hill Inn* sits regally on a hill with vertigo-inspiring views of the lake from many of the eight guest rooms and the wrap-around porch. The elaborate Queen Anne-style home was built in 1891 and is lovingly and quirkily appointed with Persian carpets and deer-antler lamps. This is a place where you'll instantly feel like you're living large. The restaurant on the premises is regarded as among the best in northern Maine. Entrees are included in a five-course menu. This revolving menu includes a wide variety of choices and is priced at a fixed rate of $59 per person. Rooms start at $399 and go up from there. For more information call (207) 695-0224 or visit blairhill.com.

Nearby is the whimsical *Lodge at Moosehead Lake*. The innkeepers have played up the North Woods theme, featuring beds suspended from the ceiling on old boom chains (once used in logging operations), stick furniture, and rustic headboards carved by a local craftsman. Rates range from $400 to $600 per night. For more information call (207) 695-4400 or visit lodgeat mooseheadlake.com.

Somerset County

The west side of Moosehead Lake falls within Somerset County, which extends westward to the Canadian border. Like many of the northern counties, Somerset is long and narrow, encompassing a variety of terrain. This is also timber country: In every Somerset township from Bingham northward, timber companies own 5,000 acres or more.

Western Moosehead Lake Area

The west side of Moosehead Lake between Greenville and Rockwood can be quickly covered on ME 15. The road is wide and fast, but it offers few glimpses of the lake until you approach the village of Rockwood. Here you'll be rewarded with a full view of what amounts to the lake's trademark: the sheer, flinty cliffs of Mount Kineo.

Mount Kineo has long been a landmark in the region. Natives traveled from afar to the cliff's base to gather its flint for weapons. One Indian legend claims that the mountain is the remnants of a petrified moose sent by the Great Spirit as retribution for their sins. In the late 19th century, the broad peninsula at the base was the site of the Kineo Mountain House, at its heyday perhaps the grandest of the Maine resorts. The stately gabled building boasted more than 500 guest rooms, and the dining room could seat 400 at a time. An immense annex was built to house the staff, some of whom tended a 40-acre garden to provide food for the table.

Alas, the Mountain House closed in 1934 and was demolished in 1938, after the automobile and the Great Depression sounded the death knell for the era of the grand resort. Various attempts to revive some of the remaining buildings foundered on an uncooperative economy and thin financing. The annex was demolished in 1996, leaving just a golf course and an array of handsome, turn-of-the-20th-century homes along the lake's edge.

Water shuttles across the lake are available from Rockwood (look for signs to the town landing), allowing visitors to snoop and explore. Once at Kineo you can wander the grounds of the venerable resort and enjoy the extraordinary views down the lake. Be sure to leave two to three hours for the round-trip hike to Kineo's 1,800-foot summit. To find the trail, walk along the golf course, then cut across the eighth fairway to the old carriage road that runs along the west side of the mountain. Follow this about a half mile to a rock with a white arrow pointing uphill. The steep ascent will take you along the cliff's face to a series of ledges looking southward toward Greenville. For a more expansive view, continue along the trail about another 0.3 mile to an abandoned fire tower, which may be ascended for a not-soon-forgotten view of the entire lake. (Not recommended for those afraid of heights or suffering from vertigo-related issues.)

One of the more popular activities in the Moosehead Lake region is to sign up for a moose safari. You can spot moose on your own, of course, but your odds are better if you head out with the experts. You can travel by pontoon boat, airplane, canoe, foot, or four-wheel-drive vehicle in search of the lanky beasts. The chamber of commerce can point you to any one of a half-dozen or more guide services offering moose-spotting trips. Among the better-known tours: the *Moose Cruise*, which is run on comfortable pontoon boats (think: floating living rooms) out of the Birches Resort just north of Rockwood. Safaris range from $35 to $70 per person, depending on time of day (and whether a meal is included). Call (800) 825-9453 or visit birches.com.

Other area moose outfitters include the *Maine Guide Fly Shop* on Main Street in Greenville (207-695-2266, maineguideflyshop.com), which runs excursions by canoe or kayak, and *Lawrence's Cabins* (207-534-7709; lawrences cabins.com).

A favorite spot for overnighting and dining in the North Woods is *Maynard's in Maine*, a sporting lodge that's been unchanged for nearly a century. The town of Rockwood has grown up around it somewhat (logging trucks rumble by on the road across the river), but it still feels like a trip back in time. The cabins ring a lawn with a horseshoe pit and tetherball and are simple and furnished with flea market vintage decorations. The meals in the Smithsonian-quality dining room are filling, basic, and inexpensive. Even if you're not spending the night ($90 per person, including all meals), it's worth calling ahead for dinner reservations (mandatory) and swinging by for a meal, which includes a choice of two entrees nightly, covering the basics from baked ham to chicken parmesan to broiled sea scallops. For more information call (207) 534-7703 or visit maynardsinmaine.com.

The northern end of the lake and the tiny settlement of *Seboomook* can be reached by logging roads in about an hour. Like Kineo, Seboomook during its glory days was the site of a fine resort, now long since forgotten. Remaining at Seboomook are a handful of summer cabins, a campground, and a small general store. There's also the *Seboomook Wilderness Campground*; call (207) 280-0555 or visit seboomookwildernesscampground.com.

Head into the store for an interesting sight: a photograph of a World War II prisoner-of-war camp constructed here in the early 1940s to hold German prisoners captured in the African campaigns. Some 250 prisoners were kept busy here cutting trees and hauling them with horses to the lake for the spring trip to the mills. Evidently the POWs, who were paid for their labor, also were treated well; many returned after the war to take jobs with timber companies. Today only the pictures remain. The buildings, including sentry towers and the icehouse, have since been reclaimed by the forest, and only an overgrown foundation or two may be found.

Nearby, where the north and south branches of the Penobscot River flow together, you'll find **Pittston Farm**, a longtime North Woods institution. This farm complex stuck deep in the woods was built in the 19th century to provide the grain for the horses used in logging. Today it's a rough backwoods lodge and campground favored by anglers and canoeists (they offer snowmobiling, hunting, fishing, food, and fuel). For more information call (207) 280-0000 or visit pittstonfarm.com.

Route 201

A pleasant drive on ME 6 and ME 15 will bring you to scenic US 201 and the town of **Jackman**, the starting point of the **Moose River canoe trip**. This 34-mile trip attracts a number of eager canoeists throughout the year not only because of its scenic merits, but also because of sheer convenience: Canoeists start and finish at the same point, linking the loop with a 1.25-mile-long portage between Attean and Holeb Ponds. A couple of smaller portages around waterfalls are involved; otherwise the river is gentle and forgiving, with only mildly challenging rapids. A number of riverside campsites are located along the way. Trip maps produced by the state are available at the several canoe rental shops in Jackman.

Heading south from Jackman along US 201 will soon bring you to **The Forks**, where many of the rafting outfitters serving the Kennebec Gorge and the Penobscot maintain offices (see "Running the Rapids" earlier in this chapter for more information on rafting). While you're at the Forks, a short side trip to dramatic **Moxie Falls** will prove rewarding. This beautiful cataract tumbles some 90 feet into a narrow slate gorge. There's a fine mix of forest trees here, with cedars and other softwoods mingling with birch. A trail skirts the gorge and offers good views. Both the brave and the foolish alike work their way down to swim in the turbulent, clear waters at the base of the cascades.

To find Moxie Falls, turn off US 201 on the road along the east bank of the Kennebec River. (If you're coming from the south, that means turning right before crossing the bridge over the Kennebec.) Travel 2.7 miles and park near the sign. A trail of slightly less than 2 miles will take you down to the falls.

Finally, before leaving the area, make a stop at the ***Floodproof Wire Bridge*** in the town of New Portland in the southwest corner of the county. This remarkable suspension bridge, built in 1841, has the aplomb and elegance of a miniature Brooklyn Bridge dropped in a wild, forested setting. The bridge's wooden deck is held aloft over the Carrabassett River on two thick cables— made in Sheffield, England—rigged between two handsome shingled pylons. The bridge was designed by F. B. Morse for the people of New Portland, who were weary of having their bridge wash out in the spring freshets. The fact that it still stands more than a century and a half later would suggest that Morse's design was successful. To find this remarkable structure, head down ME 127 onto ME 146 in the village of New Portland, then turn left at the sign indicating the way to the bridge. You can drive across through the polygonal openings, but to really appreciate the bridge, park at one end or the other and walk across. If you visit on a warm day, there's a nice place to swim in the river just downstream.

Heading south from the bridge toward Farmington, look for ***Nowetah's American Indian Museum***, located off ME 27 in New Portland. The museum and shop is owned and operated by Abenaki Indians, a tradition begun by founding namesake Mrs. Nowetah Timmerman in 1969. There are displays of native crafts from North and South America, including stone tools, petroglyph rubbings, a genuine birch-bark canoe, an authentic maple dugout canoe, old photos showing some of the ancient crafts techniques, and a collection of over 600 Indian baskets, featuring those made of brown ash and sweetgrass. This isn't a stuffy spot with everything enshrined kept away from visitors—kids are encouraged to touch a number of the displays and to try crushing corn with mortar and pestle or play drums and flutes. The museum's gift shop sells a number of items made on the premises, including porcupine quill and bead jewelry, corn-husk dolls, and hand-woven rugs.

The museum is open year-round from 10 a.m. to 5 p.m. daily and usually an hour or so earlier on weekends. Admission is free (donations are encouraged). For more information call (207) 628-4981.

Places to Stay in the North Woods

BANGOR

The Charles Inn
20 Broad St.
(207) 992-2820
thecharlesinn.com
Inexpensive
First art gallery hotel in Bangor. Featuring more than 150 original-listed artists' paintings. Free breakfast.

Fairfield Inn by Marriott
300 Odlin Rd.
(207) 990-0001
marriott.com/hotels
Moderate
Pool, hot tub, fitness room, laundry, cable television with HBO, free breakfast with waffles

THE FORKS

Inn By The River
2777 US 201
(207) 663-2181
innbytheriver.com
Inexpensive
One of the better buys around for a memorable outdoor vacation. Imagine bald eagles soaring overhead and white tailed deer grazing just outside your room.

Northern Outdoors
Old Canada Road Scenic Bwy, US 201
(207) 663-4466
northernoutdoors.com
Inexpensive
Caters to nearly all outdoor activities, with an emphasis on whitewater rafting

GREENVILLE

Blair Hill Inn and Restaurant
351 Lily Bay Rd.
(207) 695-0224
blairhill.com
Expensive
See main entry (p. 202) for full description.

Greenville Inn
40 Norris St.
(207) 695-2206
greenvilleinn.com
Moderate
See main entry (p. 202) for full description.

Lodge at Moosehead Lake
Upper Lily Bay Rd.
(207) 695-4400
lodgeatmooseheadlake.com
Expensive
See main entry (p. 202) for full description.

SELECTED CHAMBERS OF COMMERCE

Bangor Region Chamber of Commerce
2 Hammond St., Ste 1
(207) 947-0307
bangorregion.com

Jackman/Moose River Chamber of Commerce
US 201
(207) 668-4171
jackmanmaine.org

Katahdin Area Chamber of Commerce
1029 Central St., Millinocket
(207) 723-4443
katahdinmaine.com

Moosehead Lake Region Chamber of Commerce (The Maine Highlands)
480 Moosehead Lake Rd., Greenville
(207) 695-2702
themainehighlands.com

MILLINOCKET

Big Moose Inn Cabins and Campground
Barter State Park Rd.
(207) 723-8391
bigmoosecabins.com
Moderate
Closest full-service accommodations to Baxter State Park. Has most everything, from antique inn rooms, cabins, campgrounds, fine dining, and also casual dining.

MOOSE RIVER

Sky Lodge
US 201
(800) 307-0098 or
(207) 668-2171
skylodgecabins.com
Moderate
Luxurious accommodations in a rustic setting

PATTEN

Shin Pond Village
ME 159
(207) 528-2900
shinpond.com
Inexpensive
Good home base for fishing, hiking, swimming, and canoeing adventures

ROCKWOOD

The Birches Resort
218 Birches Rd.
(800) 825-9453 or
(207) 534-7305
birches.com
Moderate
Has everything for the outdoor enthusiast, including boat rentals, fly-fishing instructions, lakeside cabins, and snowmobile rentals

Lawrence's Lakeside Cabins
Village Rd.
(207) 534-7709
lawrencescabins.com
Inexpensive
Exceptional views out across Moosehead Lake. Has fully equipped cabins and a private dock.

Maynard's in Maine
131 Maynards Rd.
(207) 534-7703 or
maynardsin
maine.com
Inexpensive
In operation since 1919. Full menu breakfast and supper, with two main courses that change daily.

Rockwood Cottages
Cottage Ln.
(207) 534-7725
mooseheadlakelodging
.com
Inexpensive
A village of housekeeping cottages on majestic Moosehead Lake

Places to Eat in the North Woods

BANGOR

Dysart's Truck Stop
Exit 44 off I-95
(207) 942-4878
Inexpensive
Not just for truckers. Mainers love Dysart's. Famed for their baked beans.

Governor's Restaurant and Bakery
643 Broadway
(207) 947-3113
governorsrestaurant.com
Inexpensive
A Maine institution. Governor's devises a new burger for each gubernatorial candidate during election years.

Ichiban Japanese Restaurant
226 Union St.
(207) 262-9308
bangorichiban.com
Moderate
Quiet, dignified, and very good food

McLaughlin Seafood Inc.
728 Main St.
(207) 942-7811
mclaughlinseafood.com
Inexpensive
Some of the freshest and best seafood around. Eat in or take out.

Sea Dog Brewing Co.
26 Front St.
(207) 947-8009
seadogbrewing.com
Jumping joint on the
Penobscot River. Excellent
brews, good pub food.

GREENVILLE
Auntie M's
31 Lily Bay Rd.
(207) 695-2238
Inexpensive
Breakfast served all day,
fresh-baked bread. Great
lunch specials.

**Blair Hill Inn,
Moosehead Lake**
351 Lily Bay Rd.
(207) 695-0224
blairhill.com
Expensive
See main entry (p. 202)
for full description.

**Greenville Inn at
Moosehead Lake**
40 Norris St.
(207) 695-2206
greenvilleinn.com
Moderate
See main entry (p. 202)
for full description.

JACKMAN
Four Seasons Restaurant
17 Main St.
(207) 668-7778
Inexpensive
Home-cooked comfort
food

KOKADJO
Northern Pride Lodge
First Roach Pond
(207) 695-2890
northernpridelodge.com
Moderate
Fine dining by reservation

MILLINOCKET
Appalachian Trail Cafe
210 Penobscot Ave.
(207) 723-6720
Inexpensive
Great breakfast. Located at
the end of the Appalachian
Trail; Thru-hikers have their
names emblazoned on a
special ceiling tile.

River Driver's Restaurant
(at New England Outdoor
Center)
Old Midway Rd.
(800) 766-7238
neoc.com
Expensive
Rave reviews, including
"best food in Maine."
Special cuts of meat and
seafood. There's also a
$9.99 fish fry on Friday
nights.

ROCKWOOD
The Birches Resort
281 Birches Rd.
(800) 825-9453 or
(207) 534-7305
birches.com
Moderate
Dining is casual. Lake
views from every table,
rustic atmosphere.

Pittston Farm
53 Pittston Farm Rd
(207) 280-0000
pittstonfarm.com
Moderate
See main entry (p. 205)
for full description.

The County

This is it, folks: You've reached the top. "The County"—as **Aroostook County** is referred to throughout the state—has an uncommonly broad sweep and size for New England. Connecticut and Rhode Island together could fit inside it.

Altogether, the County doesn't square with many preconceptions about Maine. The gentle hills, broad vistas, and sprawling farmlands share little with either Maine's sparkling coast or its dense North Woods. In fact, travelers would be forgiven for thinking they missed a turn somewhere and ended up in Wisconsin. They also would be excused for believing they've wandered into another era: Aroostook often seems to have more in common with the slow pace of the 1950s than with the more hectic present.

Many travel guides tend to ignore the County or gloss over the region in a page or two. Not only does it fail to resemble the Maine many travelers seek, but there are few tourist-oriented inns or restaurants. But don't let that deter you. The County has a subtle grandeur and fascinating immigrant history that reveals itself only to those who aren't too hurried to notice. In short, Aroostook County is about as off the beaten path as Maine gets. As such, it is one of the few areas in Maine (and

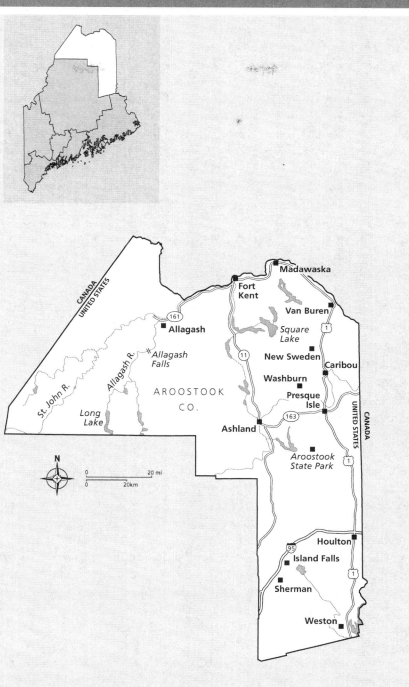

the country at-large) where the population is waning; the region has long-struggled with how best to maintain its wild identity while at the same time boosting its commerce and tourism prospects.

When heading north on US 1, the town of **Weston** offers eye-dazzling views. The eastern gateway to the County, it is bounded on the east by 16,070-acre East Grand Lake. Views from the highway include distant vistas in neighboring New Brunswick, Canada, and bird's-eye scenes of the lake and its many islands. To the west, drivers soon come upon the well-named *"Million Dollar View."* This is a breathtaking look at Mount Katahdin and neighboring mountains. A sign at a roadside parking area invites drivers to turn off and take in the lovely scenery. However, glimpses of the mountains are available at various points for many miles along the highway, so don't worry if you tend to drive right past one.

Still, in some cases, the name hardly does justice to this striking scene; surely, given the rate of inflation, the name could be changed to the "Billion Dollar View." Really, though, it's a truly priceless place. The valley between Weston and Baxter State Park stretches out like an endless oasis, and the stark ruggedness of Maine's biggest mountains is a fitting background to this panoramic glimpse of Aroostook County.

Houlton Area

Houlton, the county seat and oldest community in Aroostook, is a good jumping-off point for a ramble. Here the Maine Turnpike and US 2 both come to an abrupt end and US 1 passes directly through, suggesting Houlton's geographic importance. Despite its regional stature, this center of commerce has maintained a pleasantly drowsy character through the years.

Take some time to enjoy Houlton's **Market Street Historic District**, a tiny block-long downtown area showcasing a variety of commercial architectural styles from 1885 to 1910. Many of the fine brick buildings have happily avoided the depredations that befell other commercial districts around the nation in the name of modernization. While Houlton's downtown is fighting the same battle against the migration of retail to strip malls, it maintains its great architectural integrity. Look high along the rooflines at the intricate brickwork. Also be sure to note the elegant First National Bank building on the north side of the square. This small columned building dates from 1907 and is almost a caricature of the imposing banks that flourished at the turn of the century in many eastern seaboard cities.

A short walk from Market Square is the **White Memorial Building**, an impressive 1903 colonial revival house listed on the National Register of Historic Places. Elegantly and regally lording over Main Street, it houses the collections of the *Southern Aroostook Historical and Art Museum*. Founded in 1937 by Ransford W. Shaw, it is filled with items and artifacts representing both local industry and commerce. Of particular interest is a collection of items from the mid-1940s, when the now-defunct Houlton Army Air Base was used as a prisoner of war camp for German soldiers. (Yes, you read that right.) There are paintings and other artifacts made by the prisoners who were kept here, as well as images of the men themselves.

Meanwhile, there's a room dedicated to Houlton's ill-fated Ricker College (yearbooks, mementos, pennants, and sports jerseys) which opened in 1848 and was auctioned off after bankruptcy in 1979, while others spotlight military exploits over the years, as well as a turn-of-the-20th century kitchen. Also sprawled across both its upstairs and downstairs rooms: a dog mill-powered butter churn, badges from early Republican conventions, and a hand-carved wooden box filled with spruce gum (a typical gift of early woodsmen to their wives or sweethearts). The Edward B. White collection, meanwhile, features a collection of alluring photographs taken from 1885 to 1920.

Keep an eye out for the elaborately detailed diorama of a man sitting near his canoe at a lakeside log cabin. Spruce trees line the forest behind him, and a moose browses along the shoreline. What makes this notable is its construction entirely of matchsticks. In 1924 Leon Goodwin entered this work in a contest sponsored by a match company but was disqualified since the contest rules required that whole matches be used. (Goodwin glued his into solid blocks, then carved them.) Contest judges were sufficiently impressed, however, to award him a special $50 second prize.

The museum (207-532-4216, houltonmuseum.wixsite.com) is located at 109 Main St. and is currently open only by appointment.

The *Watson Settlement Covered Bridge* is a short detour off US 1 in *Littleton*, 5 miles north of Houlton. This bridge boasts two superlatives: It was the last covered bridge built in Maine (1911), and it's the state's northernmost covered bridge. Neither of these claims may seem particularly noteworthy, but the drive to the bridge through lush, rolling farmlands is a nice change of pace from the higher-speed travel on US 1.

The 150-foot bridge isn't in use today (a more modern concrete bridge runs parallel to it), but visitors can cross by foot and sit along the banks of the Meduxnekeag River. A farmhouse and elms stand on the crest of a hill above, and songbirds proliferate along the banks, making for an inviting picnic and lounging spot. The bridge also has the local distinction as a place for teens to express their affections (or not) for one another in ink and spray paint.

To find the bridge, turn east from US 1 at Carson Road. There's a small blue sign indicating a covered bridge, but it's easy to miss. Drive 2 miles, then bear right down the hill where the road splits. The bridge is a few hundred yards beyond the fork.

Presque Isle and Vicinity

For a high-altitude view of the region (or what passes for high altitude hereabouts), head to *Aroostook State Park*, located south of the city of *Presque Isle.* It holds a distinction, as well: It is Maine's first state park, established in 1939 a year after locals set aside 100 acres for it. The park contains 577 forested acres situated between Echo Lake and Quaggy Joe Mountain (more on that unique name below). There's swimming and picnicking at the lake (which is ringed with summer homes) and camping at several sites managed by the state at the base of 1,213-foot Quaggy Joe. Hiking trails ascend both the north and south peaks of the hill; they are connected by a ridge trail, making for a 3-mile loop that can be hiked in a couple of hours. The north summit ledges offer fine views east into Canada as well as west across a seemingly uninterrupted blanket of forest extending to the craggy profile of Mount Katahdin. If time is short, bypass the south peak, which has limited views and an unattractive cluster of radio towers on the summit.

Three primitive tent pads (no water, no amenities, and no fires allowed) are provided along the trail to the north peak. These are available on a first-come, first-served basis. However, the regular park campground has several campsites. And while no electricity or water is available at the sites, a bathhouse has hot-water showers. Also, a cook shelter, or outdoor kitchen, allows campers to cook their meals under a roof when inclement weather hits. This three-walled, wood-paneled cook shelter is unique among Maine state parks, and park officials are proud of it.

If you're wondering who Joe was and what made him so quaggy, you may be disappointed to learn that the name is merely a corruption of Quaquajo, the Indian name for the mountain. The commonly accepted translation is "Twin Peaked."

Aroostook State Park is open year-round from 9 a.m. to sunset. Admission is $3 for adult ME residenrs, $4 for adults non-residents, and $1 for non-resident

FAVORITE ATTRACTIONS

New Sweden Historical Society Museum, New Sweden

Nylander Museum, Caribou

Salmon Brook Museum, Washburn

Southern Aroostook Historical and Art Museum, Houlton

seniors (65 and older) and children (ages 5 to 11). Maine seniors and children under 5 are free. Follow park signs from Spragueville Road 4 miles south of Presque Isle on US 1. For more information call (207) 768-8341 or go to camp withme.com to reserve a campsite.

Just beyond the state park on Spragueville Road is **Maxie Anderson Memorial Park**, marking the launch point of the *Double Eagle II*, the first helium balloon to cross the Atlantic Ocean. One evening in August 1978, Maxie Anderson, Ben Abruzzo, and Larry Newman lifted off in the glare of television lights from this farmer's field. Five days and 3,100 miles later, they landed unceremoniously in another farmer's field, in Miserey, France.

For balloonists, their accomplishment was the equivalent of Lindbergh's transatlantic flight. Previously, dozens of people had attempted the crossing without success (and several died in the process). To commemorate the historic event, a committee of Presque Isle citizens and businesses created a small park in the field with some modest landscaping, a pair of flagpoles, and a row of benches. The centerpiece is a 15-foot-high tin model of the *Double Eagle II* balloon and gondola mounted atop a brick and concrete pedestal. The park is dedicated to Maxie Anderson, who died in 1983. Visit pirec.org to learn more about the park and other recreation options in town.

Just outside downtown Presque Isle at 79 Parsons St. is the classically nondescript **Winnie's Restaurant and Dairy Bar**. It's the type of place that once proliferated across the United States—before fast-food chains and microwaves put them out of business. Winnie's has managed to thrive in large part because of one item: its fabulous seafood chowder. In fact, it even recently closed and reopened under new ownership—so it's (likely) not going away anytime soon. Be sure to check out this unique (and newly-remodeled) vestige of the past when you're in town. The restaurant is open year-round, with extended hours in the summer; call (207) 760-7462.

A typical blockhouse dating from the **Aroostook War** may be viewed in the town of **Fort Fairfield**, just a musket shot from the present Canadian border. This replica was built in 1976 based on plans provided to the Maine militia by Captain William P. Parrott. The **Fort Fairfield Blockhouse**, with its heavy timbers and overhanging second floor, was designed to withstand a formidable siege. Narrow windows, barely more than slits, allowed the militia to shoot out but weren't wide enough for bullets to enter by skill—only occasionally by chance. The overhang was created to allow the occupants to defend the main doorway and first floor by firing through openings in the floor. In the case of Aroostook's blockhouses, of course, all the planning was theoretical since no shots were actually fired.

The blockhouse is maintained by the ***Frontier Heritage Historical Society***, which has filled it with sundry items of local historical merit. These include a massive early wooden canoe, an old pedal organ, a wooden sheep catcher, and a "potato wheel" used by locals to haul its namesake vegetable up from the cellar. Located on Main Street across from the post office, the museum is open the second Sat of every month from 10 a.m. to 1 p.m. It can also be visited by appointment through the chamber of commerce; call 207-472-3802 or visit fortfairfield.org.

If you're near Fort Fairfield in mid-July, plan to swing by for the week-long ***Maine Potato Blossom Festival***, which Fort Fairfield has celebrated annually for more than 70 years. The festival lauds Aroostook's principal cash crop and includes road, river, and bike races; fireworks; a parade; and the crowning of the Maine Potato Blossom Queen. The festival is always held the third week in July and attracts tens of thousands of visitors from around the region. For more information call (207) 472-3800 or visit the town website at fortfairfield.org.

Another unique and unexpected find around here is the ***Canterbury Royale Gourmet Dining Room***. It's located on Sam Everett Road—but you can't just pop in. This special dining room affords gourmets (couples or other small groups) their own intimate haute cuisine dining experience with one of the ornate dining rooms all to themselves and the chefs catering only to them (thus they get the "royal" treatment). The French menu (what else were you expecting?) features dishes from Paris, Lyon, Normandy, and beyond, and five courses comprise your meal. The setting is fittingly ornate, lit by silver candelabras and chandeliers, with sculptures, oil paintings, and elegant draperies all around you. Reservations are a must; call (207) 472-4910 or visit canterbury royale.com. All told, it is a touch of regality in this land of rusticity.

The View from Mars (Hill)

Heading north through the County on US 1, you can't miss **Mars Hill** on the right, one of the few topographical landmarks of any distinction in the area. This 1,660-foot-high mound played a cameo role early in the extended dispute between the British and the Americans over the border between the United States and Canada. Britain claimed that this mound marked the highlands dividing the watersheds between the Gulf of Maine and the Gulf of St. Lawrence, the agreed-upon boundary in the Treaty of 1782. The United States disagreed and eventually prevailed on the issue, however. In reaching a final settlement, the US negotiators later conceded extensive territory farther to the north. Today Mars Hill is the home of a modest ski area on its west side. It can be hiked for a bird's-eye view of the once-disputed terrain (and beyond).

Intergalactic Journey

Along US 1 between Houlton and Presque Isle is a unique attraction to the County (and, we can fairly assume, the solar system). Here you'll find the largest scale-model solar system in creation. The community project, organized by the University of Maine at Presque Isle, is built on a scale of 1:93,000,000, putting the Earth exactly 1 mile from the Sun. All the planets are appropriately sized—the Sun is based at the Northern Maine Museum of Science at the university and has a diameter of 50 feet (it's actually represented by a proportional section); the Earth (on a pedestal in front of a car dealership) is just 5.5 inches. In between, you'll find Mercury in orbit at the Leisure Gardens retirement center in Presque Isle and Venus at the city's Budget Traveler Motor Lodge. Mars stands guard at a "Welcome to Presque Isle" sign 1.5 miles from the sun, Jupiter (complete with its four major moons) is predictably enormous, and Saturn weighs nearly half a ton. (These two have their own parking lots.)

Uranus is in Houlton; Neptune at Houlton High School; and the golf-ball-sized Pluto, although stripped of its designation as a planet, remains on display at the Houlton Information Center just off I-95 at ME 1 (Thus about 43 miles from the "Sun.")

What about Charon, Pluto's largest moon? "We included it because it's exactly the size of a BB," says Kevin McCartney, who teaches at the university. The project is run by volunteers, including high school students who built and painted the planets. For more information contact the **Northern Maine Museum of Science** or visit their solar system website at pages.umpi.edu/nmms/solar.

Caribou and Environs

Driving on ME 161 from Fort Fairfield to *Caribou*, you'll pass by a rambling complex of farm buildings at *Goughan's Strawberry Farm*. This family farm is open to the public between May 1 and Christmas, with pick-your-own opportunities emerging as each season unfolds. The farm is perhaps best known for its 20 acres of strawberries, which are open for picking for several weeks beginning at the end of June. There's also asparagus and rhubarb early in the spring; raspberries in July; and corn, pumpkins, squash, and gourds later in the fall. For visiting children the Goughans also maintain an animal barn with mountain sheep, turkeys, geese, pigs, and ponies. When in the hundred-year-old barn, be sure to notice the "ship's knees" construction—brackets hand carved from massive tree roots and used to hold the rafters in place. A small snack shop on the premises offers hot dogs, hamburgers, ice cream, and—what else?—strawberry sundaes and shortcake when berries are in-season. Goughan's is 4 miles east of Caribou on ME 161. Call for more information: (207) 498-6565.

Anyone with an interest in natural history will enjoy the *Nylander Museum* in Caribou. This small city-owned museum houses the collections of Olaf Nylander, a Swedish-born amateur naturalist who was an inveterate

A Quiet War

In your travels through the County, you're bound to come across periodic references to the **Aroostook War of 1839**, certainly one of the more obscure and unremembered conflicts in American history. Hostilities—such as they were—were provoked by Canadian lumbermen venturing into territory that both the United States and England claimed as their own. The American government responded to this encroachment by sending thousands of troops to construct and man blockhouses in the St. John and Aroostook River valleys. Emotions ran high, but reason prevailed before things intensified. After many tense months, the Webster–Ashburton Treaty of 1842 settled the boundary matter between the two nations once and for all.

collector of just about everything, but especially shells. (The curator says that he was "really big on mollusks.") Nylander came to Maine in 1880 at age 16. While earning his living as a housepainter, he spent his free time exploring and amassing vast collections of rocks, plants, and fossils from the local hills and forests, eventually exchanging many specimens with scientists around the world. Much of what is known about the Devonian geologic period in Maine is due to Nylander. The museum, housed in a low building resembling a schoolhouse, was built to display Nylander's collections by WPA New Deal laborers in 1938–39. Nylander served as curator until his death in 1943.

The museum today still has an Old World feel to it, its extensive collections identified with labels written in a tight, cramped hand and displayed in old glass cases. There are stuffed birds and mounted butterflies (including a wonderful display of tropical birds that borders on the garish), and Nylander's beloved mollusks are amply represented. A small gift shop offers field guides and other natural history items for sale; more serious naturalists can inquire about using the reference collection in the basement. Also take time to poke around the herb garden in the back, where you'll find eighty different species of medicinal and culinary herbs.

The Nylander Museum is at 657 Main St. in Caribou. It is open on Sat and Sun in the summer from 1 to 3 p.m., and other times by appointment. Admission is free, but donations are accepted. For more information call (207) 498-6156 or visit nylandermuseum.org.

If there's any one product that defines Aroostook County, it's the potato. The humble tuber has long been cultivated in Aroostook, and after World War I the industry boomed wildly. With prodding from Maine's Department of Agriculture, the production of certified seed potatoes grew from a mere hundred bushels in 1920 to more than five million bushels in 1942. Although the region's potato industry has been in decline since those golden days, about 90

TOP ANNUAL EVENTS

MARCH
Can–Am Sled Dog Races
Fort Kent, early Mar
(207) 543-7515
can-am-crown.net

JUNE
Midsommar Festival
New Sweden
Held the weekend closest to June 21

Acadian Festival
Madawaska, late June
(207) 728-7069
acadianfestival.com

JULY
Maine Potato Blossom Festival
Fort Fairfield, mid-July
(207) 472-3800
fortfairfield.org

Northern Maine Fair
Presque Isle, late July and early Aug
(207) 764-1884
northernmainefairgrounds.com

OCTOBER
Bigrock Octoberfest
Mars Hill, early Oct
(207) 425-6711
bigrockmaine.com

NOVEMBER
Scarecrow Festival
Fort Kent, early Nov
(207) 834-5354
fortkentchamber.com

percent of Maine's potato crop still comes from the County. It makes for an unexpectedly beautiful backdrop in late June and early July: This is when the potato plants blossom with flowers of pure white. As you explore by car, bike, or foot, acres and acres of white intermingled with lush green roll and dance all around you.

Given the central role of the potato, it's a bit disheartening to discover there's no potato museum anywhere in the state. But don't despair. One place that serves as a commendable substitute (until some visionary fills the gap) is the ***Salmon Brook Museum*** in ***Washburn***, southwest of Caribou on ME 164.

Maine: The Coldest

More often than not, Aroostook County, Maine, is the coldest place in the nation. If your favorite television weather forecaster includes the national high and low temperatures, take note. You'll soon notice that day in and day out, Maine has the distinction of being the most frigid. And yet northern Maine woodcutters routinely work outside with nothing but a sweater or sweatshirt for outerwear.

Unique Plants of the St. John River

The **St. John River**, with its amazing 200-mile stretch of free-flowing water, is home to many rare and delicate plants. For example, it is the only place in the world where Furbish's lousewort lives. A rather sparse-looking plant, the lousewort grows to a height of 3 feet. The St. John River's spring floods and giant ice floes that scour and grind the riparian habitat make the area well suited for these rare plants because the ice keeps trees and their accompanying shade off the riverside. Other special plants growing here include the St. John tansy, grass-of-Parnassus, bird's-eye primrose, and prairie rattlesnake root. It is a veritable jewel for horticulturalists.

This sleepy town, home to a handful of general stores and cafes, can itself claim a place in the history of the potato: The frozen french fry was invented in Washburn and first manufactured by Taterstate Frozen Foods. (Another unexpected Maine first!)

The Salmon Brook Museum is housed in an 1852 farmhouse in the center of the village, just off the town green. The simple but graceful home and its outlying barn was purchased by the Salmon Brook Historical Society in 1985 and carefully restored to its earlier appearance. Its rooms display nearly 3,000 items of historical interest, from a foot-powered dentist's drill to the town's original postmaster's desk. The exhibits are well presented and neatly organized, making Salmon Brook one of the better community museums in the state (as well one of its northernmost).

For exhibits related to the history of the potato, go to the agricultural museum in the barn behind the farmstead and head upstairs. You'll find a selection of turn-of-the-20th-century potato harvesters and early potato planters, as well as several different versions of potato seed cutters and other agricultural implements. There's also a beautiful carpenter's chest from 1870 with a set of antique tools and a ca. 1950 chainsaw that appears as unwieldy as it does menacing.

The museum is open in the summer on Wed from 8 to 11 a.m. and on Sun from 1 to 4 p.m. (or by appointment). Admission is free, but donations are encouraged. For more information call (207) 540-1154 or (207) 429-9359, or visit the Salmon Brook Historical Society's Facebook page.

New Sweden and Vicinity

Northwest of Caribou along ME 161, signs of Swedish infiltration start to appear (thus, it's not difficult to discern where the name came from). You don't need to be an ethnologist to notice it: Towns like Jemtland, Stockholm, and New Sweden crop up along the way, and mailboxes are lettered with names such as Sandstrom, Wedberg, and Johannson. On some homes you'll even notice painted detailing of the Swedish flag (a Nordic cross against a backdrop of blue).

To learn more about how the Swedes came to settle in the region, stop by the **New Sweden Historical Society Museum** in **New Sweden**. The museum is housed in a convincing replica of the community's early Kapitoleum, or meetinghouse (the original burned down in 1971). Dominating the entrance-way is a bronze bust of William W. Thomas of Portland, who established the community in 1870. An American diplomat in Sweden under Abraham Lincoln, Thomas watched as thousands of Swedes packed off to the Great Plains and other western points to establish communities and build lives away from New England and Maine. Convinced that hardworking Swedes would contribute much to the area, Thomas persuaded the Maine state legislature to grant each willing Swedish immigrant one hundred acres of "rich and fertile soil." The first group, numbering fifty-one men, women, and children, arrived in New Sweden in July 1871.

The historical society's three-floor museum is filled with items from the settlement's early days, along with portraits, an early bicycle with wooden rims, wooden skis (including one pair more than 9 feet long), a wreath made of human hair intricately woven and tied to resemble flowers, and a handsome tuba. Behind the Kapitoleum is the Lindsten Stuga, a typical early settler's cabin. This was moved from nearby Westmanland in 1982 and contains many of the original furnishings from the Lindsten family. Next door is a schoolhouse, and beyond that is the town cemetery where the local history is preserved on tombstones.

On the weekend closest to June 21, New Sweden celebrates the summer solstice with its annual **Midsommar Festival**. Each year hundreds of locals and others attend this two-day pageant, which features costumed dancing, a maypole decorated with local wildflow-ers, and a festive procession to W. W. Thomas Memorial Park. The park is located on a hilltop with endless views across rich, undulating countryside, and

northernmaine trivia

Students at the University of Maine at Fort Kent get an orienta-tion seminar in "Franglais," the English–French hybrid that's often used around the region. Among the best words: *gadang-gadang*, which translates roughly as "a bit too fancy."

features a distinctive wooden bandstand in a stately grove of trees. The celebra-tion ends with a folk dance encouraging audience participation.

The Historical Society Museum is on Station Road just east of ME 161 and is open in the summer, Mon through Fri from noon to 4 p.m., and Sat and

Sun from 1 to 4 p.m. No admission is charged. For more information about the museum or pageant, call (207) 896-5200 or visit nshs.maineswedishcolony.info.

Acadian Maine

As you head toward the Canadian border, the Scandinavian influence fades and the Acadian presence grows. And grows. By the time you reach northernmost Maine between Van Buren and Madawaska, you're as likely to hear French spoken as English when you stop at a store or restaurant.

Maine's Acadians are descended from the early French settlers who made their home in French-ruled Nova Scotia in the 17th century. The British drove the French rulers out in 1710 but allowed most Acadian settlers to remain for the time being. The two cultures got along on fairly good terms until the French and Indian Wars got hot in the mid-1700s. Fearing that the French-speaking settlers would support the enemy, the British dispersed the Acadians to far-flung destinations, including Louisiana ("Cajun" is a shortened slang version of "Acadian"), New Brunswick, and other locales. New Brunswick initially welcomed the immigrants, but eventually turned hostile and drove them inland to the St. John River Valley around 1785. The trials and tribulations of the Acadians were captured in verse by Maine poet Henry Wadsworth Longfellow in his epic poem *Evangeline*.

A good place for a quick course on Acadian culture is in **Van Buren**, home of the **Acadian Village**, or Village Acadien. This privately-run museum consists of a dozen or so buildings, most of which were moved from other locations in the valley or are replicas of historic structures. Representative buildings span a broad time period, from the earliest days of settlement to the late 19th century. The structures are arranged in a field off US 1 and include a shoe repair shop, an iron shop, a small railroad station, and a barber shop. The most interesting edifice is the **Notre Dame de l'Assumption**, a log-cabin chapel complete with a bell tower and a cross. Also on the grounds are a collection of baby carriages, an early post office, and the Emma LeVasseur Dubay Art Museum. Guided tours help explain the intriguing history behind the buildings.

The Acadian Village is open from noon to 5 p.m. daily from mid June through mid Sept. Admission is $7 for adults and $4 for children. For more information call (207) 868-5042 or visit acadianvillage.mainerec.com.

In the tiny village of **Lille** (on US 1 between Van Buren and Grand Isle), look for the handsome and prominent **Notre Dame du Mont Carmel Church** (you really can't miss it), built in 1909. The pair of handsome domed belfries are capped with a pair of trumpeting golden angels; these are foam-and-fiberglass replicas of the wooden originals and were installed by crane in 2000. The church, which was deconsecrated in 1978, has served as an Acadian cultural center since then. If it's open, be sure to stop in for a look.

Read All About It

French descendants predominate in the river valley near Allagash as they do to the east. But within this sea of French influence there are also islands of descendants of Scottish settlers. There's little evidence of these contrasting cultures to the outside observer, but a series of novels by author Cathie Pelletier (an Allagash native) chronicle the picaresque adventures and misadventures of the Catholic and Protestant characters in the fictional town of "Mattagash." The tales—included in *The Funeral Makers, Once Upon a Time on the Banks,* and *The Weight of Winter*—span four decades from the 1950s to the present. Pelletier's entertaining accounts are available in paperback wherever books are sold (as well as in a number of Maine stores). Or visit the author's website at cathiepelletier.com.

Continuing north on US 1, you'll soon hit ***St. David Church*** and the ***Tante Blanche Museum*** in the scarcely noticeable town of ***St. David*** (it's almost a suburb of ***Madawaska***, a major mill town to the north). The Romanesque-style church dominates the countryside with its ornate brick facade and handsome stained-glass windows, suggesting the strong presence of the Catholic Church. The church building was begun in 1911, with its first mass held in 1913. Next door is the Tante Blanche Museum (open irregularly), housed in a small log cabin and named after an early Acadian heroine. The collections include an assortment of articles of early commerce, industry, and entertainment. Behind the house are an early schoolhouse and a 19th-century home representative of an Acadian settlement.

Follow the dirt road down the hill from the museum and toward the river; shortly after you cross the railroad tracks, you'll arrive at the ***Acadian Cross***. Erected in 1985 for the bicentennial of the arrival of the Acadians in the St. John River Valley, the cross is believed to mark the spot where the first settlers landed after coming down the river by canoe. Also present are a series of seventeen memorial markers commemorating the original St. John's Acadians.

Fort Kent Region

Another remnant of the Aroostook War (see "A Quiet War" earlier in this chapter) may be found in ***Fort Kent***, at the confluence of the St. John and Fish Rivers. The ***Fort Kent Blockhouse*** may look familiar; in fact, it's the same size and shape as the one described earlier in Fort Fairfield. But this isn't a replica. It's the real deal, constructed in 1839 by Maine militia dispatched to defend the frontier against British encroachments. Some 10,000 troops were stationed in the region for four years before the matter was finally resolved. The blockhouse, which is managed jointly by the state and a local Boy Scout troop, has a scattering of local artifacts and articles about the Aroostook War. A picnic area and tenting sites are located along the Fish River adjacent to the blockhouse and travel information is also available in a nearby building.

The blockhouse is open daily in the summer from 9 a.m. to 5 p.m. and on weekends in Sept. Admission is free. Call (207) 941-4014.

Near the international bridge crossing from Fort Kent to the Canadian town of Edmunston, look for the sign marking the end of US Route 1. This meager marker seems a bit anticlimactic for the ending of one of America's more notable highways. On the other hand, you can walk around and view the notice from the other side, which seems suitably humble and hopeful: THIS MARKS THE BEGINNING OF U.S. ROUTE 1 ENDING IN KEY WEST, FLORIDA, 2,209 MILES SOUTH.

The *Outdoor Sport Institute* (formerly the Maine Winter Sports Center) brings Olympic-caliber winter sports training to northern Maine, a region blessed with consistent snow throughout the cold-weather months (and often beyond). Olympic biathlon contenders race along cross-country ski trails, periodically swapping poles for rifles to shoot at small targets. The Winter Sports Center is open year-round. Trails are well maintained for cross-country skiing in the winter and offer easy hikes in the summer. Visitors are always welcome, as are donations. The *Fort Kent Outdoor Center at 10th Mountain* is located south of Fort Kent off ME 11. Maps and information are available at the entrance. For more information call (207) 492-1444 or visit outdoorsportinstitute .org, or 10thmtskiclub.org.

Following ME 161 westward from Fort Kent provides access to the northernmost timberlands managed by the North Maine Woods consortium, a network of businesses, nonprofits, government agencies and other organizations dedicated to economic, environmental and community initiatives in Maine's furthermost region. Through routes to other parts of Maine or into Canada are available only by way of roads that cross these private lands, and a sturdy high-clearance vehicle is recommended. (Among the consortium's efforts is to enhance that by developing a network of rural destination areas; visit maine woodsconsortium.org.) Those inclined to explore this interesting cul-de-sac can drive the 29 miles to *Allagash* and back on the gently dipping and curving paved road. In midsummer you're likely to see more vehicles with canoes on top along the way. Allagash is the northern terminus of a popular 100-mile canoe route from Telos Lake in Piscataquis County. The drive is pleasant and pastoral, following a gentle river valley framed with fields that terminate abruptly at a forested edge. You'll pass several small villages along the way, each with a general store or two and little else.

Before arriving at the town of Allagash, hikers and other adventurous sorts may choose to strike south on logging roads to reach the *Deboullie Unit*. This

A Giant Ploye

Fort Kent used a 450-pound griddle and an 8-foot bed of charcoal to cook the world's largest *ploye* in 2000. A *ploye* is a French–Canadian dish made with buckwheat flour that falls somewhere between a pancake and a crepe. Fort Kent's *ploye* was 10' 2" in diameter, topping the record set in 1989 by Edmonston, New Brunswick, a town just across the border.

Getting the giant *ploye* into the *Guinness Book of World Records* is contingent on convincing Guinness that a *ploye* is actually not a pancake. (The largest pancake is twice as big as Fort Kent's *ploye*.) The major difference? A *ploye* is cooked only on one side, while the flapjack is flipped.

rugged, undeveloped parcel of public land is made up of 21,000-plus acres traced with 30 miles of hiking trails and dominated by a half-dozen scenic ponds. (And this is a prime example of the Franco influence in full effect, as *deboullie* is a rough translation of the French verb "debouler," to come or go quickly from a place.) After the town of St. Francis, turn left after the Chamberlain store to the checkpoint. It's $8 per person per day for non-residents and $5 for Maine residents; ask for a map and directions to the trailhead. Plan on a two-hour hike from Red River Camp to the summit of **Deboullie Mountain**, which includes a steep half-mile stretch. Near the summit you can explore an old warden shack, or climb the fire tower for a magnificent view of the northern forest. You can easily fill a day or more exploring here; there are boat launches and 10 miles of snowmobile trails, too, and 30 small primitive campsites. Bring a canoe and tent to really settle in if you're so inclined. For information call (207) 435-7963 or visit maine.gov/deboullie.

Maine Route 11

South of Fort Kent, **Route 11** unspools endlessly through farmlands and dense forest. The road follows the route originally blazed hastily through woodlands in 1839 during the US military buildup to defend the frontier at Fort Kent. The road's relatively ancient lineage is reflected in the surprisingly sheer climbs up hillsides that today would be leveled, blasted, and contoured by road engineers. The northern 37 miles between Fort Kent and Portage are designated as a Maine scenic highway, but the entire 98 miles between Fort Kent and Patten are about as picturesque as you'll find anywhere in the state.

Island Falls, slightly east of Patten, hosts a combination store/museum, Emerson Store and the attached **Tingley House Museum**, on the Nina Sawyer Road. The store brims with locally produced craft items, including lovingly crafted quilts and knitwear. The museum is a mid-19th-century country house featuring two full floors of period furnishings. There are no guided tours and not even an admission fee. Instead, visitors are welcome to peruse the building on their own. The store and museum share the same hours, those being 9 a.m. to 1 p.m., Wed through Fri. However, the museum will open by appointment at other times. For more information or to schedule a tour, call the Island Falls historical society at (207) 463-2264. To reach the store and museum, take the Island Falls exit (No. 59) off I-95, and then two rights; look for a sign for the store and museum.

Places to Stay in The County

CARIBOU

Crown Park Inn
30 Access Hwy.
(207) 493-3311
crownparkinn.com
Inexpensive
Lots of accommodations, attentive staff. Also offers extended-stay rooms.

Northern Door Inn
356 West Main St.
(207) 834-3133
northerndoorinn.com
Inexpensive
A community fixture for decades. Comfortable rooms, free breakfast, Internet, and laundry.

Old Iron Inn Bed and Breakfast
155 High St.
(207) 492-4766
oldironinn.com
Inexpensive
Early 1900 house furnished with period antiques. Has collection of old irons, thus the name. Also features an extensive library filled with books about Abraham Lincoln, mystery, and the history of aviation.

SELECTED CHAMBERS OF COMMERCE

Central Aroostook Chamber of Commerce
3 Houlton Rd, Presque Isle
(207) 764-6561

Fort Fairfield Chamber of Commerce
18 Community Center Dr.
(207) 472-3802
fortfairfield.org

Greater Fort Kent Area Chamber of Commerce
291 West Main St.
(207) 834-5354
fortkentchamber.com

Greater Houlton Chamber of Commerce
109 Main St.
(207) 532-4216
greaterhoulton.com

HOULTON

Ivey's Motor Lodge
241 North Rd.
(800) 244-4206 or
(207) 532-4206
iveysmotorlodge.com
Inexpensive comfy rooms,
Irish pub. Canadians
know a thing or two about
comfortable places to stay,
and this is one of their
favorites when in Maine.

Shiretown Motor Inn
282 North Rd.
(800) 441-9421 or
(207) 532-9421
shiretownmotorinn.com
Inexpensive
Pool, health club, centrally
located, just minutes from
downtown Houlton

OAKFIELD

**Yellow House Bed &
Breakfast**
1040 Ridge Rd.
(207) 757-8797
Moderate
Home-cooked breakfast
served in a glass atrium in
the summer and in their
travel library in winter

PRESQUE ISLE

**Arndt's Aroostook River
Lodge and Campground**
95 Parkhurst Siding Rd.
(207) 764-8677
arndtscamp.com
Moderate
Ideal stay for upland
hunters, snowmobilers,
ATV riders, and canoers

**Budget Traveler Motor
Lodge**
71 Main St.
(207) 796-0111
thebudgettravelerinn.com
Inexpensive
Clean rooms, friendly staff,
can't beat the price

SHERMAN

Katahdin Valley Motel
32 Main St.
(207) 365-4554
katahdinvalleymotel.com
Inexpensive
Offers packages, including
guide service. Good place
to stay before entering
Baxter State Park from the
North Entrance.

Places to Eat in The County

FORT KENT

Rock's Family Diner
378 West Main St.
(207) 834-2888
Inexpensive
Interesting lunch specials
(Chinese pie, for example)

HOULTON

Courtyard Cafe
61 Main St.
(207) 532-0787
thecourtyardcafe.biz
Moderate
Ever-changing menu
features local fruits and
vegetables, seafood, meat,

poultry, and vegetarian
offerings

Houlton Farms Dairy Bar
131 Military St.
(207) 532-2628
houltonfarmsdairy.com
Inexpensive
Generous portions of
ice cream, no growth
hormones used.
Considered the best ice
cream in Maine by people
from The County. Also has
a dairy bar at 98 Bennett
Drive, and a location at 792
Main St. in Presque Isle.

PRESQUE ISLE

Riverside Inn Restaurant
399 Main St.
(207) 764-1447
Inexpensive
Good, old-fashioned home
cooking

**Winnie's Restaurant and
Dairy Bar**
79 Parsons St.
(207) 760-7462
Inexpensive
See main entry (p. 215)
for full description.

STOCKHOLM

Eureka Hall Restaurant
5 School St.
(207) 896-3196
Moderate
Offers home-made baked
goods. Try their pizza.

Index

About the Author

Taryn Plumb is a freelance writer who has also authored *Haunted Boston: Famous Phantoms, Sinister Sites, and Lingering Legends*, and *Haunted Maine Lighthouses*, both by Globe Pequot Press. She enjoys exploring her home state whenever she can—and "discovering" hidden gems and off-beat places.